WHO WON WATERLOO?
THE TRIAL OF CAPTAIN SIBORNE

+

www.whowonwaterloo.net

Who Won Waterloo? – The Trial of Captain Siborne © Copyright 2006 by Barry Van Danzig

Cover design by Tony Lindfield Design, Bexhill

Scotland For Ever! 1881 (oil on canvas) by Butler, Lady (Elizabeth Southerden Thompson) (1846-1933) Leeds Museums and Galleries (City Art Gallery) U.K./ The Bridgeman Art Library
Field Marshal Prince Von Blucher (1742-1819) c.1816 (oil on canvas) by Dawe, George (1781-1829) © Apsley House, The Wellington Museum, London, UK/ The Bridgeman Art Library
Cuirassiers Charging the Highlanders at the Battle of Waterloo on 18th June 1815, 1874 (oil on canvas) by Philippoteaux, Felix (c.1815-84) © Apsley House, The Wellington Museum, London, UK/ The Bridgeman Art Library
Napoleon Bonaparte (1769-1821) by David, Jacques Louis (1748-1825) (after) © The Crown Estate/ The Bridgeman Art Library
The Morning of The Battle of Waterloo: the French Await Napoleon's Orders, 1876 by Crofts, Ernest (1847-1911) © Sheffield Galleries and Museums Trust, UK/ The Bridgeman Art Library
Wellington's March from Quatre Bras to Waterloo by Crofts, Ernest (1847-1911) © Sheffield Galleries and Museums Trust, UK/ The Bridgeman Art Library
Sir Thomas Picton, by Shee, reproduced by kind permission of the National Portrait Gallery, London.
Pictures of the Siborne model by kind permission of the National Army Museum

Every effort has been made to contact the copyright holders of work included in this publication. If you are the owner of the copyright of a work not credited, please contact the publisher below.

A catalogue record of this book is available from the British Library

First Edition: November 2006

ISBN: 1-84375-300-6

To order additional copies of this book please visit: www.whowonwaterloo.net

Published by: UPSO Ltd
5 Stirling Road, Castleham Business Park,
St Leonards-on-Sea, East Sussex TN38 9NW United Kingdom
Tel: 01424 853349 Fax: 0870 191 3991
Email: info@upso.co.uk   Web: http://www.upso.co.uk

WHO WON WATERLOO?

THE TRIAL OF CAPTAIN SIBORNE

by
Barry Van Danzig

UPSO

I dedicate this book to my wife Liz whose help and tolerance over the years has enabled me to complete the study of the battle without having a battle of our own.

Contents

Section One
The Documentary Evidence

Section Two
The Evidence from the New Model

Section Three
The Evidence from the Battle Re-creation

APPENDIX

Acknowledgements

My thanks go out to all those who have assisted me over the years in the study of military history. In particular I would like to thank Brian Hilton and Mike Beard for their proof reading skills that corrected more grammatical errors than I would like to admit to. In addition I would like to thank David Pearman of UPSO Ltd for his advice and assistance. I would also like to thank the staff at the photographic library at the National Army Museum for their assistance in publishing the photos of Siborne's model.

Foreword

History is the story of that which has passed, usually told by those who were not there. As such what we believe we know is not always the truth. History has political significance. Its interpretation can affect future generations views upon the world and it is therefore important that historians get it right. But what is right? History can inspire people to do great things or it can provide excuses for people to do wicked things.

Afro Caribbean Englishmen and women often feel that history portrays them in a poor light, or ignores them. History tells us that they came as slaves from Africa and then as immigrants to Great Britain during the 1950's and 60's. History also tells us of the Great Britons of the past, one of whom was Horatio Nelson. There is a famous painting of the moment when Nelson was shot on the deck of the Victory at the Battle of Trafalgar. On the deck of the Victory there are eighty men, two of whom were young black Englishmen. These men were not slaves but gunners serving the guns as part of the gun crew, part of the team. The ratio of black Englishmen to white Englishmen on the deck of the Victory is 2.5%, about the same as it is today nationwide. Perhaps if history was interpreted in this way those young men would feel much more part of the team than the perceived history makes them feel.

Therefore read history with these cautions in mind. This book sets out to explain what most probably happened on a single day nearly 200 years ago and to set before you those possibilities so that you can be better informed, take part in the debate and conclude with others what happened. History is a live subject, a debate, a mystery, a puzzle. It is fascinating but it is also dangerous. I trust that the readers will benefit from the experience and perhaps take a harder look at history in the future and ask the question; "Is that really how it happened?"

Introduction

"No one Englishman, not even the Duke of Wellington himself, has had so great an influence on the English-language historiography of The Battle of Waterloo as Captain William Siborne."

So begins the introduction to Captain William Siborne contained in David Hamilton-Williams' book *Waterloo – new perspectives* published by Arms and Armour Press a Cassell Imprint and BCA in 1994.

The premise of this book is that Captain William Siborne committed a *crime* when he wrote his book *"The History of the Waterloo Campaign"* in 1842. He published three editions, in which he altered some of the points made in the earlier editions.

The *crime* Siborne is accused of is distortion of the historical facts for financial gain. The accusation is supported by no less a personage than the Marquess of Anglesey, a descendent of the famous cavalry commander Lord Uxbridge who commanded the British and Allied cavalry on 18th June 1815.

The consequences of the *crime* are that since 1842 all histories have referred back to Siborne's original source documents and have therefore compounded the *crime* by perpetuating the myths Siborne created.

The debate gathers pace later when in 1998 Peter Hofschröer's book *The Waterloo campaign – The German Victory* was published by Greenhill books. Later still Peter Hofschröer wrote another book entitled *"Wellington's Smallest Victory"* which confirms Siborne's distortion of history but rather than his *crime* being for financial gain, asserts that it was caused by pressure from the Duke of Wellington himself so that the battle remained a British victory and down played the Prussian role.

This is the stuff of history.

History is after all 'His-Story'. The victor is not necessarily the person who carried out the great deed but rather the person who is credited with the achievement by historians. Throughout history this has been the case and we do not need to look as far back as 1815 to find examples of historical distortion, for whatever reason. We need only look to Hollywood to see historical distortion at its finest.

It is however the responsibility of historians to seek out the truth or at least set out the most plausible description and explanation of any event in history.

So what to do?

Well if a crime has been committed then a trial must surely ensue. Unfortunately all of the participants are long dead. Nevertheless Siborne's good name and reputation has been challenged and so has that of the Duke of Wellington and other famous officers in the British Army at that time. Therefore the issues raised by David Hamilton-Williams and Peter Hofschröer challenge the accepted view of the Battle of Waterloo and bring into sharp focus the actual events of that day casting doubt upon the established version of history.

To find out who is right and who is wrong is an immense task. Both sides have ample evidence to support their views. One or both parties have interpreted the evidence to support their views, but both views cannot be right as they conflict so dramatically. The fact is we do not actually know exactly what did happen on that day and therefore any version must be open to interpretation.

The solution I propose is to put Siborne on trial and in doing so put the conflicting views on trial so that the truth or at least the most probable sequence of events is proven as best as it can be.

What is proof? Siborne has been accused of a **crime** but no crime in the legal sense has been committed. Siborne put forward his views on the battle that were formed by gathering together hundreds of eye-witness accounts. If we wish to regard his views as a criminal act then we would have to apply criminal law to the process. Criminal law requires proof beyond all reasonable doubt. If this test is applied then Siborne is innocent. After a period of 189 years with all of the witnesses dead, proof beyond reasonable doubt cannot be achieved. Therefore we shall apply the other, lesser, requirement of proof used in civil courts, the balance of probability.

In this book I hope to set out the facts and will put the case for the prosecution and defence as fairly as I can. Other books mentioned here in the text and in the bibliography will be useful in forming your opinion.

You are the jury; you will decide the verdict, guilty or not guilty to the various accusations and versions of events concerning Siborne, Wellington, Vivian, Blucher, Bulow, Ziethen and of course Napoleon himself.

We have created a web site ***www.whowonwaterloo.net*** and you, the reader, are invited to put your point of view and to vote on guilt or innocence of the accused persons and events.

The wheels of justice grind ever slowly and we should not look to a quick solution to the matter. Hopefully many readers will pass their opinions on the issues. It is hoped that the book will get a wider audience in both the German and French-speaking countries as well as the English-speaking world. The final outcome of the jury will be published one year after publication but the web site will remain open after that time in case new evidence comes to light and the verdict can be appealed.

There are, however, rules of court to be applied.

You, the reader, are required to be polite in your responses. Any response that is phrased in a racist or offensive manner will be deleted from the site and such opinions will not form part of the eventual judgement.

Your co-operation in determining the truth is sought, for this is the first time as far as I am aware that the reader's view has been sought in such matters. I hope you will take part and enjoy the experience. History is His Story; how we interpret it is our story. I look forward to a lively debate and eventual outcome that may influence history beyond the confines of the great battle of 18th June 1815 in a field called Waterloo.

THE CHARGES AGAINST SIBORNE, WELLINGTON, VIVIAN AND THE HISTORY OF THE BATTLE OF WATERLOO.

The controversy over Siborne's history is nothing new. It started as soon as he began to write his history. On the models it revolved around the precision Siborne required to picture accurately the moment when the Imperial Guard were defeated by Wellington's army. Who stood where? Who did what? Wellington thought the task impossible and, knowing more than most about it, thought that it was best left alone.

This may have been because he wanted to keep the history of the battle as it was, his victory and no-one else's. Or it may have been a genuine comment about the complexity of the task.

When the model was displayed the 'British' viewer thought that the 'Prussians' were too far forward and complained to Siborne that he had got it wrong. British and Prussian does not refer to the birth place of the individual but rather the side where their opinion lay. Sir Hussey Vivian the British born cavalry commander who fought in Wellington's army may be viewed as a Prussian in this context as he supported the Prussian view of what happened at the end of the battle.

When Siborne's history was published the arguments arose about his treatment of Wellington's allies, namely the Dutch Belgium army and the Prussians' part in the battle. This was bad enough in his lifetime but recently, following the discovery of the 'unpublished' Waterloo letters, (unpublished that is until Gareth Glover published them in 2004), led to the accusations of deception, hiding the truth, fraud for financial gain and crimes against history. These can be distilled down to the following charges against Siborne.

1 That William Siborne deliberately suppressed evidence and distorted the true historical events in order to enhance the British performance at the Battle of Waterloo to the detriment of the Prussian army.

2 That William Siborne deliberately suppressed evidence and distorted the true historical events in order to

enhance the British performance at the Battle of Waterloo to the detriment of the Netherlands army.

3 That William Siborne committed these acts for financial gain.

4 That Sir Hussey Vivian and others paid Siborne in order to have their part, and the part played by their regiments, highlighted in the history and distorted in order to appear that their actions were greater and more decisive than they really were in fact.

5 That the Duke of Wellington indirectly brought pressure on William Siborne to amend his model of the battle in order falsely to place the Prussian army further back than originally placed in order to make the Prussian contribution to the final victory appear less pronounced that it would otherwise have been.

6 That the 1st Corps of the Prussian army commanded by Lieutenant-General von Ziethen arrived in more decisive fashion on the afternoon of 18th June 1815 and was the main cause of the French rout.

7 That the 4th Corps of the Prussian army commanded by Lieutenant-General Count von Bulow and the 2nd Corps of the Prussian army commanded by General-Major Von Pirch were further advanced towards Plancenoit than shown on the revised Siborne model and that they captured the village at about the same time or very soon after the defeat of the French Imperial Guard on the ridge between Hougoumont and La Haye Sainte.

Other controversial incidents are covered in this book but the crux of the matter is contained in the seven points of accusation outlined above.

Analysis of the new Waterloo letters can answer the charges about Siborne's integrity. However to determine whether Siborne got it right in his history and his model will require a more detailed study of the battle, using a new model and photography so that we can see what most probably happened on that day nearly one hundred and ninety years ago.

The popular sequence of events at the Battle of Waterloo.

The detail of the battle will be gone into in great depth later in the book but it will be necessary for any reader who does not know much about the battle to have a brief understanding of the popular view of the day's events so that he or she can follow the rather complex nature of the controversies that sprang up after the battle took place.

The battle of Waterloo took place on 18th June 1815 on the plain of Mont St. Jean twelve miles south of Brussels. Napoleon with an army of 125,000 men had marched north from France on 15th June and arrived at Charleroi, which was the junction between the Prussian army of 116,000 men commanded by Prince Blucher and the Anglo Netherlands army of 92,000 men commanded by the Duke of Wellington. Napoleon was therefore outnumbered by 83,000 troops. By arriving at the junction between the two armies Napoleon hoped to drive them apart and hold one army off with a detachment of 30,000 to 40,000 men whilst he destroyed the other enemy army with the remaining 85,000 to 95,000 troops.

Napoleon achieved strategic surprise catching both the Prussian and Anglo Netherlands armies with their forces spread over a wide area. The French drove the Prussians back north eastwards and held off Wellington's forces to the north and west with a detachment under the command of Marshal Ney.

On 16th June there were two battles; one with the Prussians at Ligny and the other against the Anglo Netherlands army at Quatre Bras. At Ligny the Prussians were defeated and driven from the field. At Quatre Bras the Anglo Netherlands army was contained and later, on the 17th, was driven back north by the numerically superior French forces under the command of Napoleon himself. The victories would have been more decisive if the 1st French Corps under de Erlon had not been poorly directed, marching uselessly between each battlefield and taking part in neither battle.

Napoleon despatched 33,000 men under the command of Marshal Grouchy to prevent the Prussians from joining up with Wellington so that Napoleon could decisively defeat Wellington's army in the field and drive the British out of mainland Europe.

If Napoleon could defeat Wellington in battle or force him to withdraw from

The battle of Waterloo depicting a British infantry square facing a French cavalry charge

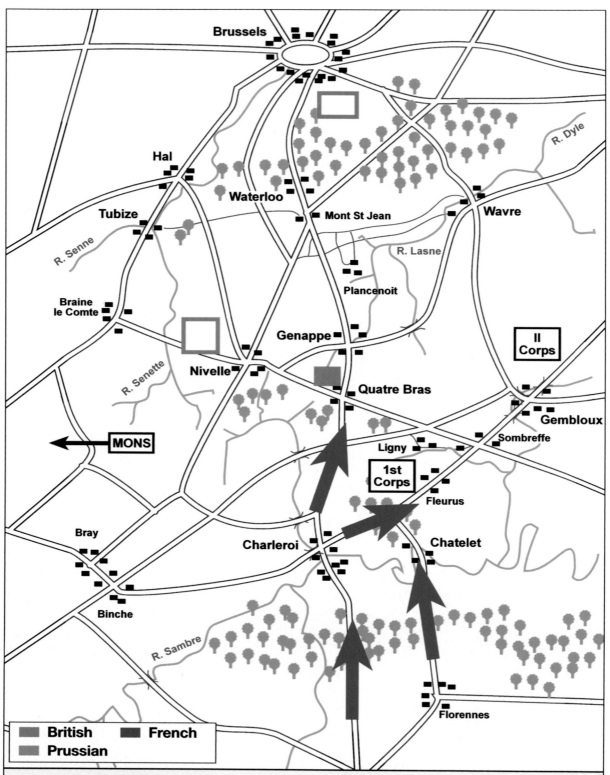

The opening of the campaign. Napoleon breaks through at Charleroi. Wellington, aware of this still attends the Duchess of Richmond's ball believing that this was a diversion from the real attack which would come through Mons. When news arrived at the ball that no troops were attacking through Mons Wellington exclaimed, "By God Napoleon has humbugged me!"

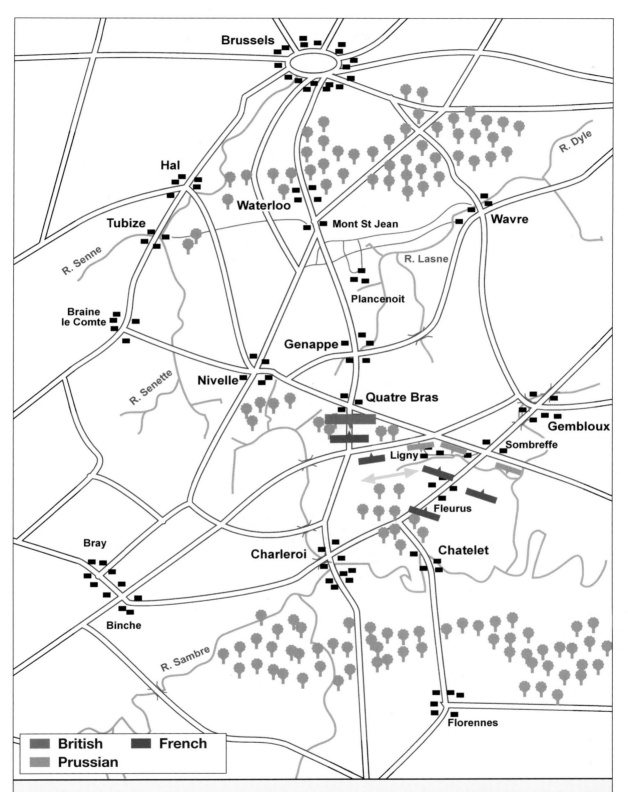

The battles of Ligny and Quatre Bras fought on 16th June. Napoleon held off Wellington with Ney's forces whilst he crushed the Prussians at Ligny. The double headed arrow denotes the abortive march of de Erlons corps between the two battlefields.

Belgium back to England then it was feasible that a peace of sorts could be negotiated which allowed him to stay on the throne of France. If, however, Wellington and Blucher defeated him then Napoleon would be in real difficulty. France was exhausted and wanted peace and whilst he did have other troops left in France a defeat would make Napoleon's position impossible and he would eventually have to abdicate.

This is the fascination of Waterloo, the stakes were extremely high, and the decisions made by each commander were of national and international importance. A wrong move, a poor decision might lead to defeat and disaster for any one or more of the commanders of the three armies.

The Prussians did not retreat eastwards towards Prussia but rather northwards towards Wavre. This enabled them to keep in touch with Wellington and hopefully join up with him on 18th June. Wellington retreated back to the Waterloo position and prepared to give battle on the proviso that Blucher would support him with the aid of at least one Prussian Corps, about 30,000 men.

Wellington's army had reduced to 67,000 men as 17,000 were detached to Hal in the west to protect the approach to Brussels from that direction, a further 4,000 had been killed or wounded at Quatre Bras and the remainder were left defending Brussels and other towns in

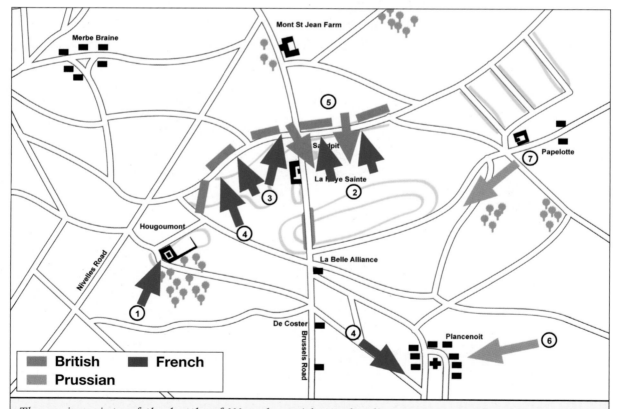

The main points of the battle of Waterloo with (1) the diversionary attack on Hougoumont, (2) de Erlon's attack, (3) the cavalry attacks and (4) the two attacks of the Imperial Guard. Also shown is (5) Uxbridge's cavalry attack and (6) the advance or attacks of both Bulow's corps and (7) Steinmetz 1st. brigade of Ziethen's corps.

the area.

Napoleon had an army of 72,000 men after losing 7,000 at Ligny and Quatre Bras and having detached 33,000 men to pursue Blucher. Girard's division was also left at Ligny to assist the wounded.

Blucher had retreated faster than Grouchy pursued him and was able to leave a rearguard at Wavre whilst he marched to Waterloo.

During the 17th and into the early hours of the 18th it rained heavily making the ground sodden. This and the late arrival of some of Napoleon's troops at Waterloo delayed the start of the battle until 11.30am.

The battle opened with an attack on the Allied right at the Chateau of Hougoumont. This was a diversion designed to pin down Wellington's right whilst the main attack was made on the centre left of Wellington's line. Just before the main attack went in the French noticed Blucher's troops approaching from the direction of Wavre. Napoleon despatched troops to delay the Prussians whilst he attacked Wellington.

The attack on Wellington's line was repulsed. Napoleon was now in some difficulty with his main attack driven back and the Prussians advancing on his right flank. Under such circumstances one would expect the outflanked army to withdraw, but Napoleon would not even consider this. He believed that he could still beat Wellington and then turn on Blucher. The French then attacked Wellington's line with massed cavalry, which was also repulsed.

About 4.30pm the Prussians began to arrive on the battlefield and were pressing the French right wing, bending

The Prussians meet up with Saxe Wiemar's Nassau troops at Papelotte

it back. Napoleon detached more troops to defend his right flank whilst maintaining the pressure on Wellington with the remainder of his forces. These forces finally captured the centre of Wellington's line and victory seemed to favour the French. But there was a pause. Napoleon had to detach more troops to deal with the Prussians who were about to capture the village of Plancenoit, which would open the right rear of the French army to an attack by the numerous Prussian forces massing on that flank.

The troops sent by Napoleon to deal with this threat were part of his Imperial Guard, his most elite troops. They drove the Prussians out of the village and back to their start line beyond their artillery batteries. This left the way open for a final attack with the rest of Napoleon's Guard on Wellington's line. This attack, like the others, was repulsed but this time Wellington counter attacked and drove the French back. The French panicked and left the field in rout. The Prussians swept in from the eastern flank and completed the rout.

Or was it that the Prussians broke through on the right flank just as the Guard were making their final assault and it was this breakthrough that caused the panic and the rout of the French army?

After the battle, the controversy. Did Wellington win the battle?

Or did Blucher arrive in the nick of time to save the British from defeat?

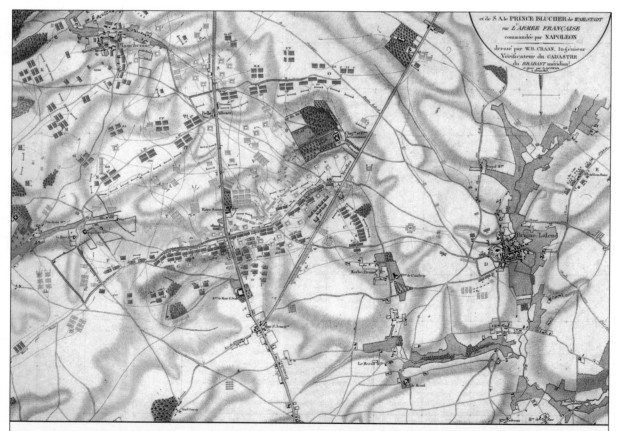

De Craan's (original) map showing the various deployments of the troops of each nation during the battle.

Section One

The Documentary Evidence

Chapter One

Siborne and his Models

William Siborne was born on 15th October 1797 in Greenwich. His father was an officer in the 9th Foot (East Norfolk) regiment and William himself joined the army in 1811 as a Gentleman Cadet at the Royal Military College. William had seen military models in Paris and was much impressed by them. William Siborne was commissioned by the army to build a model of the battle and visited the battlefield of Waterloo in 1830. He carried out a detailed survey of the ground. From this survey Siborne designed a terrain model and sought funds from His Majesty's Government to build the model. Lord Hill was at that time head of the army and Wellington was Prime Minister, both veterans of Waterloo. Permission had already been granted and some funding already paid. Siborne, confident that he had both the

Siborne's large model looking south from Merbe Braine Allude towards Hougoumont.

permission of Government and the promise of sufficient funding to complete a model of the battlefield, set about writing to surviving participants of the battle in order to gain from them information about the terrain and the position of the respective regiments, battalions and batteries present on the day of the battle.

What came back was the most comprehensive collection of eyewitness reports ever compiled of any battle up until that date. Never before had so much been written by participants about a single action. Waterloo was the last and most decisive battle of the Napoleonic wars although no doubt other battles, Austerlitz, Borodino, Jena were decisive encounters in their own right. But from those battles we have little in the way of written eyewitness accounts compared with the hundreds of letters written to Siborne. Perhaps the amount of data was too much. Letters conflicted about the same events viewed from differing perspectives. The battles of Austerlitz, Borodino and Jena do not attract anything like the controversy Waterloo does. Is this because Waterloo was so different from the other battles, or is it because we have so much more data about the battle of Waterloo than we have about the others?

The archive of the Waterloo letters is a national treasure, no, they are an international treasure. Siborne had to decipher these hundreds of letters in order to place the regiments of each nation on the model at the exact time he had chosen to represent, i.e. the so called *crisis* when the Imperial Guard attacked the British line and was repulsed and

routed. We can imagine the difficulty Siborne must have had when reading for the first time the letters he received. The letters did not agree with each other. Different officers had different views and it fell to Siborne to decide who was right and who was wrong. Wellington's words of advice suddenly seem to be wisdom itself. As he expressed later, the task was a folly. As more and more facts are discovered "what will happen to the reputation of those officers who had made something of their part in the battle who may now be found out?"

The terrain model began to take shape. This was the easy part as the terrain is not controversial. Save for the crops growing at the time of the battle and the altered ridge line caused by the building of the lion mound, the ground was much as it had been fifteen years earlier. The difficult part was establishing the correct numbers of troops in each regiment at the precise time the model represented and their exact location on the field.

This was an impossible task. Memory changes as time passes and it is only the overall picture that remains. It is quite remarkable that the memory of the events is as clear as it is in the Waterloo letters. Memorable as the event must have been, the minute details still fresh in the memory of soldiers anything up to twenty years after the event is to me both remarkable and wonderful. But were they true? And was Siborne's interpretation of them accurate?

Siborne had the permission of His Majesty's Government, and the promise of financial support to finish the model, from the then Commander in Chief of the army, Lord Hill. However, before the model was even started the Government changed and the new Government reneged on the deal leaving Siborne in a fix. He no longer had the money but was still forced to finish the model at his own expense. Mr. Ellice, the Secretary of War, wrote to Siborne in 1833 declining to advance any further funds for the model's completion. Furthermore, Mr. Ellice stated that the Lords of the Treasury would only allow Siborne to keep the £380 already advanced if Siborne agreed to finish the model at his own expense; otherwise they wanted it back! If only Siborne had the sense to employ a lawyer he might have faired better. The £380 had already been advanced in payment for legitimate expenses; it was not recoverable in law. Furthermore Siborne had a legitimate claim against the Government for the rest of the costs of the model but alas he was too awed by Lords, Peers and Governments to stand up to them. He was after all a serving officer in the army, and thus a military servant himself.

Siborne was in a tight spot. He felt that if he stopped he would have to pay back the £380 and the only way he could do that was to sell his commission, thereby losing his only means of income for his family. Alternatively he could borrow or raise the money himself and finish the model that he believed would be a financial success. He took the gamble

Siborne's first and larger model showing the village of Plancenoit heavily defended by infantry from the Imperial Guard but not under attack from the Prussians.

and finished the model.

To raise the funds he turned to the soldiers who had written to him in reply to his circular, asking for investment or gifts of money so that the work could be completed. The model cost some £3,000 to create, a vast sum in those days, a sum sufficiently vast to cause a mere Captain to become bankrupt.

Siborne stands accused of 'selling' places in history in exchange for money. Siborne wanted the model finished and he needed the financial support of many benefactors in order to raise the funds to complete his task. Benefactors may have felt that they had the right to influence Siborne as to the position of the troops on the model. It would be quite possible for someone in Siborne's position to give way to these demands, as he could not finish the model without the benefactor's funds.

We will examine in detail whether Siborne did in fact give into this natural impulse later but for now I wish you to consider the plight of a well intentioned man meeting the solid wall of Government opposition and establishment displeasure. The accusation that some officers said yes they would contribute and others said no is clearly true. The fascination is did some officers say "Yes I will help you Siborne, I was over there behind that tree during the battle, but on your model would you put me there right in the middle of the action"? Siborne stands accused of answering "Yes alright, that will be ten pounds please"! You will need to decide whether Siborne was an affable rogue who sold places in history in exchange for cash or a serious historian who

studied and evaluated the facts before him and produced an accurate portrayal of the day's events.

From this simple event it is claimed that the whole history of the battle has been distorted.

Eventually the model was completed and put on show to an eager public. The controversy started immediately. Here again natural human reaction that resides in us all came to the fore.

Siborne had discovered some unsavoury facts in his research on the battle. Regiments, British regiments, ran in panic from the attack of the Old Guard. Some soldiers in those regiments did not view the retirement of their regiment as anything other than a 'redeployment to the rear', not a panicked rout. But run they did. Other regiments, in particular the British Guard regiments, felt certain that they alone had driven back the Old Guard and could not accept that Colborne and the 52nd Foot had attacked the flank of the Imperial Guard Chasseurs. Many letters testified to the retreat of the Netherlands troops in the face of de Erlon's attack. Others complained about all of the Netherlands and any other non-British troops under Wellington's command, excepting of course the King's German Legion.

Siborne had selected one precise moment in time and had placed the troops in accordance with his research and his opinion of what had happened at that moment. This was bound to cause disagreement; it did and still does. Wellington criticised the concept of the model, and he never visited it in case he gave it his seal of approval. Wellington said that he thought the task to be impossible; "it would be like trying to describe a moment in a ball when all is movement and is suddenly frozen in time". Who was where and who was with whom? An impossible task. Wellington was of course technically correct. The model represented some 180,000 men at a single second in time. Of course they were not all in the right place but only as near as Siborne's researches could determine. However the overall impression such a model produces can be regarded as 'accurate' in the general sense of the word provided that the location of the troops on the model is reasonably correct and stands up to scrutiny.

Naturally the participants in the battle wanted to show their relatives and friends the position of their regiment on that day and *may* have exaggerated their part in the action only to find that they were now found out and placed in a less important location on the field. Or worse, found that they were misrepresented by Siborne's interpretation of events.

But the greatest controversy was the location of the Prussian troops at the moment the French army panicked and fled the field.

When the model was first displayed in 1838 it showed the Prussians close to Plancenoit. 48,000 Prussian troops were represented by 24,000 tiny lead figures. After the controversy had raged for several years Siborne revised the model and removed 20,000 lead soldiers representing 40,000 Prussian troops. This

Siborne's model viewed from behind the allied lines showing the eastern side of the battlefield, from La Haye Sainte to Papelotte.

moved the Prussians' front line some 300 metres further back from Plancenoit and off the model altogether.

This, it is claimed, enhanced the British and diminished the Prussian role unfairly. This again we will examine in detail later on. The fact that the figures were removed is incontrovertible; Siborne makes a considerable effort to explain why he did it in his third edition of his book on the Waterloo campaign. Whether it was right to do so is another matter.

The model now resides in the National Army Museum in Chelsea, London. It is without doubt a work of art. It is most beautiful to look at and admire. It does give an impression of a battle of the period but the figures appear to be too small. I believe that when it was first displayed there were opera glasses mounted around the model so that a close inspection of the figures could be made. The model shows the battle at approximately 7.30pm part way through the Imperial Guard's attack on Wellington's line.

The model went on display on 8th October 1838 and was seen by nearly 100,000 people, each paying one shilling (five new pence) to see it. The exhibition continued until the end of 1839 and then, sometime before July 1840, Siborne decided to create another model.

I have a mental picture of his long suffering wife reaching for a pistol to blow her brains out when William told her of his plans. They had suffered years

Siborne's model showing a close-up of Hougoumont burnt-out after the fire. French troops can be seen in the wood, in the meadow and beyond.

Another view of the large model (above) showing Plancenoit from above without any Prussians attacking it as it is displayed now after the removal of the Prussians after 1838. Below is how it might have looked in 1838 when it was first displayed from documents and plans showing where the Prussians were initially displayed on the model and recreated on my model.

of anxiety, debt, vilification and argument and had survived it together. Now as the controversy fades as do the money worries, Siborne decides to do it all over again.

Siborne's second model depicts the moment when the British cavalry charged de Erlon's Corps scattering it

The Duke of Wellington. Did he bring undue pressure to bear on Siborne to alter his model and his opinion of the role the Prussians played in the battle?

back to the French lines. This model was different from the first one in that the scale of the figures was one inch to six feet (25mm to 1.8m). The terrain model covered a smaller portion of the field but was still a considerable undertaking. Once again the controversy started anew, although proportionally less as fewer regiments were engaged. This model is now in Leeds Armoury Museum but was for a long time in Dover Castle.

The issue of money bedevils the history of the models.

Siborne was always complaining about being low on funds. In a letter on 26th October 1836 from Mr. F.H. Lindsay who was secretary to the Duke of Wellington, Lindsay offered an invitation from Wellington to meet Siborne to discuss the model. Lindsay told Siborne

to keep the object of his journey quiet but advised him that he would do well to come to London or Walmer castle for a meeting with the Duke.

Siborne's reply on 29th October 1836 is a litany of woes and complaints about money. He cannot come for he is completely ruined; he has starved to finish the model but still needs five hundred pounds which he cannot see any chance of getting. So Siborne declined the invitation to meet the most important eyewitness to the battle because he could not afford the fare to London. This is very odd, very odd indeed. The fare cannot have been much but Siborne is adamant that it is quite out of the question. He must have been severely impoverished at that time, so much so that he missed such a golden opportunity to meet Wellington

Another view of Siborne's second model showing the charge of the household cavalry.

himself and to converse with him about his model.

In January 1837 in another blow to Siborne's pocket, Lord Howick of the War Office declines to pay Siborne any money in order to allow him to finish the model.

On 7th March 1837 Lord Somerset wrote to Siborne stating his opinion that the model was flawed as the Prussians were too far forward towards Plancenoit. He also declines to offer any money but says that a Colonel Egerton or a Colonel D'Aguilar will write to Siborne on the subject of Lord Hill's subscription.

Then suddenly on 19th April 1837, only six weeks after Somerset's letter Sir Hussey Vivian writes to Siborne rejoicing in the fact that Siborne's prospects are so bright and he truly hoped that they might never again be clouded. What happened between 7th March and 19th April 1837 to change so dramatically Siborne's financial state? The answer would appear to be that a benefactor or investor came up with the money. There is no letter to prove who the benefactor was but it is possible that it was Lord Hill who gave the money to Siborne in order to allow the model to be finished in time for its exhibition in October 1838.

It could have been an investor, perhaps the agent who later threatened to sell the model if his debts were not repaid, but there is no evidence of this in the letters.

There are two points of interest here. One, who paid the piper, two, why did he not call the tune?

We know that when the first model went on show the Prussian figures were in close proximity to Plancenoit. We also know that Somerset and therefore Wellington knew that to be the case before the model was finished. Lord Hill, if it was Lord Hill, was firmly in Wellington's camp on this matter. He had served with Wellington throughout the Peninsular War and at Waterloo and yet if he paid he did not, and by implication neither did Wellington, interfere with the layout of the model in exchange for financial support.

It certainly was not Sir Hussey Vivian who sorted out Siborne's finances during this period for it was he who wrote rejoicing in Siborne's good fortune. If he had been the cause of it why write and rejoice in it? Who else could it have been? It was a considerable sum of money. Only a rich person or a collection of people, or a Government could have raised the funds. If it had been a collection of people then they would all have to have been of a like mind in order to influence the model. They might be those who raised it except that Siborne had written to them before without success. Also it would be extremely lucky for Siborne that a number of people had got together and raised the funds between 7th March and 19th April.

It is unlikely that a Government would have paid the money. It certainly was not the British Government who paid. Could it have been the Prussians? This also seems to me to be unlikely for the same reasons as the British Government's refusal to pay. The refusal was not a decision made by Government to refuse to pay but rather it was the civil service mentality of not making a positive decision for fear of retribution. You cannot be criticised in the civil service for not spending money but you can be criticised for making a decision to spend Government funds on any project without due authority. It might even have taken a Parliamentary vote to get the money from Government to fund Siborne's model. The same would probably have been true in Prussia. This would have taken time to get the decision made. It could not have been made in a few weeks.

It is equally unlikely that a commercial investor paid the money as there would have been considerable documentation and correspondence in Siborne's files.

The most likely benefactor has to be a rich man, possibly a Lord. In the absence of any other suspect, I suggest that it was Lord Hill who provided the funds out of his own pocket. He had commissioned the first model and he may well have felt duty bound to assist.

If this is the case then it is clear evidence that no pressure was brought to bear on Siborne to alter his first model by Wellington, or his supporters, before it went on display in October 1838. It shows instead that the establishment of the British Army paid for the first model to be completed even though it showed the Prussians much further forward and appearing to be more decisive than the later model showed them to be.

This is in direct conflict with Peter Hofschröer's claims in his book 'Wellington's smallest victory' that it was Wellington's determination to maintain the established view of the battle that

Siborne's second model showing the advance of Kempt's infantry in line behind the cavalry which has just defeated the French column.

brought such great pressure to bear on Siborne that he had to alter his model to conform to the Wellington line. Surely if this was the case then Wellington could have stopped the model from ever being seen by anyone by suggesting to Lord Hill, or whoever paid the money, that nothing should be paid.

Siborne would then have gone bust; the model would not have been finished. It would have been scrapped as an unfinished model has no value, and that would have been the end of it. That did not happen, someone paid. The model was finished with the Prussians further forward than Wellington is alleged to have liked and was then put on display in London in October 1838 in front of 100,000 visitors.

Therefore the question for you to ponder is this;-

Does the accusation that Siborne accepted money in exchange for altering his model at the behest of Wellington's camp stand up to scrutiny in the light of the fact that he did receive funds from someone but did not alter his model to suit Wellington's views?

But let us not forget that two years later he **DID** alter the model and took the Prussians off the field and three hundred yards further back. Could it be that the person who paid for the first model to be completed did not see the model nor a plan of the model before he paid the bill? Could it be that having paid the bill and

Detail from Siborne's second model showing the fine detail on the uniforms of the figures.

Siborne's second and smaller model depicting the moment of the British cavalry charge

then seen the model he was horrified by what had been produced as it showed the Prussians too far forward in his opinion? Could it be that he then brought pressure to bear on Siborne to make the alterations that he eventually made to the model in 1841?

We shall see.

Chapter Two

Siborne and his Letters

In 1891 William's second son Herbert published some 180 of the letters written to his father between 1829 and 1845. This archive contains the best eyewitness accounts together with maps showing where the various troops were at the selected time. I have read and re-read these letter dozens of times and each time revel in the detail they reveal. When I first read David Hamilton-Williams' book 'Waterloo New Perspectives' I was shocked to discover that there were not 180 letters but actually 480. The remaining 300 were in the British Library to which the whole collection was bequeathed by the Siborne family during the 1950s.

It was my plan to publish these letters on the web as documentary evidence in this trial. Then in May 2004 I discovered another book, 'Letters from the Battle of Waterloo' by Gareth Glover. I knew instantly what these were just from the title; they were the missing 300 letters, or rather 200 with a list of the other documents some of which are only the envelopes. This is an excellent book

painstakingly edited, translated and produced by Gareth Glover and published by Greenhill Books. Here was the missing evidence needed for the trial.

David Hamilton-Williams bases most of his accusations against Siborne on these missing letters. In here is the 'evidence' that proves that William Siborne sold his soul for a few coppers and corrupted history to boot.

Gareth Glover in his foreword points out that *"following recent books"* on the subject he was determined to read all of the letters in order to establish the truth.

Clearly David Hamilton-Williams' claims provided the inspiration to get the rest of the letters published by Gareth Glover and we must thank both authors for this new evidence.

David Hamilton-Williams' claims are quite alluring especially when they are backed up by the existence of documentary evidence and the support of such eminent people as the Marquess of Anglesey.

Gareth Glover on the other hand has also read the unpublished letters and cannot find any evidence to support David Hamilton-Williams' claims. I too have now read them and cannot find any evidence to support David Hamilton-Williams' claims either.

Both books are excellent reads but only one of them can be right on this point. The full argument put forward in David Hamilton-Williams' book on the cause of the rout of the French army will be examined later when we examine in detail the battle itself. But on the point of whether Siborne took bribes to alter his model we have two new books that conflict. We need to examine this issue carefully for the integrity of Siborne is challenged and even on the balance of probability he may not be guilty.

We have already established that Siborne was not influenced to change his model by whoever paid him to finish it. But there is evidence in Gareth Glover's book to suggest that he was willing to change it if the Government bought the model from him. This is contained in a letter dated 16th September 1841 to Major General Sir Henry Hardinge, Secretary of War. In this letter he says that, if the Government buys the model, he, Siborne, is prepared to change it so that the Prussians are further back from Plancenoit which he believes is in line with the "Highest military authorities" views.

This has been condemned by Gareth Glover and of course David Hamilton-Williams and Peter Hofschröer and is used as evidence of Siborne's malpractice. I see things differently. In this letter Siborne says that he is willing to amend the model to suit the views of the new owner, in this case the British Government. What he says is that "the moment the work ceases to be my property and I am no longer obliged to adhere to those impressions, I shall be most willing to make any alteration that may be suggested in this or any other respect". In other words if you buy the model it no longer represents my views but rather your views and it can be amended to suit those views, BUT they will not be my views which will remain the same as they are today. Viewed in this light Siborne's integrity seems to be intact. He would not alter the model to conflict with his own views whilst he owned it but sees no reason why someone else with different views from his should not have them displayed if they then owned the model.

This of course ensured that the model could not be sold and then changed for it would not then carry with it the all-important support of Siborne's opinion. By this time Siborne had become the leading authority on the battle. His view was of paramount importance. The offer to sell the model to the Government was rejected.

Siborne was prepared to alter the model but not, at that stage, his views.

Siborne was also in the process of writing his history of the campaign in which he explains at great length why he decided to alter the model and remove the offending Prussians from around Plancenoit.

What happened to make him change not only the model but also his valuable opinion?

The new letters contained in Gareth Glover's book do throw light on other areas of the battle not previously discovered. Most intriguing is a letter from Captain Charles Gore of the 85th Foot (letter number 175) who was an aide de camp to Sir James Kempt at the Battle. He enclosed three sketches showing the position of troops at the time of de Erlon's attack which clearly shows, not only that the Dutch Belgians of Bijlandt's Brigade were **behind** the hedged road running along the front of Wellington's position, but that they were in fact almost adjacent to the crossroads separated only by the deployment of two companies of the 95th rifles. This does conflict with other reports of the battle. Conventional reports, including Siborne's, claimed that Bijlandt deployed his troops on the forward slope in the face of the enemy and then took the full brunt of the French cannonade. This barrage so devastated them that when the French columns advanced they turned and ran away. Later reports claim that they did deploy initially on the forward slope but then moved back when the battle began.

When I built my first model of Waterloo and deployed the troops in accordance with conventional wisdom Bijlandt's Brigade stuck out like a sore thumb. The deployment made no sense at all. Wellington was only yards away at the elm tree on the crossroads. Wellington was a master of deployment and of the use of terrain. It is inconceivable that Wellington would allow a brigade to be so poorly placed until the first shots were fired. Furthermore the troops themselves would have thought it odd to be stuck out in front of the front line. Bijlandt in my view, did not deploy his troops on the forward slope but rather

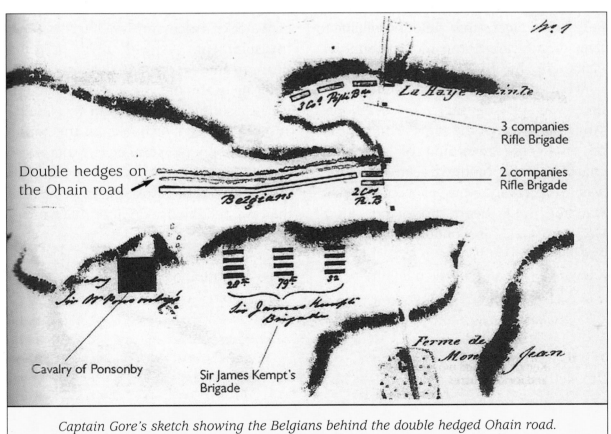

Captain Gore's sketch showing the Belgians behind the double hedged Ohain road.

behind the hedge as Gore's sketch shows from the outset.

Taken together the 380 published letters are the best collection of eyewitness accounts of any battle up until that date and probably are not surpassed until the American civil war, or maybe even until the First World War. This is a splendid archive and, largely because of the controversy raised by David Hamilton-Williams' book, the letters are now all in print for all to read and study. Together they make fascinating reading and it is only when you try to piece together the events of the day that it becomes clear that the issues are complex and do not quite tie up as you might have hoped. Siborne took the view that he had to choose who was telling the truth and who was not. This is in my view a little harsh for in fact they were all telling the truth from their own perspective. It is these differing perspectives that cause the confusion not deliberate untruths.

What is evident from the letters is that time was playing tricks on everyone. Time then was not the same as time now, or rather the recording of time has changed. Time or the tracking of time was a relatively new concept. Pocket watches had been perfected after Harrison made his wonderful clocks that assisted Captain Cook in charting the known world but that was only fifty years before. At about this time it was still not unheard of for different towns in England to have their own set time of day. Time did not have the importance it does today. There were no trains to catch or appointments to keep at certain times of day, things were slower then, more relaxed, less stressed. It is doubtful whether all officers synchronised their watches to correspond with each other. Why would they?

Orders were not always sent out with times noted on them. They did not say move your brigade to this location and arrive there at a precise time. Much is made of the timing during the battle and the campaign but it is my view that this might lead to error. If one man's watch was different from another's then they are bound to conflict as to when an event occurred. The other difference is of distance. On de Craan's map of the battle of Waterloo there are five different scale measurements. Two of these are the Prussian mile and the English mile each differing from the other by about 250 yards. Using testimony from the letters, and other letters or books on the battle, on time and distance is, therefore, fraught with danger. If we are to establish the truth or the most plausible events then we need to use another mechanism that more precisely determines what most probably happened on 18th June 1815 at Waterloo.

Chapter Three

Siborne and his History

Siborne's book entitled ***History of the War in France and Belgium in 1815*** was first published in 1844. It was later republished as the ***History of the Waterloo Campaign*** with the third edition coming out in 1848.

If he thought that his model was controversial then his book must have been a shock to the system. He was vilified by a Captain Knoop of the Netherlands army. Knoop denounced Siborne as a liar and a slanderer over his treatment of the Dutch Belgian troops in the army at Waterloo. Historians today regard Siborne's book as jingoistic and patriotic, sycophantic towards Wellington and too praiseworthy towards the British army to the detriment of both the Netherlands and Prussian armies.

The only criticism from the Prussians contained in the newly published Waterloo Letters concerns two points early in the campaign on whether Von Ziethen sent a message to Wellington early in the morning of the 15th or later in the day and whether it arrived in Brussels on the morning of the 15th or the evening. No mention is made about Plancenoit except a letter written on 15th March 1837 by Captain Wagner of the Prussian Staff who states: "There exists neither in German nor the French language a work that contains more details about the fighting in the village of Plancenoit than the description signed by you which I received."

This description must have been sent to Captain Wagner by Siborne before March 1837 and was the basis of Siborne placing the Prussian figures close to Plancenoit on the model of 1838. It would also be the basis of Siborne's history published in 1844. As these are one and the same, and as the representative of the Prussian staff praised it so much, it cannot, therefore, be the description of the action at Plancenoit that Siborne described in his book which caused offence. The controversy is the movement of the Prussian figures that took place sometime between 1838 and 1845 when it was later exhibited.

However in 1848, some three to six years after the location of the Prussians around Plancenoit was altered on the model, no fewer than five letters from the Prussian Ambassador to Britain, the Department Chief on the Prussian Staff and General von Canitz survive in the newly published 'Letters from the Battle of Waterloo' challenging the accuracy of Siborne's work. These challenges centre wholly on the actions of von Ziethen, not at Waterloo on 18th June, but rather his communications with Wellington on 15th June at the commencement of the campaign. Siborne amended his history accordingly in the third edition and states on page 36 that Wellington received the report from Ziethen at 9.00 in the morning of 15th June.

There is no complaint about the description of the action around Plancenoit on the 18th June. Nor is there any mention of von Steinmetz, Commander of the 1st Brigade of von Ziethen's Corps, attacking as described in David Hamilton-Williams' book.

Nevertheless on page 398 and 399 of the third edition of his history Siborne goes to great lengths to explain why he has altered his views on the location of the Prussians at the precise time that is depicted on the revised model of the battle. Peter Hofschröer reports that the changes were first mentioned in a letter from Francis Egerton, a politician and close adviser to Wellington, which was dated 23rd September 1842. This means that the decision to amend the location of the Prussians on the model was made between 1839 and 1842. If this is the case, and the accusation that he made the alteration in exchange for money is true, then Siborne's money worries would from that time be over. Clearly this

is not the case since as late as 1846 a Major Basil Jackson is still trying to assist Siborne in raising funds to buy the model for the nation.

There is no evidence whatsoever that proves, even on the balance of probabilities, that Siborne received money for changing the model. Peter Hofschröer claims that he did it to curry favour with the Duke of Wellington in order to oil the wheels of Government so that his model could be purchased.

Today we might consider that the expenditure of a mere £3,000 to buy such a treasure would be a trifling sum to a Government and that the Government was meanness itself not to purchase the model from Siborne. Peter Hofschröer points out in his book, 'Wellingtons Smallest Victory', that £2.2s, two guineas, then equates to several hundred pounds today. If we take several as being three then the first edition of Siborne's book would today cost £330.00. The £3,000 it cost to build the model would be a staggering £450,000 in today's terms. This is no small sum for a civil servant, even in the War Office, to approve. There was no chance of the Government buying the model with or without Wellington's support. Wellington, it should be remembered was an ex prime minister, Waterloo was his battle. Imagine Margaret Thatcher pressing the current Labour government to authorise the spending of £450,000 to build a monument to the Falklands war, or, more particularly, to the sinking of the Belgrano.

I believe that the charges made against Wellington in this regard are without substance. Peter Hofschröer has made several claims that it was Wellington who orchestrated a campaign against Siborne out of spite and that it was Wellington that stopped the money becoming available to buy the model. There is no evidence that Wellington effectively brought any influence to bear on the matter. Equally the King of Prussia had no influence either. He recommended that the model should be purchased by the Prussian Government but was over ruled on the matter by them.

Government funds are the nation's money. Governments are all about money and its expenditure. They must spend it wisely to ensure that they are not voted out of office at the next election. In the 1830s and 40s this was in even sharper focus than it is today. In those days only men, and only property owning men at that, had the vote. They were also the principal taxpayers. Can you imagine the uproar if Wellington had pressed to have the model purchased using taxpayers' money? The Opposition would have had a field day!

*"Lord Wellington has had the temerity to use some £3,000 of **our money** to buy 'for the nation' a model whose only benefit is to heap glory on Wellington himself for the victory at Waterloo."*

Wellington had to keep out of it; he would never have risked his reputation by getting involved in either promoting the model or in punishing Siborne and being confronted with this by the Government of the day.

Wellington had his enemies in the Parliament; they would have loved the prospect of throwing this up in his face. There is no direct evidence that he did interfere; only innuendo and that will not suffice.

The letters and documents in the archive and those referred to in the books mentioned deal with the issue of whether Siborne changed the model either for financial gain or because of unsavoury and undue pressure from Wellington and the British military hierarchy. There is no evidence whatsoever to show or even hint at the suggestion that Siborne took money from anyone in exchange for altering his model, absolutely none. Nor is there any credible evidence that he altered his model to curry favour with the Government. Successive Governments were indifferent to the model and what it portrayed.

I would ask you to consider therefore the following accusations and comments:

1 That William Siborne deliberately suppressed evidence and distorted the true historical events in order to enhance the British performance at the Battle of Waterloo to the detriment of the Prussian army. ***This is not substantiated by any written evidence.***

2 That William Siborne deliberately suppressed evidence and distorted the true historical events in order to enhance the British performance at the Battle of Waterloo to the detriment of the Netherlands army. ***This is equally not substantiated by any written evidence.***

3 That William Siborne committed these

acts for financial gain. ***This is certainly not true.***

4   That Sir Hussey Vivian and others paid Siborne in order to have their part, and the part played by their regiments, highlighted in the history and distorted so as to appear that their actions were greater and more decisive than they really were in fact. ***This is also not true***.

5   That the Duke of Wellington indirectly brought pressure on William Siborne to amend his model of the battle falsely to place the Prussian army further back than he originally placed them in order to make the Prussian contribution to the final victory appear less pronounced that it would otherwise have been. This is not supported by any documentary evidence ***but still might be true if the Prussians were in fact closer to Plancenoit as Siborne originally thought.***

The case for the prosecution has been best made by David Hamilton-Williams and Peter Hofschröer in their books 'Waterloo New Perspectives' and 'Wellington's Smallest Victory'. In Siborne's defence it must be said that there is no evidence in the unpublished Siborne letters to show that Siborne suppressed anything in order to enhance the British performance to the detriment of the Prussians or the Netherlands contingent of Wellington's army at the battle.

In my view there has been a lot of individual 'interpretation' and 'gap filling' by both authors in order to enhance their point of view on the battle. For example David Hamilton-Williams assumes that, because Siborne said that he was willing to alter the model **if** it was purchased by the Government, that he did in fact alter it for that financial reason. This is not the case. For whatever reason he did alter the model it was not because he was paid to do so, for the only evidence of money becoming available to him 'out of the blue' was in March April 1837 which was *before* the model was first exhibited.

There is no evidence that he suppressed evidence at all. The newly published letters do not contradict the previously published letters in any important fact, save for the letter by Captain Gore mentioned above. Nor is there any evidence that new letters exonerate the Netherlands army from the accusations made by Siborne in his history of the battle; the evidence simply is not there. Siborne acknowledges that he was harsh on the Netherlands army but says that he is only repeating the numerous eyewitness reports given to him. After all, the Dutch Belgian regiments of Bijlandt's brigade did break and run away from the French advance. It may not be politically correct today to mention it but in those days it was quite acceptable to make statements such as these. We may discover in the next section that Siborne was wrong in his assessment of the Netherlands army but we do know now that any such error was not deliberate, nor was it malicious. Siborne presented the facts as told to him by people who were there and he took them at their word and printed his history in good faith, based upon his researches.

The same is true of the Prussians. He certainly did not write in his history anything detrimental to the Prussians but rather praised them, possibly over praised them. No evidence exists to show that Siborne had evidence that he suppressed in order to cast the Prussian performance in a bad light for the sake of enhancing the British performance. Sir Hussey Vivian did support Siborne financially but there is no evidence to support the claim that Vivian then used that support to pressurize Siborne into accepting his view over others, in fact quite the reverse. In many instances he disagrees with Vivian and does not accept his version of events.

Finally where is the evidence to prove that Wellington himself brought pressure to bear on Siborne to alter the model and that he then spitefully ruined Siborne financially, by using his influence on others to boycott the book and not buy it?

Almost every famous character of the age bought Siborne's book, even the Queen herself, but not, or at least not directly, Wellington himself. If he had any influence, and we must assume that he did, then his alleged use of it was pretty ineffective if everyone ignored him and bought the book anyway.

But Siborne **DID** alter the model and it is easy to see how one might imagine that Siborne did so for his own gain. If he did not then he did it for some other reason and if we are to find out what that reason is then we need to use a method other than documentary evidence.

The testimony of the letters can only go so far to prove the truth, for in the end we have to interpret what they say and we then fall into the same trap as Siborne. Many of the letters do conflict but each tells the truth from a certain point of view. That was the truth as they saw it at the time. The Prussians in Plancenoit could not see the British on the ridge and neither could the British see what was happening on the Prussian front.

The most contemporary document of the battle is of course Wellington's Waterloo despatch. This was written during the night after the actual day of the battle when the events were fresh in Wellington's mind. This document comes under much criticism and is often almost disregarded in the debate. I have copied the despatch in Appendix 'A' of this book and I recommend that you read it with the knowledge that Wellington still had the grime of battle upon his face when he wrote it.

I suggest that if we wish to know the true, or most probable, sequence of events during the various stages of the battle then we need to construct another model, a different model, that can provide us with a clear image, minute by minute if necessary, of what happened or what most likely happened during the day of the battle.

Section Two

The Evidence from the New Model

Chapter Four

My Waterloo Model

William Siborne's models of the Battle of Waterloo are infinitely superior to mine in every respect except one. That one respect is that on my model the figures can be moved and on his they could not. A battle, like a dance as Wellington said, is a fluid affair with everything happening all of the time and at the same time.

I have re-fought the battle three times in great detail. The first time took fifty-six days at an average of three hours per day to complete, spread over a nine-month period. In these battle re-enactments I sought to determine what Napoleon was thinking throughout the day; why did he attack the way he did on that day; what was the thinking behind the great cavalry charges and why send in the Guard against Wellington when he had so much success with so few Guardsmen against the Prussians at Plancenoit?

Next I re-fought the battle without the Prussians arriving, to see whether Wellington was defeated if the Prussians did not arrive. The final battle was to see what would have happened if Napoleon had outflanked Wellington's right early in the day and had attacked through Merbe Braine Allude towards Waterloo village.

The results of these detailed re-enactments were very interesting. In the first battle a long study of the field and the deployment led me to understand that in fact Napoleon knew what he was doing in both his diversionary attack on Hougoumont and de Erlon's attack on Wellington's left and indeed during the massed cavalry charges. As will be seen this was an excellent plan well executed but which came to nothing for an equally excellent reason.

This only becomes obvious from the use of a large-scale model because a map does not show clearly the important points. The use of a model assists in understanding the actions and the decisions the Generals made on the day. It is not clear from one-dimensional plans or maps but it is clear, as we will show when the various stages of the battle are seen, in three dimensions.

My model is something of a 'T' shape

extended down the road towards Charleroi to include Rossomme and as far north to include Mont St. Jean Farm. It is 7.2 metres wide by 2.4metres to

A view of my model showing Reille's Corps deployed south of Hougoumont.

3.6metres deep. My model does differ from Siborne's in that it extends eastwards to the Bois de Paris from which the Prussians debouched in the afternoon of the battle. The model then extends westwards to include Merbe Braine Allude, which was about as far west as Wellington deployed the troops he used on the day.

The figures I have used are 25mm high, greatly over vertical scale and each represents 36 men so that the Footprint the figure covers in width is approximately equal to the ground thirty six men would occupy in a three deep line. To represent a two deep line the figures can be spread further apart. Drill regulations allow a width of two feet six inches per foot soldier and six feet per cavalry trooper to deploy. Front to back, a line will have a gap of three feet between it and the next line. Therefore a three deep line would be twelve feet from front to back; that is two feet for the first line, a three foot gap, two feet for the second line, a three foot gap and two feet for the third line. This is about four metres front to back. As the ground scale I have used is one millimetre to the yard, or metre then the fact that the foot troops occupy a depth of twelve yards instead of four is clearly wrong. This however is not so important as the frontage of the troops, which is as close to accurate as I can get. The model is definitely not perfect but it is equally imperfect for all sides. It also gives a good impression of the battlefield and I shall use the model to determine

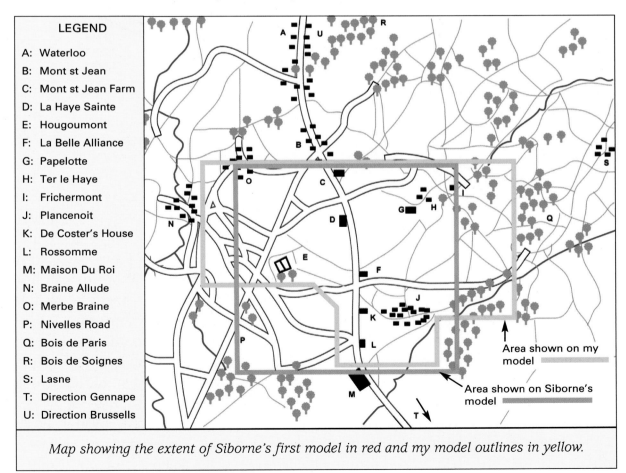

LEGEND

A: Waterloo
B: Mont st Jean
C: Mont st Jean Farm
D: La Haye Sainte
E: Hougoumont
F: La Belle Alliance
G: Papelotte
H: Ter le Haye
I: Frichermont
J: Plancenoit
K: De Coster's House
L: Rossomme
M: Maison Du Roi
N: Braine Allude
O: Merbe Braine
P: Nivelles Road
Q: Bois de Paris
R: Bois de Soignes
S: Lasne
T: Direction Gennape
U: Direction Brussells

Area shown on my model

Area shown on Siborne's model

Map showing the extent of Siborne's first model in red and my model outlines in yellow.

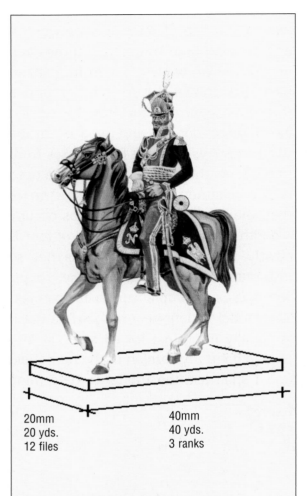

20mm
20 yds.
12 files

40mm
40 yds.
3 ranks

One cavalry figure represents 36 troopers in three ranks of twelve men. The depth of a figure is 40mm. This is grossly over scale. But in width 20mm representing 20 yards is approximately correct.

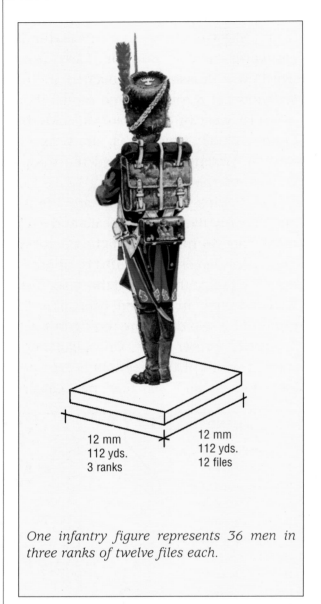

12 mm
112 yds.
3 ranks

12 mm
112 yds.
12 files

One infantry figure represents 36 men in three ranks of twelve files each.

the most likely outcome of the events of the day. The model contains some five thousand figures, all hand painted using dress uniforms rather than just greatcoats and mud, for although Wellington said "I don't care how they look but rather how they fight" they certainly look better in dress uniform than in drab greatcoats!

Every battalion of infantry, every regiment of cavalry and every artillery battery that took part in the battle is represented on the field at some time;

hopefully at the right time and the right place.

The number of troops in each army does vary from author to author. Casualties on the 16th and 17th include 'missing', many of whom would have turned up before the battle on the 18th. The charts in the army chapters (pages 74-113) detail the estimated troop strengths on the day.

The purpose of the model is to examine the testimony in order to determine the likelihood of which of the differing interpretations of the battle is the most likely to have occurred. This is important in answering the charges set out against Siborne, Wellington, Vivian and others.

If we are to agree on anything then we do need to agree on the non-contentious parts of the battle and the model.

It is generally agreed that Siborne's model was accurate in the terrain features. Therefore I have followed his maps and field layouts except that I have used a vertical scale of 1mm equals 1 foot. Therefore where it says on Siborne's plan that the ground is 150 feet high and elsewhere it says that it is 125 feet high, then on my model the former is 25mm higher than the latter. Buildings are also grossly over scale in height but they cover the same footprint that they and their surrounding gardens etc. did in reality. Therefore, whilst La Haye Sainte is over scale in height it does cover the same amount of ground that the real building, its gardens and orchards did in length but it is a bit too wide from east to west.

The second point is the number of troops in each regiment deploying at the beginning of the day. Much has been written about this but I have used 'The Waterloo Companion' written by Mark Adkin and published by Aurum Press as the basis for each regiment's strength on the day.

The third point is the initial

The centre of Wellington's line showing the farm of Mont Saint Jean at the top centre of the picture.

deployment and for this I have used Mark Adkins' deployments, except for the deployment of Bijlandt's brigade which will be explained later.

The whole length of the model shown from west to east with La Haye Sainte in the centre.

THE PURPOSE OF THE MODEL

Siborne says, in short, that it was the defeat of the Imperial Guard infantry that caused the panic and disruption of the French army. It was Wellington's counter attack, using Adam's Brigade supported by Halkett and the Hanoverian battalions, which was followed up by Vivian's cavalry charge into the centre of Napoleon's line, that caused the rout of the French army.

David Hamilton-Williams says in his book *Waterloo New Perspectives* that it was Steinmetz's 1st Brigade of Ziethen's Corps that came up out of the Smohain dip in a Prussian brigade attack column, that broke through the French line at its junction between de Erlon's and Lobau's Corps and by driving back Durutte's Division drove a wedge between these Corps, outflanking both. This caused panic to ripple along the French lines giving rise to cries of 'treason, save yourselves' and 'The Prussians!' and it was this action that caused the French rout, destroying Napoleon's army utterly.

This view is supported by Peter Hofschröer in his book '*The Waterloo Campaign*' *The German Victory*, together with the view that at the same time as the attack of the Imperial Guard on Wellington's line, Bulow's Corps broke through at Plancenoit. This break through was also a major cause of the French rout.

So we have two diametrically opposed views on what happened at the end of the battle of Waterloo. Siborne is no longer here to defend his version. The opposed views have caused an expansion of the accusations into a *crime* against history, accusations of fraud for financial gain and the deliberate suppression of evidence.

The fundamental question that we hope to answer using the model is :-

Did Siborne move the 40,000 Prussian troops back from Plancenoit on his model because:

He had been persuaded, as he claims in the third edition of his history of the Waterloo campaign, that it was right that the Prussians were further back from Plancenoit than he previously thought?

Or

Were the Prussians in the position he originally thought they were and he moved them back against his better judgement because of pressure from Wellington and other senior British Army officers and politicians?

Whether he changed the position of the Prussian troops for financial gain has, I believe, already been thoroughly examined. You must decide whether this accusation is proven or not.

Remember it is you, the reader, who has the final say on the true or most probable outcome and you can post your opinion on the website in order to influence the final verdict.

I hope to set out the known facts and trust that the clarity of the model will show what did actually happen, or what most probably happened, on that eventful day in June 1815.

Chapter Five

The Approach to Battle

'There is nothing more risky than a battle' quoted Wellington. He and any other General in charge of an army does well to keep this in mind. A battle should only be fought for very specific reasons. In all other cases it should be avoided if possible. Salamanca is a good example of this. For three days the two armies of Wellington and Marmot marched and counter marched in order to gain a victory without an engagement. It was only when Wellington saw a huge gap open up in the French line of march that he could see the opportunity of a victory with minimum loss. He launched his attack and 'defeated forty thousand men in forty minutes'.

The reason for the battle of Waterloo being fought was a coming together of the perceived opportunity for success at the same time in the minds of Napoleon, Blucher and Wellington. It was not to protect Brussels that Wellington fought the battle, the **_army in being_** was more important than the city of Brussels, Nor was Napoleon fighting for possession of the city. A city is of no use if the enemy army is still in the field, as he learnt to his cost in Moscow.

Wars are essentially fought over resources, not religion, not ideals, not territory, just resources. One might consider that territory is a worthy cause for a war but it is not the territory that is worth fighting over; only the resources that can be exploited in that territory. From Napoleon's point of view he wanted peace and to trade but obviously on his terms. These were for him to be recognised as the legitimate Emperor of the French and then to be left in peace to trade with the rest of the world as he saw fit.

From everyone else's point of view, including a significant number of French men and women, they wanted the restoration of a monarchy. The Bourbons were conveniently in line of succession; their parliament was elected in some semi-democratic way. The rest of the world wanted to deal with France on equal terms without the risk of a French army coming to negotiate trade terms with them at bayonet point.

Napoleon's re-capture of France in March 1815 was most remarkable. It was not just chance that it happened. It was planned by Napoleon, 'a coup d' état' carried out with meticulous skill, both political and military, that resulted in his resuming his role as Emperor of the French on 20th March. It had taken less than three weeks to capture a whole country, and he did it without a shot being fired by his troops or a casualty suffered. Between 21st March and 14th June he raised a considerable army. Part of this became the *Armee Du Nord*, which he would lead into Belgium to attack Wellington and Blucher.

The allies, Britain, Prussia, Austria, Russia, Sweden, Spain, Portugal (and a host of others) joined forces with one single aim, to rid the world once and for all of Napoleon's influence on world affairs. These countries raised armies of over a million men at enormous cost in order to achieve their objective. Their strategy was the same as in the previous year, mass the armies on the borders of France, march on Paris, restore the Bourbon Government and capture or kill Napoleon at the same time.

From Napoleon's point of view he needed to defeat each army in detail before they crushed him with their numerical superiority. Strategy in war, as

A view of the model showing the village of Plancenoit before the fighting began. At the top of the picture are the backs of light cavalry of the Guard as they face north towards Wellington's line.

one American general once said, is all about getting there 'the fastest with the mostest'. If Napoleon could use the advantage of his central position, working on interior lines of communication to move his troops from one front to another defeating each enemy in turn before they could combine their efforts, then he would win. Equally the allies using their advantage of working on exterior lines could control more resources than Napoleon and should in the long run win by this strategy.

This strategy worked in 1814. Napoleon defeated each army tactically but not strategically. He won each battle but the allies simply withdrew away from him and advanced elsewhere where he was not present. When he rushed across the land to confront the new menace, those he had just defeated advanced on Paris again. This went on until Paris, and then Napoleon, fell in the spring of 1814.

Now Napoleon believed he had the chance to defeat decisively both the Anglo allied army of the Netherlands and the Prussian army of the lower Rhine long before the Austrians and Russians could enter the field. Defeating England was his main aim. If he could defeat the *English army,* (which had more Scots, Welsh, Irish and Germans in it than English), then it was quite conceivable that Castlereagh's Government would fall. This would end their roles as the paymaster of European coalitions created to oust Napoleon from power. Napoleon thought that he could then sue for a peace on his terms, making concessions where necessary, and remaining in power for the foreseeable future.

The allies of course would have none of it; they wanted him out and would spend whatever it took to achieve that aim. But Napoleon did not know this. Or if he did then he ignored it. For him to accept it was to accept ultimate defeat.

Wellington was duly appointed to command the army of the Netherlands stationed in Belgium. Blucher was chosen to command the army of the Lower Rhine assembling on the Belgium border. All was set for the battle to commence. Napoleon was trapped by his political aims into seeking a battle and the sooner the better. The Anglo-Prussian armies were sitting and waiting for the Austrians and Russians, Spanish and Portuguese to advance in order to repeat the 1814 strategy of numerical superiority. Neither Wellington nor Blucher wanted to fight a battle if they could possibly avoid it. They did not need to risk a battle as in the end numbers would tell and win the war for them. If battle were joined then it would have to be on extremely advantageous terms or be unavoidable in order to make the risk worthwhile.

It is no easy task to bring to the battlefield an enemy army that does not want to fight. Napoleon had this problem to overcome; if he attacked and they retreated then he might not be able to catch them. Napoleon had to find something to force, or entice them to fight. That something was not the defence of a city but the enticement of the prospect of defeating Napoleon in the field by allowing the allied armies a combined numerical superiority over him.

Napoleon planned to separate and

defeat each in detail by having a local numerically superior French army. Napoleon therefore had to deploy an army of only 125,000 men against a combined Anglo-Prussian army of 215,000 men. His plan was to attack at the very junction of the two armies and keep one busy with a smaller proportion of his army whilst the bulk of his troops defeated the other army. He could then turn on the remaining enemy army and deploy a numerically superior force to ensure victory. This was classic Napoleon. He was the master of the battlefield and his opponents were ideally placed to be defeated in this classic manner.

In this respect Belgium for the allies was a poor choice for a theatre of operations. It was small and flat with no natural barriers to the advance of an enemy army. Nor was there a position such as the lines of Torres Vedras in Portugal behind which Wellington was able to wait in comfort throughout the winter of 1810/11, whilst Massena starved on the other side of this impregnable series of defensive lines he had created for just such a purpose. What if Napoleon did drive between the allied armies and defeated each in turn? The Prussians would be forced back into Prussia and could be pursued as they were after Jena in 1806. This would have destroyed the Prussian army of the lower Rhine. Equally if this were achieved then Wellington would be forced back to the coast in a rehearsal of the Dunkirk evacuation of 1940.

Both Wellington and Blucher could only be forced to fight, and then be defeated, if Napoleon attacked them at the junction of each army and drove them apart but only then if he used a numerically inferior force. It would not work to attack the outer flanks of each army, that is the Eastern flank of the Prussians or the Western flank of the Anglo Netherlands army. That would simply cause the army attacked to withdraw to link up with the other allied force. Equally it would not work if Napoleon attacked with an army of equal strength. The allies would have declined the invitation to join in battle.

The Anglo-Prussians armies had to be convinced that they had a real chance of defeating Napoleon by being able to combine their forces and use their numerical advantage to overcome Napoleon's superior quality army. As it turned out the army of the Netherlands proved to be equal to the task, man for man, principally because of Wellington's tactical brilliance. But on paper it looked like the allies would need a numerical advantage of at least 1.5 to 1 to stand a chance of winning a set piece battle against the greatest commander of the age, Napoleon Bonaparte.

Estimates of the size of the armies at the beginning of the campaign do vary slightly but in general they comprised 116,000 to 125,000 French against 116,000 Prussians and 106,000 Anglo Netherlands troops. Napoleon was therefore outnumbered by almost two to one. Why did Napoleon only take with him into Belgium 125,000 or less troops when he had another 150,000 available in France? Why not 150,000 or 175,000 or even 200,000 men? The reasons cannot be because he could not arm that many or could not assemble that many or could not control that many troops. Of course he could. Nor is it the case that he needed the troops on the frontiers to defend against the Austrians and Russians for they would not be on the French frontier for another two months. So why so few?

It was a planned and calculated number of men Napoleon felt was large enough to defeat each army in detail and yet was small enough to tempt both Blucher but more especially Wellington into accepting battle in the hope that their numerical superiority would be sufficient to ensure a victory. Never mind Brussels, or Antwerp, it was the annihilation of the enemy armies that Napoleon sought as a strategic aim. From my studying of the event I think that he deliberately chose an army of small enough size to tempt the opposition into accepting battle where he was confident that he could defeat each in turn.

To support this idea Siborne lists in his book, appendix X (see below).

This is very detailed information released or discovered just before the commencement of hostilities. I would

---

Appendix X

'The strength of the French Army according to information received at the Prussian headquarters shortly before the commencement of hostilities.'

This list is quite detailed and accurate giving the following information;

1st Corps under D'Erlon at Lille	22,000 men
2nd Corps under Reille at Valenciennes	24,000 men
3rd Corp under Vandamme at Mezieres	18,000 men
4th Corps under Gerard at Thionville	16,000 men
6th Corps under Lobau at Laon	14,000 men
Imperial Guard under Mortier in Paris	21,000 men
The 4 corps of reserve cavalry	15,000 men
	———————
	130,000 men
	———————

suggest that this was not gleaned by a spy although Fouche or Talleyrand would no doubt have been willing to give out this information. But rather it looks to me as though Napoleon released the information in order to tempt Blucher and Wellington into accepting battle on the frontier of France and Belgium. Just suppose the report had said that Napoleon's army was another 100,000 men stronger and was deployed both further east and west of the above positions. In this case would Wellington and Blucher have stayed in Belgium or retreated eastwards to link up with the Russians and Austrians? We will probably never know but whatever the reason it was a gamble based upon his confidence in his and his army's ability to defeat both Blucher and Wellington on the field of battle.

In any event Napoleon marched north with an army of 125,000 men to fight two armies with a combined strength of 226,000 men. Blucher and Wellington had decided, possibly because of, or partly because of, the above information, to stand and fight in Belgium close to the frontier and they intended to combine their armies and defeat Napoleon in the field.

Napoleon drove through Charleroi and pushed the Prussian 1st Corps away from the river Sambre towards Gilly where a small action took place. The Prussian's 1st Corps under the command of General Ziethen then withdrew towards Fleurus to join up with the rest of the Prussian army, which was concentrating along the Ligny stream in the villages that straddled this small brook.

At the same time the French left wing advanced on Quatre Bras and was engaged and stopped by Saxe Weimar's Netherlands Division. The following day, 16th June, the battles of both Ligny and Quatre Bras took place. It is not in the scope of this work to offer a detailed study of either action. In summary, after a difficult fight and with Blucher himself unhorsed and injured, the Prussians withdrew north towards Wavre. At Quatre Bras Wellington's army arriving piecemeal managed by the skin of their teeth to drive off every attack Marshal Ney made on his position. At the end of the day Wellington's strength was greater than Ney's and he was therefore able to hold his position.

Three controversial incidents took place during this period.

Firstly there is the matter of Wellington's despatch claiming that he did not receive news of the French advance against the Prussian's until the evening of the 15th June. It was for this reason that he could not despatch his troops towards Quatre Bras until early on the 16th. Ziethen was adamant that he had despatched a rider at 4.30am by his watch. No matter how slowly he rode from around Fleurus to Brussels he certainly got there before 9.00pm. In fact all of the evidence shows that he got there by 9.00am and that Wellington was aware that the French had attacked across the Sambre by early to mid morning on 15th June. Wellington was clearly not, however, ready to commit his forces towards the Charleroi area and Quatre Bras without first knowing what was happening further west towards Mons. When Wellington said that Napoleon had humbugged him what did he mean? Was it that Napoleon had also released information to the effect that the Charleroi attack was a feint and that the real attack would come via Mons, thereby cutting Wellington off from Ostend, a route out of Belgium if all else failed? Whatever the reason, Wellington was accused of not telling the truth in his Waterloo despatch when he said that he did not know of the attack until the evening of the 15th; he might have known in the morning.

The second incident was the movement of de Erlon's Corps marching back and forth between the battles of Ligny and Quatre Bras. This was a disaster for the French and was caused by arrogance on the part of Ney and poor communication on the part of Napoleon. Ney, the bravest of the brave, a Marshal of France, countermanded Napoleon's order to de Erlon to march from Quatre Bras to Ligny. Ney's arrogance at having his subordinate given a direct order from an aide de camp of the Emperor's without first clearing it with Ney himself caused de Erlon's Corps to march uselessly between the battlefields. Napoleon's failure to impress on Ney the importance of pushing the two opposing armies apart (although Ney should have known this himself) aggravated the problem. Had de Erlon continued to advance on the Prussian right flank from the direction of Quatre Bras there is no doubt that Blucher would have had to retreat and retreat towards Namur not Wavre, thereby separating the two armies as Napoleon had planned.

The third incident was that during the night of 16th/17th June a messenger, Major Graf Winterfeld, was sent by von Gneisenau, Prussian chief of staff, to Wellington with the news of the Prussian defeat and their withdrawal towards Wavre. On the way Winterfeld ran into some French soldiers who shot and severely wounded him. The message did not get through although Winterfeld managed to escape capture and make his way to Wavre. This does not ring true at all. If the information sent was important enough why was only one messenger sent? Furthermore the wounded Winterfeld was unable to ride the five to eight kilometres from the Prussian's position to deliver the message and get medical assistance but chose instead to fail in his mission and then ride 16 to 20 kilometres north to Wavre, bleeding all of the way, to get medical aid.

When Wellington knew the truth his face turned stony in anger. It was clear to him that Gneisenau had used Wellington to cover his retreat by not informing him. With Wellington left at Quatre Bras as bait, Gneisenau knew that the Prussian army stood a better chance of escape than it would if their allies were retreating as well. Wellington was now in a fix. He faced the full might of Napoleon's army in a position that was not a particularly good one. He had a village and a stream in his rear across his line of retreat through which his army would have to defile. It was likely that whilst retreating through the bottleneck he would be engaged and cut to pieces.

The French were not however in a rush. They were cooking breakfast. Wellington slipped away whilst maintaining a bold front, until suddenly Napoleon himself appeared on the skyline and forced a frantic flight to take place. Divine intervention in the form of a massive thunderstorm came to Wellington's rescue. The downpour was almost tropical; nothing like it had been seen before except for those troops who had seen action in India, The storm brought the pursuit effectively to an end. Both armies slithered into their respective positions drenched to the bone and in no way looking for a fight that night.

Chapter Six

Napoleon's and Wellington's Plans for the Battle

As dawn broke on the morning of 18th June the sodden bivouacs of both armies came slowly to life. Fires were lit using whatever was available. It was unfortunate that someone decided that the western wooden gate to La Haye Sainte would be better used to dry his clothes than defend the farm and cut it up for firewood. It took time to dry out men and equipment. This would delay the battle's start until sometime around 11.30am. Much is made of this and Napoleon is often much criticised for delaying the battle until that time. Jac Weller in his book 'on Waterloo' gives the clearest explanation of why Napoleon could not attack earlier. His troops were still strung out down the Charleroi road almost all the way back to Quatre Bras.

During the rain-soaked previous night Napoleon had stood on the Rossomme heights and surveyed the battlefield. In the rain and gloom of evening he decided upon his plan of battle. Here again Napoleon is much criticised for the battle plan he used at Waterloo.

"Napoleon should have manoeuvred to the left and outflanked Wellington's position in the west."

This plan does not work. I have tried it out on the model.

The problem is that Wellington's position is so well thought out for defence. Between Hougoumont and Braine Allude is a frontal battlefield with a strongpoint at either end, which funnels an attacking force into the centre right into the mouths of the cannons and musket lines of Wellington's finest troops. Furthermore the 17,000 troops at Hal would be in the rear of such an attacking force making any such attack fraught with danger.

"Napoleon should have concentrated his forces on his right and driven Wellington westward by attacking through Papelotte and Smohain then driving him westward towards his ships and back to England."

This was not good enough for Napoleon's strategic needs. If Wellington and Blucher escaped back to their respective countries they could be re-equipped and sent back into the fight. Napoleon needed a battle of annihilation that destroyed Wellington's army, his reputation and even his life so that it was not possible for the British to interfere directly in the war again. To achieve a battle of annihilation Napoleon had to make a frontal attack, smashing his way through Wellington's line then sending the heavy cavalry left and right to disperse his forces. Wellington's army would be an army no more, just a clutter of scattered units with no hope of reorganising into an effective force. When you consider this as Napoleon's aim then his plan makes perfect sense. His plan was simple. Clearly Wellington was nervous about his right, western, flank as this was heavily defended. Napoleon decided to pin his right with an attack on Hougoumont, then mass his cannon and drive through Wellington's left centre with de Erlon's, and possibly Lobau's, Corps; establish himself on the Mont St. Jean plateau and then scatter Wellington's forces from front and flank with the cavalry and the Guard. It is a splendid plan. It is the only plan that works to fulfil his strategic aim and it very nearly worked out for him.

The plan is however much criticised and in particular the attack on Hougoumont with Jerome's and then Foy's Divisions is seen as being a

British horse artillery deployed on the retreat from Quatre Bras to the Waterloo position.

mistake. Equally de Erlon's attack is regarded as a mistake but in fact it was well planned, even down to the use of columns. It was also well supported by cavalry on both flanks and was preceded by the biggest artillery barrage even the most experienced of Wellington's troops had ever witnessed.

No wonder Napoleon was confident of success on the morning of 18th June. Even the rumour of the Prussian advance to Waterloo, gleaned from the waiter in the hotel Roi de Espagne, did not alarm him. It did not even matter about the weather and the late start, the affair would be nothing more than a picnic, pin Wellington's right, crush his left centre, scatter his reserve on the Mont St. Jean plateau and drive the remainder of his force westward into the sea.

It would only take three to four hours to win the battle. By 3.30pm he would be driving Wellington towards the sea and if the Prussians dared to risk approaching him from the east, strung out on poor roads for ten miles or more, then more fool them for they would also be crushed by a lightning advance right down their throats. Such an eventuality was nonsense. Blucher was not mad enough to try it. It would be a picnic, over by mid afternoon.

Across the battlefield, a mere 2,000 yards away, stood Wellington. His view of the affair was very different from Napoleon's.

Wellington had studied the French system of war before he went to Portugal to fight them there. His view was that before a battle had begun in earnest Napoleon had already won a great victory. He had established his moral ascendancy over the battlefield. "On the field of battle his hat is worth 40,000 men". This neat remark sums up the reputation of Napoleon throughout the Napoleonic wars. His tactics echoed this reputation. His battles opened in the main with a concentrated artillery barrage on one sector of the enemy line. At the same time Tirailleurs (French light infantry) crept forward to close range with the enemy line and picked off the officers and sergeants thereby disrupting the 'command and control' of the enemy army. Next came the impressive columns of infantry, drums playing, troops cheering, muskets popping and bayonets gleaming, the Napoleonic equivalent of 'shock and awe'.

To an enemy line already showing great and bloody gaps where the round-shot had smashed their way through flesh and bone, with officers wounded or dead and even sergeants out of action, the sight of a solid block of enemy troops confident of victory and marching straight towards 'you personally' was often enough to make the whole line break and run away. Once this happened, and it might take a volley from the column followed up by a bayonet charge to make it happen, the heavy cavalry burst into the gap and attacked left and right cutting up the remaining troops and driving the enemy army into ruin and defeat.

Now of course it did not happen like this every time and often they had a real fight on their hands, but overall the French had won many more times than they had lost and their reputation as gods of war was on the whole well deserved; everywhere that is except in Spain and

Portugal when they had faced a British army under Wellington.

Wellington and General Moore, who died at the battle of Corunna in northern Spain, had devised the antidote to the French system in battle. In the first instance they placed their troops on a reverse slope, behind a hill. This meant that the solid iron round-shot passed over their heads causing little harm. Secondly they deployed their own light infantry in front of the infantry line to stop the French Tirailleurs from doing their job. Finally the British infantry Commanders had developed the two deep line and had trained their troops to fire faster and more accurately than the French. In a column versus line duel the British had come off best every time. The British two deep line was just as much a psychological formation as was the column.

A French officer vividly described facing it in battle. In this instance the French column advanced from a thousand yards away from the line with much shouting, drumming and firing of muskets into the air. The British line was impassive, unimpressed by the storm that was about to break upon them. As the French closed on the British their nerves began to jangle. Why are the British so confident? They seemed

French column attacking a non British infantry line.

French light infantry pick off officers and NCOs weakening the line before the solid block of infantry smash through scattering the enemy left and right.

unmoved, their muskets at the port position, everyone began talking at once wondering what was going to happen. Then as they got even closer there was a shout from the British line and the muskets came down to the fire position in a single well-drilled movement. Now the French were anxious; it seemed as though every musket was aimed at 'you personally' but still the British did not fire. More anxiety in the French column, for god's sake fire, the waiting is intolerable, and then another shout, Fire!

The British army fired its muzzle-loaded muskets by platoon, starting at the left hand company and ending with the right hand grenadiers of the battalion. The idea was that by the time the grenadiers fired, the first platoon had re-loaded and was ready to fire again. Thus the firing was continuously rolling from one end of the line to the other. British infantry could load and fire three rounds a minute. The guards and some line battalions could manage four rounds. Six hundred men in a two deep line had a frontage of 250 yards and would fire 1,800 rounds a minute. That is equivalent to three modern machine guns each firing 600 rounds a minute. The concentration of firepower was enormous, although the accuracy was very poor.

French column attacking a British line of infantry.
The line has been protected from enemy fire by being hidden behind a reverse slope of a hill. British light infantry have forced the French skirmishers to fall back leaving the column to face the full force of a two deep line firing three to four rounds per minute.

Even so, as many as 100 men could fall in the first volley and their bodies caused more confusion and panic in the French column. Another volley, and then another would bring the column to a halt and then a cheer from the British line followed by a screaming charge scattered the column at the point of the bayonets.

Now of course it did not work that way every time. Often the line did not appear until the last minute, which was even more startling to the attackers. But what did work every time was that the disciplined volleys from well trained troops brought the column to a confused halt, which was then easily broken by a well timed bayonet charge. Wellington

was therefore confident that if he could induce or force Napoleon to attack him frontally then his superior tactics would drive away the French columns every time. What he now needed was a battlefield that delivered this vital condition.

The battlefield of Waterloo is remarkable in that it does not look much to the untrained eye. It is not marked by steep hills or outstanding features, deep rivers or impassable terrain. It is a series of gently rolling fields intersected by two main roads and crossed by a few cart tracks. Three major buildings stand out as bastions. But these are domestic farm buildings, not military fortifications, and

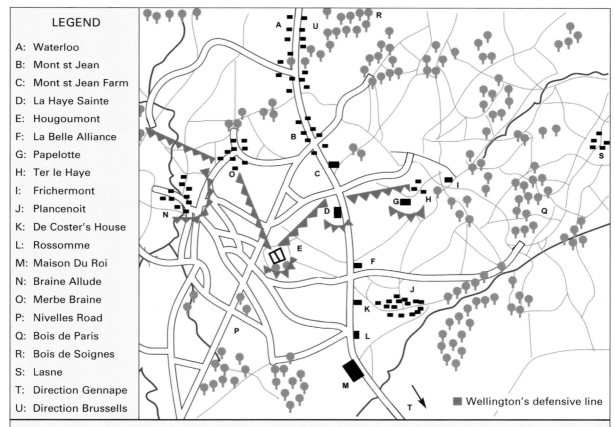

LEGEND

A: Waterloo
B: Mont st Jean
C: Mont st Jean Farm
D: La Haye Sainte
E: Hougoumont
F: La Belle Alliance
G: Papelotte
H: Ter le Haye
I: Frichermont
J: Plancenoit
K: De Coster's House
L: Rossomme
M: Maison Du Roi
N: Braine Allude
O: Merbe Braine
P: Nivelles Road
Q: Bois de Paris
R: Bois de Soignes
S: Lasne
T: Direction Gennape
U: Direction Brussells

■ Wellington's defensive line

Map showing the strength of the Waterloo position. Outflanking to the west is not possible and to the east is too boggy. Only a frontal assault is possible. If the chosen field had been further south with its left on Plancenoit then its right could have been outflanked. Rumours that Wellington chose the more southerly field cannot be correct.

they could easily be reduced to rubble by the French artillery. It was said that the field was actually selected by de Lancey, Wellington's chief of staff. Although Wellington had seen the battlefield in the previous year he is supposed to have chosen the French ridge with La Belle alliance as the centrepiece of the battlefield rather than La Haye Sainte. I find this difficult to accept.

The field from La Belle Alliance to Genappe does not offer the 'vital condition' Wellington needed to ensure that the French made a frontal assault on his line. The battlefield would be too wide. From west of the Nivelles road to the Lasne brook east of Plancenoit is a distance of some three miles as opposed to the two-mile front of the more northern position. Furthermore this width would bring into play the roads from Nivelles to Mont St Jean and the road from Nivelles to Hal, thus widening the right flank of Wellington's army and opening it up to a tactical manoeuvre much more easily than the actual battlefield chosen. The strength of the Waterloo position is that no matter what Napoleon does he must, at the crucial moment, come face to face with Wellington's infantry line. Look at the map on page 61. If Napoleon manoeuvres to his left, westwards, and outflanks Hougoumont he then comes face to face with a line drawn from Braine Allude to Hougoumont. If he moves further northwest then the line is drawn from the Forest de Soignes to Braine Allude.

Wellington therefore had little fear of a tactical outflanking manoeuvre but he was concerned about a strategic manoeuvre through Hal towards Brussels.

Nothing much is ever said about the Hal force, except that it was a mistake for Wellington to deploy so many troops seventeen miles west of the main battlefield. This was not a mistake. Wellington's Waterloo despatch clearly shows that he thought that he was facing almost all of Napoleon's army at Waterloo.

"The enemy collected his army, with the exception of the third corps, which had been sent to observe Marshal Blucher...."
Waterloo Despatch.

Clearly Wellington thought that he was not only facing the army that actually fought at Waterloo but also Gerard's Infantry Corps and Exelmans' 2nd Cavalry Corps. Wellington was confident enough to face an extra 12,000 infantry and 5,000 cavalry than he actually had to on the day.

If you look at the map on page 63 you will notice that there is a road that runs from Genappe to Nivelles then north to Hal and further west to Braine le Comte. From Braine le Comte there is a road that runs north to Tubize and Hal. Tubize controls the crossing of the rivers Senne and Senette and Hal controls the only other crossing of the river Senne further north from Tubize. The road through both Tubize and Hal heading north runs right into Brussels and is therefore the only practical route that outflanks the Waterloo position. If you wish to outflank the Hal and Tubize position then you would have to march further west to Enghien. That is just too far for a detached force to be certain of achieving a strategic outflanking manoeuvre within

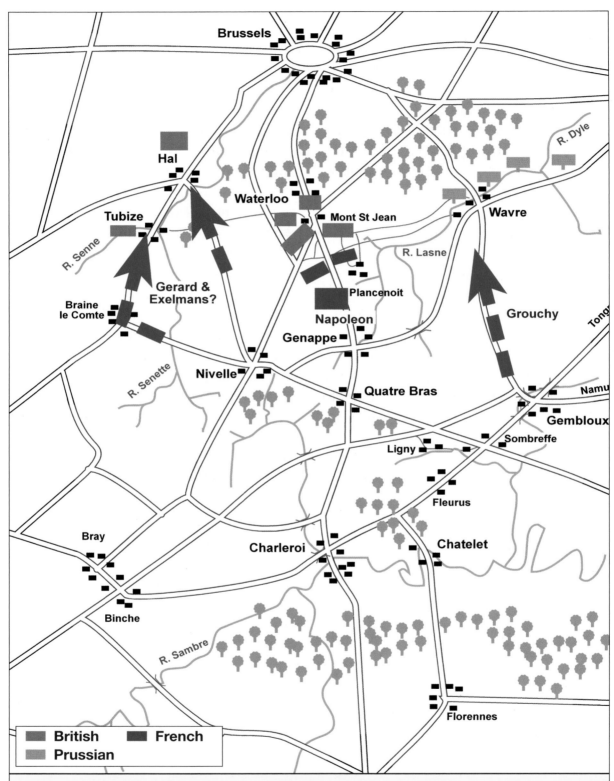

Wellington's nightmare was for the French to position a corps at Hal and Tubize thereby cutting him off from the sea, whilst Exelmans' Cavalry Corps moved on Brussels cutting off his northern escape route. This was why 17,000 troops were left defending the eastern route to the sea at Hal and Tubize where they could also forestall any move on the capital.

the day's battle time frame. Wellington placed 17,000 men and 28 guns at Hal and Tubize to forestall any expected outflanking manoeuvre by Napoleon with a proportion of his army, perhaps the corps of infantry and a corps of cavalry Wellington actually thought he was facing.

Could Napoleon have outflanked Wellington's position to the east? Look at the map again. To the east the roads run west to east not south to north. Furthermore we know that the roads were in poor condition and the Lasne valley was a boggy swamp because of the overnight rain. There was no point in an outflanking manoeuvre to the east as this would bog down the French troops in a position of little tactical value and even less chance of battlefield success.

In any event Napoleon would have to make a frontal assault on Wellington's position with battlefronts of one thousand yards or less between the outposts of Papelotte, La Haye Sainte,

Hougoumont, Merbe Braine, Braine Allude and the Forest de Soignes. If, however, either La Haye Sainte or Hougoumont fell into French hands then the battlefronts would open up to two thousand yards or more. This would increase the possibility of a local tactical flank attack on part of the line, which could open up a gap to allow the cavalry through. The vital defensive positions were therefore Hougoumont and La Haye Sainte. It is perhaps fitting in light of the accusations about whether it was a German or British victory to ponder on the fact that Hougoumont was principally defended by British troops supported by some Nassaus and Hanoverians. La Haye Sainte was principally defended by the King's German Legion, Nassaus and Hanoverians supported outside the farm by the 95th Rifles. Clearly Wellington had as much faith in his good quality German troops as he had in his good quality British troops.

Chapter Seven

Blucher and the Decision of the Century

Wellington said that Blucher's decision to retreat north to Wavre from the defeat at the battle of Ligny was the most decisive decision of the age. I am not so sure about that. The decision was made by Gneisenau, Blucher's Chief of Staff, as Blucher was recovering from his fall from his horse when the French dragoons rode over him at the end of the battle of Ligny.

Let us look at the decision he made.

Napoleon had attacked on 15th June arriving at Charleroi, which was effectively the junction between the two armies of Prussia and the Netherlands. The Prussians were driven back north-eastwards and took up a position along the Ligny brook occupying the villages of Wagnalee, Le Haye, Ligny, Tongrenelle, Boignee and Balatre. Behind the brook the main Prussian forces deployed in full view of the French artillery, which numbered 230 guns. The battlefield of Ligny extends to nearly six miles from east to west and on this field Blucher deployed 83,000 men and 224 guns. This is a ratio of 14,000 men and 37 guns to

the mile. If we compare this to Wellington's deployment at Waterloo we see that Wellington managed to concentrate 30,000 men and 75 guns to the mile, more than twice that of the Prussians at Ligny.

Against the Prussians at Ligny Napoleon deployed 63,000 men and 230 guns.

Remember our American general who once said that strategy was getting there the 'fastest with the mostest': In other words it is the concentration of forces at the decisive point that wins battles. Wellington visited Blucher on 16th June before the battle began and he commented that if Blucher fought there on that battlefield then he would be 'damnably mauled'.

Blucher's army was more than 30% larger than Napoleon's. Furthermore Blucher had taken up a defensive position and the French would have to attack and winkle him out of his fortified villages along the Ligny brook, before they could get to grips with the main Prussian force deployed in the rear of the defensive front line. Normally it is reckoned you need to have a numerical superiority of three to one if you wish to be certain of success when attacking a fortified position. Napoleon had an overall inferiority but was able to concentrate his forces around the village of Ligny faster than Blucher could and did gain a local superiority of 1.5 to 1 at this decisive point.

In the later stages of the battle Blucher, in desperation, ordered a cavalry charge, which was countered, by the French and Blucher himself was knocked from his horse and ridden over by the French cavalry.

Prussian losses were horrendous. Between 20,000 to 25,000 troops and 22 guns were lost. This includes an estimate of 10,000 deserters who fled east towards Namur. It was nearly much worse. At the climax of the battle Napoleon had ordered that de Erlon's Corps, which was under the command of Marshal Ney who was engaged with Wellington at Quatre Bras, should march east along the old roman road and attack the right flank of Blucher's army. Just as they appeared on the battlefield an enraged Ney sent a message to de Erlon ordering him to return to Quatre Bras. Despite the presence of one of Napoleon's aide de camps de Erlon duly obeyed the order from Ney and turned around and marched back westward. Napoleon was furious. He had seen the approach of de Erlon's corps and was confident that the Prussian army would be virtually annihilated. Furthermore, had de Erlon attacked the right flank of the Prussian army then the retreat away from this attack, combined as it would

have been with the attack of the Guard at Ligny, would have to have been towards the east and not the north. This would have effectively prevented Blucher from retreating on Wavre and thereby maintaining contact with Wellington.

Ney's reason for ordering de Erlon back towards Quatre Bras? The order had been given directly from Napoleon via his aide de camp to de Erlon himself and not through Ney, the proper channel of communication. Ney was affronted and in that fit of pique robbed Napoleon of his best chance of winning the campaign outright. Two days later at Waterloo Ney himself would ignore the proper channels of communication and give orders directly to the brigade or divisional commander for the cavalry to move forward. When challenged about the lines of communication he roared at the underling "The salvation of France is at stake!" Pity he did not say that to himself on the 16th.

Further Prussian losses in effective men were suffered over the next day or so as scattered units failed to re-group. This reduced the effective strength of the Prussian army from 116,000 men under arms on the 15th to 80,000 on 18th June. Worse still in fact, for 30,000 of the effective Prussian troops came from Von Bulow's 4th Corps who took no part in the battle of Ligny. Therefore, after the battle of Ligny, Gneisenau had a reduced and disorganised army of some 50,000 men which had been driven north from the battlefield. He had to decide on what to do next in light of what was best for Prussia and its army.

Gneisenau was distrustful of Wellington. After all, he claimed, the

Prussians had only fought at Ligny on the promise of the support of 20,000 allied troops coming from the west to bolster the Prussian right flank. Wellington did not keep his promise and the Prussians were defeated. This of course is just scapegoat hunting. The Prussians lost the battle of Ligny because they deployed their army badly over too wide a battlefront. This allowed the French to gain a local tactical superiority and defeat them. But having suffered such a defeat Gneisenau was feeling somewhat aggrieved. He was all for retreating towards Liege and linking up with the Prussian corps under Kleist which was posted in Luxembourg. Blucher, although injured, was adamant that they should maintain contact with Wellington. But it was Gneisenau's own Chief of Staff, Karl von Grolmann, who persuaded Gneisenau that Wavre was the best place to head for.

At Wavre they could link up with von Bulow's 4th Corps, 30,000 men, and use that corps as the vanguard on which the rest of the army could rally. From Wavre they could still retreat east to Prussia if necessary or march west to Wellington if they were confident that the British were going to fight the French. If they chose to retreat eastward from Ligny then the option of supporting Wellington was lost. They could only re-group and then face Napoleon alone or link up with the Austrians and Russians further south sometime later if, that is, the war was not over by then. Despite his chagrin over the loss of the battle and his suspicion of Wellington, Gneisenau decided to march north and concentrate on Wavre thereby keeping his options open. To assist in his

disengagement from Napoleon he contrived to keep Wellington's army at Quatre Bras for as long as possible, in order to tempt Napoleon to attack Wellington there so that the Prussians could get clean away. The officer sent with the despatch informing Wellington von Muffling, (the only despatch sent by Gneisenau), was wounded and then retreated north so the message never got through.

One must wonder whether the message was ever sent at all. Or if it was it was not intended to arrive. For if such a message was important, and clearly it was, then why send only one courier? Nevertheless the trick worked for Wellington was unaware that the Prussians had been defeated on the 16th at Ligny and was in his own mind preparing to make a joint attack on the French with the Prussians on the 17th. As the Prussians had withdrawn then Wellington had to withdraw and take up a position at Waterloo just south of Brussels.

Both armies retreated throughout the 17th and reached their respective positions later that evening. Napoleon did indeed advance against Wellington. But he had escaped in the nick of time using his cavalry in textbook fashion under the command of Lord Uxbridge and under cover of a timely thunderstorm, which made rapid pursuit impossible.

So by the evening of 17th June both Wellington and Blucher had fallen back seventeen miles to their respective positions at Wavre and Waterloo. Napoleon had pursued Wellington to Waterloo with 72,000 men. He had despatched 33,000 men under Marshal Grouchy to pursue the Prussians and prevent them from interfering with his planned attack on Wellington on the following day.

Marshal Grouchy, who had only just been appointed a Marshal of France, was an experienced cavalry commander who had fought with Napoleon throughout Europe. He was not used to independent command but all he had to do was pursue a beaten foe and keep him from joining up with Wellington south of Brussels. On paper this looked an easy task. Look at the map on page 63, from Gembloux Grouchy expected the Prussians to retreat either south towards Namur or eastwards towards Tongres.

When he discovered that they were in fact retreating north towards Wavre he was not too alarmed as they could then still retreat eastwards, either via Louvain or Tirlemont and then onto Tongres Liege etc. There are connecting roads between Wavre and Waterloo and another road north to Brussels but this would mean cutting themselves off from Prussia. This seemed to Grouchy to be an unlikely course of action to follow.

Grouchy's pursuit therefore was dilatory and enabled the Prussians to gain a sufficient distance for them to re-group during the night of 17th/18th June, so that by dawn on the 18th they were an effective fighting force once again. This was an incredible feat of organisational

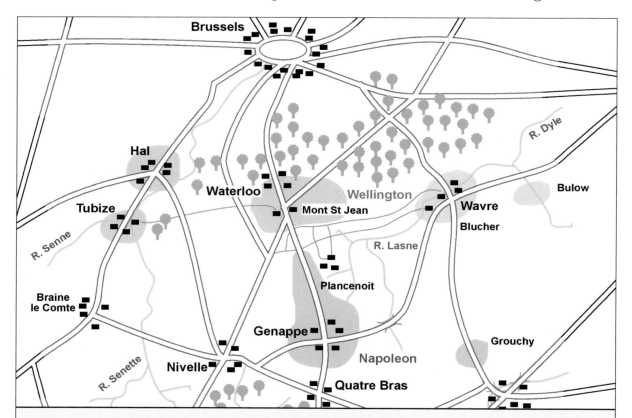

Map showing the area of the campaign with the roads running east to west from Wavre to Waterloo. Had Blucher been caught along these roads by a victorious Napoleon then he would have had no escape route.

skill. The Prussian army had been defeated at Ligny and scattered with some 15,000 dead and wounded and as many as 20,000 deserters. Yet two days later they were an effective fighting force, organised and with high morale ready for another battle. Napoleon had every reason to believe that the Prussians were a spent force after the battle of Ligny. Whilst he should have made absolutely certain of this by ordering Grouchy closer to his right flank earlier, his optimism on the morning of 18th June is understandable.

Now we come to the decision of the century. It was not the decision to march north to Wavre but it was the decision to march west from Wavre to Waterloo.

If we consult the map on page 68 we can see that the roads between Wavre and Waterloo run east to west with no roads running north to south. Blucher, with Gneisenau's support, was going to march his army along these roads to support Wellington by attacking the right flank of Napoleon's army whilst another French army under Grouchy was manoeuvring in his rear. What would happen if Napoleon defeated Wellington on the 18th and then Grouchy captured Wavre on the same or next day? What would happen was the certain annihilation of the Prussian army. It had no escape. It would have had to surrender as the Austrians did at Ulm ten years earlier. This was a truly decisive and extremely brave, or even foolhardy, decision. We should not underestimate the nature of the decision they made. This was a total commitment decision. Win or die were the only possible outcomes for the Prussians.

Would Wellington have made the same decision had circumstances been reversed? We will never know. Little is written about the debate that must have gone on in the evening of 17th June at Wavre. The whole of the Prussian army had not yet assembled, the ammunition train did not arrive until six pm and Blucher feared that it might have been captured. Up until that point no decision was possible. Until the army assembled and the ammunition arrived they had no army to move on Napoleon's right flank. But now the men, the guns, the bullets were all assembled and Blucher, Gneisenau, the Prussian general staff and the corps commanders needed to make the decision to march west and put their heads into the lion's mouth or east to safety and further reinforcements. In the debate they must have assessed Wellington's chances of standing up to Napoleon at Waterloo the following day.

They would have a reasonable idea of the forces likely to face each other and would have guessed that Wellington would have no more than 70,000 to 80,000 men against which Napoleon was likely to have a similar number of troops. Only twenty-four hours previously they had seen Napoleon smash through their army, which had a numerical superiority of 1.3 to 1. Now Wellington faced the same army with at best parity but possibly a numerically inferior army. Did they consider that he would be able to fend off the French where they had been unable to? They must also have known that Wellington's army was not a very good one. It comprised a mixture of British and King's German Legion, Dutch, Belgian, Hanoverian, Nassau and

Brunswick troops. Some of these had recently fought for Napoleon. Others, like the Nassau troops, were still in French uniforms. If those troops deserted the field, as they well might, then Wellington would have to face Napoleon with a much-reduced army making the likelihood of survival even less likely.

Yet despite this they decided to march west into the lion's mouth and risk all on Wellington standing and fighting long and hard enough for the Prussians to arrive in strength and thereby tip the balance in the allied favour.

It is likely that the decision was the lesser of two evils. Wellington made it clear to Blucher on 17th June that if he did not get the support of one corps then he would retire beyond the Scheldt river as far west as Ghent. This would only be a holding action allowing time for the evacuation of the continent by the British. There was no possibility of an invasion of England. Trafalgar, the truly decisive battle of the Napoleonic wars, had seen to that. So Britain was safe although politically it would have been a disaster. British trade would remain largely unaffected even if they had to come to some compromise with Napoleon.

Not so Prussia. Prussia had been occupied after the war of 1806 and until 1813 was a vassal state. Prussia did not want to risk any possibility of a return to subservience to France, which would have been the outcome if Napoleon remained in control of France and its army.

Ultimate defeat of Prussia would be the most likely outcome of a victory by the French in Belgium in June 1815. The British would have evacuated the continent. The Prussians would have had to retreat deeper into Prussia and that would leave only the Austrians and Russians in the war. Both Austria and Russia had come to terms with Napoleon before. The French had been soundly beaten in 1812, 1813 and 1814 by the combined forces of Russia, Austria, Prussia, Sweden and Great Britain. If now Great Britain was out of the war and Prussia was a spent force would it not be better for the remaining allies to be pragmatic and come to terms with the French, who would not want a repeat of the last three years, and live in peace? Would the Prussian King prefer to side with Blucher and Yorke and fight on alone against Napoleon or would he prefer to revert to being the vassal king of a protected Prussia?

Russia would certainly be at no risk of another invasion like the 1812 debacle. Austria had fought well in the campaigns of 1813/14 and was strong enough to deter the French from further aggression. Prussia was a small state by comparison, unable to stand alone against the French. They must have feared that if Napoleon won at Waterloo or if the British left them to their own devices then they would ultimately become a subservient nation to France. They could even become absorbed into a confederation of the Rhine type structure under French control. Blucher no doubt fully understood this as he had lived through the horror of the past nine years. He knew that only by defeating Napoleon could his nation thrive in independence and grow into a formidable nation in its own right. To defeat Napoleon the

Prussians needed Wellington to take the risk of defeat at the hands of the French and to keep the French engaged for long enough so that when the Prussian army did arrive they could fall onto an exposed flank, and crush the French army once and for all.

Strategy is forcing your opponent to conform to your will. In this case it may have been that Wellington was forcing Blucher to commit his army to a dangerous position under the threat that if they did not then they would be abandoned to their fate. If this was the case then it was indeed Wellington who was calling the tune and directing each army, French, Prussian and his own Anglo Netherlands army to conform to his plan, get the French to commit to a frontal assault and stand firm until the Prussians arrived on the French flank, thereby causing them to withdraw or be defeated.

Blucher conformed; the Prussians would march at dawn.

Chapter Eight

The Armies at Waterloo

Since Siborne wrote his history there has been an incredible amount of detail produced on the number of troops present in each army at the battle. Much of this data refers back to Siborne and numbers do differ slightly but not significantly. I am using Mark Adkin's figures from his book 'The Waterloo Companion' for this investigation. I am also using details from his book regarding the 'Footprint' a unit would occupy in order to establish a scale for each figure. Overall the model has 5,446 figures on it representing 196,000 men and over 600 guns.

Casualties

The army lists contain the number of troops present on the day, the number of figures represented on the model and the casualties reported by each regiment on the following day. These casualties are Killed, Wounded and Missing.

'Missing believed killed' was a term used in the First and Second World Wars. This was used because casualties from high explosive artillery rounds often left no trace of a casualty. It was therefore 'assumed' that a soldier missing was also killed. In the Napoleonic wars missing simply meant that the soldier was not present at roll call when it was held. In terms of the cavalry it might have meant that the trooper did not have a horse and was therefore 'missing' from the effectiveness of the regiment.

Casualty calculation was quite precise in those days. Sergeants calling the roll asked what happened to any soldier who was not present at that time and recorded it. Generally someone would have seen what happened to a missing soldier, the man standing next to him or near him would have seen if he had been wounded or killed. Those missing and not identified as wounded or killed were reported as missing. In most cases the missing soldier would turn up later, either in a hospital or simply by returning to the unit. Missing also meant 'ran away'. Running away was not unusual. Missing also included those who assisted a wounded comrade or better still an officer from the field.

What is interesting from the casualty figures is that you can see that those units placed out of harm's way did not suffer many casualties and even fewer missing troops. It is also evident that those elite units such as the British Guard Infantry had few troops go missing, four out of 3,826 Guardsmen at the battle. Although heavily engaged only one in a thousand went missing, point one percent.

Equally interesting is the number missing from Bijlandt's Brigade. This brigade was not heavily engaged but did break and run when the first French attack was made, more of this later. But they suffered 146 killed, 626 wounded and 621 missing out of 2,931. However these are the casualties for both the battles of Quatre Bras and Waterloo. Casualties on 16th June at Quatre Bras amounted to 685 for killed, wounded and missing, and it would appear from the figures that 336 went missing on the 16th but had returned on the 18th. On the 18th at Waterloo the brigade suffered 708 killed, wounded and missing, almost the same number. But at Quatre Bras the brigade stood and fought well whilst at Waterloo they ran away. Clearly the number of casualties suffered did not necessarily cause the situation at Waterloo. It may have been another factor that caused them to run away from the enemy.

The casualty returns are not always accurate however. One anomaly in the figures below shows that the 1st Dragoon Guards suffered 20 more casualties than it had men in the line! I have not corrected this error for I do not know which of the figures is wrong.

Chapter Nine

The Anglo Netherlands Army

Commander in Chief Field Marshal the Duke of Wellington

1st Infantry (Guards) Division
Major General George Cooke

	Troops	Figures on model	Casualties (in men) K	W	M

1st Brigade – Major General P. Maitland

	Troops	Figures on model	K	W	M
2nd/1st Foot Guards	781	22	51	101	0
3rd/1st Foot Guards	847	24	84	251	0

2nd Brigade – Major General Sir John Byng

	Troops	Figures on model	K	W	M
2nd/Coldstream Gds.	1098	31	55	249	4
2nd/3rd Foot Guards	1100	31	42	197	0
Captain Sandham's 9 Pounder Foot battery 6 guns		1 model			
Major Kuhlmann's 9 Pounder horse battery 6 guns		1 model			

3rd British Infantry Division – General Count Alten

5th Brigade – Major General Sir Colin Halkett.

	Troops	Figures on model	K	W	M
2nd/30th Foot	635	18	51	165	14
33rd Btn. Foot	576	16	35	102	48
2nd/69th Foot	565	16	18	53	15
2nd/73rd Foot	498	14	52	187	41

2nd King's German Legion Brigade – Colonel Baron Ompteda

	Troops	Figures on model	K	W	M
1st Light Btn.	519	14	41	91	13
2nd Light Btn.	403	11	43	129	30
5th Line Btn.	529	15	38	50	74
8th Line Btn.	636	18	47	84	16

1st Hanoverian Brigade Major General Count Kielmannsegge

	Troops	Figures on model	K	W	M
York Btn.	632	18	24	72	45
Grubenhagen	643	18	16	78	48
Bremen Btn.	533	15	12	124	35
Verden Btn.	559	16	63	101	53
Luneberg Btn.	617	17	32	142	48
Jaeger Coys.	331	9	12	41	19
Major Lloyds' 9 Pounder Battery 6 guns		1 model			
Captain Cleeve's 9 Pounder KGL Battery 6 guns		1 model			

2nd Netherlands Infantry Division Baron Henry Perponcher Sedlintzky

Troops		Figures on model	Casualties (in men) K	W	M

1st Brigade Major General Graf Van Bijlandt

Troops		Figures on model	K	W	M
27th Dutch Jaeger	550	16	4	45	40
7th Belgian Line	701	19	12	84	51
5th Dutch militia	220	6	4	8	7
7th Dutch militia	675	19	20	64	201
8th Dutch militia	566	16	9	93	61
Dutch Horse Battery	8 guns	1 model	2	16	0

2nd Brigade Major General Prince Bernard Saxe Weimar

Troops		Figures on model	K	W	M
1st Bt. 2nd Nassau	889	25	27	97	59
2nd Bt. 2nd Nassau	885	25	21	95	38
3rd Bt. 2nd Nassau	899	25	18	113	3
1st Bt 28th Or. Nas.	893	25	5	36	20
2nd Bt 28th Or.Nas.	688	19	6	46	52
Nassau Jaegers	177	5	0	0	0
Belgian Foot Battery	8 guns	1 model	15	89	14

3rd Netherlands Infantry Division Lt. General Baron Chasse

1st Brigade Colonel H. Detmers.

Troops		Figures on model	K	W	M
35th Belgian Jaeger	605	17	8	63	0
2nd Dutch line	471	13	6	28	57
4th Dutch militia	519	14	6	26	38
6th Dutch militia	492	14	5	15	22
17th Dutch militia	534	15	1	27	30
19th Dutch militia	467	13	1	28	50

2nd Brigade Major General A. D' Aubreme

Troops		Figures on model	K	W	M
36th Belgian Jaeger	633	18	3	10	41
3rd Belgian Line	629	18	1	24	56
12th Dutch Line	431	12	2	13	9
13th Dutch Line	664	18	6	20	34
3rd Dutch militia	592	16	5	26	2
10th Dutch militia	632	18	7	15	3
Belgian Foot battery	8 guns	1 model	3	5	22

Netherlands Cavalry Division Baron J.A. de Collaert

	Troops	Figures on model	Casualties (in men) K	W	M

Heavy Brigade Major General A. D. Trip

	Troops	Figures on model	K	W	M
1st Dutch Carabineers	446	12	12	75	15
2nd Belgian Carabineer	399	11	58	68	30
3rd Dutch Carabineers	392	11	37	29	26

1st Light Brigade Major General Baron de Ghingy

	Troops	Figures on model	K	W	M
4th Dutch Light Dr.	647	18	54	143	52
8th Belgian Hussars	439	12	11	151	122

2nd Light Brigade Major General J.B. van Merlen

	Troops	Figures on model	K	W	M
6th Dutch Hussars	470	13	12	70	132
5th Belgian Light Dr.	271	8	10	76	71
Horse battery	8 guns	1 model	8	9	4

British Reserve Artillery.

	Troops	Figures on model		
'A' troop RHA	6 guns	1	(casualties)	
'D' troop RHA	6 guns	1	(not listed by Digby Smith)	

2nd British Infantry Division Lt. General Sir Henry Clinton
3rd British Brigade Major General F. Adam

	Troops	Figures on model	K	W	M
1st/52nd Foot	1130	31	17	182	0
71st Foot	936	26	25	174	3
2nd/95th Rifles	666	19	34	193	20
3rd/95th Rifles	205	6	3	40	7

1st Brigade King's German Legion Colonel G.C.A. du Platt

	Troops	Figures on model	K	W	M
1st Line KGL	478	13	23	75	17
2nd Line KGL	527	15	19	81	7
3rd Line KGL	589	16	18	98	31
4th Line KGL	478	13	14	84	14

3rd Hanoverian Brigade Colonel H. Halkett

	Troops	Figures on model	K	W	M
Bremervorde Ldr.	655	18	18	22	9
Osnabruck Ldr.	633	18	20	68	6
Quackenbruck Ldr.	609	17	2	10	2
Salzgitter Ldr.	644	18	20	62	1
Bolton's Battery RFA	6 guns	1 model			
Sym! her's Battery KGL	6 guns	1 model			

4th British Infantry Brigade Lt. General Sir Charles Colville

	Troops	Figures on model	Casualties (in men)		
			K	W	M
4th British Brigade Lt. Colonel H.H. Mitchell					
3rd/14th Foot	640	18	7	22	0
1st/23rd Foot	741	21	15	84	0
1st/51st Foot	626	17	9	22	0
Von Rettberg's Hanoverian battery	6 guns	1 model			

5th British Infantry Division Lt. General Sir Thomas Picton

	Troops	Figures on model	K	W	M
8th Brigade Major General Sir James Kempt					
28th Foot	557	15	19	158	0
32nd Foot	503	14	28	146	0
79th Foot	445	12	31	143	1
95th Rifles	418	12	21	135	1*

It is now known that some 100 went missing on the day but are not recorded as such in the battalion records.

	Troops	Figures on model	K	W	M
9th Brigade Major General Sir Denis Pack					
3rd/1st Foot	453	13	15	129	0
1st/42nd Foot	338	9	5	45	0
2nd/44th Foot	494	14	4	60	0
1st/92nd Foot	412	11	14	102	0

	Troops	Figures on model	K	W	M
5th Hanoverian Brigade Colonel Von Vincke					
Gifhorn Ldr	640	18	15	72	0
Hameln Ldr.	689	19	9	64	7
Hildersheim Ldr.	640	18	3	21	0
Peine Ldr.	635	18	8	42	6
Rogers RFA Battery	6 guns	1 model			
Braun's Hanoverian Battery	6 guns	1 model			

6th British Infantry Division Lt. General Sir Lowry Cole
10th British Brigade Major General Sir John Lambert

	Troops	Figures on model	K	W	M
4th Foot	677	19	12	112	0
27th Foot	750	21	105	373	0
40th Foot	862	24	32	169	18

4th Hanoverian Brigade Colonel C. Best

	Troops	Figures on model	Casualties (in men) K	W	M
Verden Ldr.	642	18	12	101	46
Luneberg Ldr.	647	18	10	42	0
Munden Ldr.	680	19	12	103	17
Osterode Ldr.	700	19	14	98	14
Sinclair's Battery RFA	6 guns	1 model			

The Brunswick Contingent Division (acting Commander) Colonel Olfermann

Light Infantry Regiment Lt. Colonel von Buttlar

Avant-garde	635	18	7	21	28
Leib Lt. Inf.	565	16	14	37	51
1st light Inf.	688	19	4	44	48
2nd Light Inf.	621	17	39	75	114
3rd Light Inf.	691	19	36	80	50

Line Infantry Regiment Lt. Colonel von Specht

1st Line	586	16	9	46	55
2nd Line	500	14	3	7	10
3rd Line	667	19	10	53	63
2nd Hussars	684	19	28	50	78
Uhlan's	235	7	0	15	15
Horse Battery	8 guns	1 model	3	6	9
Foot Battery	8 guns	1 model	0	18	18

Nassau Contingent Brigade Major General Von Kruse

1st Battalion	951	26	85	130	0*
2nd Battalion	943	26	85	130	0*
Landwehr	947	26	85	130	0*

*The Nassau casualties are recorded for the whole brigade not individual battalions. I have divided up the casualties equally between the battalions.

1st British (Household) Cavalry Brigade Major General Lord Edward Somerset.

1st Lifeguards	255	7	18	43	4
2nd Lifeguards	235	7	17	41	97
R.H.G. Blues	246	7	17	60	21
1st Dragoon Gds	255	7	43	104	128*

*Clearly an error in that there are 275 casualties for 255 men most probably 28 missing

The 2nd British (Union) Cavalry Brigade Major General Sir William Somerset.

	Troops	Figures on model	Casualties (in men)		
			K	W	M
1st Royal Dragoons	435	12	89	97	10
2nd Nth. Br. Dragoons	444	12	102	97	0
6th Inniskilling	453	13	73	116	28

The 3rd British Cavalry Brigade Major General Sir William Dornberg.

23rd Light Dragoons	341	9	14	28	32
1st Light Dragoons KGL	540	15	33	111	10
2nd Light Dragoons KGL	520	14	20	55	2

The 4th British Light Cavalry Brigade Major General Sir John Vandeleur

11th Light Dragoons	442	12	12	28	23
12th Light Dragoons	433	12	47	64	0
16th Light Dragoons	440	12	10	20	0

The 5th British Brigade Major General Sir C. Grant

7th Hussars	362	10	56	99	0
15th Hussars	450	13	23	51	5
13th Light Dragoons	455	13	12	78	18

The 6th British Cavalry Brigade Major General Sir H. Vivian

10th Hussars	452	13	22	46	26
18th Hussars	447	12	12	73	17
1st Hussars KGL	605	17	1	6	0

The 7th British Cavalry Brigade Colonel Sir F. Arenschildt

3rd Hussars KGL	712	20	44	86	0

The Hanoverian Cavalry Brigade.

Duke of Cumberland
Hussars   516   14 figures on model
(All fled the field during the French massed cavalry charges)

Royal Horse Artillery batteries attached to the Cavalry Corps.

Major Bull's Battery	6 guns	1 model
Major Ramsay's Battery	6 guns	1 model
Webber Smith's Battery	6 guns	1 model
Whinyates' Battery	5 guns	1 model
Whinyates' Rocket troop	1 frame	1 model
Mercer's Battery	6 guns	1 model
Gardiner's Battery	6 guns	1 model

Wellington's army was a mixed bag of different nations comprising the following national units.

Nation	Infantry	Cavalry	Guns
British & KGL	21,112	7,255	102
Dutch/Belgian	9,381	3,064	26
Hanoverian	11,129	516	12
Nassau	7,272	0	0
Brunswick	4,953	919	16
Total	**53,847**	**11,754**	**156**

The total allied casualties suffered during the day amounted to 17,589 including 3,579 troops who went missing. In killed and wounded the figures are 14,010. However most authorities have the allied casualties at around 15,500. Some 2,000 of the missing must therefore have turned up in the days following the battle. The analysis of the casualties including those who went missing and including the Cumberland Hussars who fled the field on the day is as follows;-

Nation	Killed	Wounded	Missing	fled
British & KGL	1,592	5,575	794	0
Dutch/Belgian	421	1,717	1,368	0
Hanoverian	320	1,296	371	463
Nassau	331	843	172	0
Brunswick	154	456	544	0
Total	**3,136**	**10,874**	**3,579**	**463**

The nationality of the troops taking part is not wholly relevant and serves to show not so much the geographical location of the soldier's birth but rather the military training and doctrine of each participating group. The British army was not composed exclusively of people born on mainland Britain. It was often referred to as the English army but this force was composed of Irish, Scots, Welsh and English plus numerous other nationalities who made up the ranks. There was even an American, de Lancey, who was the Quartermaster General of the Army and was born in New York.

The Waterloo medal roll has the following names in the ranks of the 33rd Regiment of Foot.

Private Hoheima
Private de France
Private de Puton
Private Prideaux
Private Kinsella
Private Monkettrick

These are hardly the usual English names. But they could nevertheless have been British. In any event they were British trained. The point is that it was not where they were born that made the difference it was the system of turning them into soldiers that made them what they were.

In the Peninsular War General Beresford had set about training the Portuguese army to British army standards with British drill sergeants and officers as instructors. The result was what Wellington called his "Fighting Cocks", troops that were respected by their British allies as first class troops.

There were three distinctly different types of troops on the field of Waterloo in all armies.

Firstly there were those who had been trained to fight in the French style. Napoleon had swept away the rigid discipline of the Prussian school of Frederick the Great at the battle of Jena in 1806. The Prussians, Austrians and Russians had by 1815 all adopted the French style of combat because Napoleon had beaten each of them in battle. It was natural for them to follow the successful practices he had developed.

Secondly there were militia units, Landwehr in the Prussian army, who were poorly armed and lacked proper training. Nevertheless these troops if handled well and not put in too risky a position could fight effectively.

Finally there was the British Army system that was nothing like either of the other two.

The British army had developed from the Prussian principles of Frederick the Great through to a more formidable fighting force. This resulted partly because of the American War of Independence and also the war of 1745 against Scotland, known as the Jacobite rebellion. In the American war the British army was introduced to the effectiveness of the Kentucky Rifle and the use of light infantry in weakening an enemy line by knocking out its officers. In today's modern parlance this is known as knocking out the enemy's command and control system. It was just the same in 1776. Skirmishers would pick off officers and thereby cause confusion in the enemy ranks. The British countered this by using more and more light infantry of their own.

After the war there was much debate, as there always is, on the best way for the army to be trained to operate. The argument revolved around the use of a two or three deep line, the number of light infantry to be deployed and whether a rifle or musket was the better weapon. A compromise solution was the outcome. The British army would still fight in a three deep formation but would have both musket and rifle armed light troops. Wellington and General Moore were in the two deep line camp as this gave greater firepower than the three deep line. They argued that the advantage of the third rank of troops, who could not fire, was countered by the extra firepower of the two deep line. The third rank served to reduce the length of the line so that the sergeants and officers were closer to the men than they would be in a longer line of troops.

Wellington and Moore argued that if the discipline of the troops was sufficient to allow the officers to be further away from the men then the extra fire power of the two deep line would be decisive. The British system of discipline and regimental honour was designed to enable the troops to be trusted not to run away if they found themselves in a fog of gun-smoke and without a sergeant or officer in sight.

Wellington in particular saw the system of the French army being best dealt with by the following tactics. The French began their battles with a massive artillery bombardment using roundshot at about six hundred yards range. To counter the effects of this cannonade he suggested deploying the troops on the reverse side of a hill. In this way the roundshot would fly harmlessly over the heads of the infantry lying down in cover.

The French then sent in clouds of skirmishers who were trained to pick off the enemy officers and sergeants. To counter this Wellington suggested having better armed and as numerous light troops deployed in skirmish order on the forward slope of the hill to keep the enemy skirmishers out of range of the main line and its officers and NCOs.

Finally the French sent forward their main infantry assault in columns that looked invincible as they marched in great blocks across the battlefield towards the already shaken enemy line. To counter this Wellington adopted the two deep line deployed on the reverse slope awaiting the French columns deadly approach. The French advanced and were suddenly brought to a halt by the appearance of a red wall of deadly muskets firing platoon volleys into the packed ranks of the French column. The column remained under fire until the British officers, trained to recognise the signs, judged that the column was shaken and would break if charged at bayonet point. They had learnt this from the Scots in 1745.

The Highland charge was a feature of the Jacobite battles that caused panic in the English ranks and caused them to run away. Equally the Scots when faced by a solid rank of musketry were cut down in great numbers, making the eventual Highland charge less effective because of the losses sustained. If these two weapons, firepower and shock, could be combined then the British Army would have a war-winning tactic that would beat the French columns, whenever they came up against a line of well trained infantry.

If we now look at Wellington's army from the style of fighting and the training point of view we see the following differences.

INFANTRY

	British trained	French trained	Untrained Militia
British & KGL	21,112	0	0
Dutch/ Belgian	0	4,684	4,697
Hanoverian	3,315	0	7,814
Nassau	0	6,235	947
Brunswick	4,953	0	0
Total	**29,380**	**10,919**	**13,458**

Wellington had therefore just under 30,000 infantry of various nations who had all been trained to varying degrees to defeat a French column. He also had almost as many troops who had no idea how to fight a French column since they were either poorly trained militia or they had themselves been trained by, and fought for, the French. What they knew was the power of a French column as they had seen it in victorious action. Mercer thought that the Brunswick troops were mere boys but some of the Brunswickers had been with Wellington

in Spain and had seen his system in action.

The cavalry and artillery were much the same as the French, except that in the cavalry control was far worse in the British army than in the French. In the artillery the British did have a couple of novelty weapons, shrapnel and rockets. The former was an air burst shell that sometimes did work effectively, the second was a giant firework that whooshed off in all directions and was disliked by Wellington himself.

The other great difference between the British, French and Prussian armies was in organisation. The French army was organised on a corps system whereby a General would have under his command a corps comprising infantry, cavalry, artillery and support services. This system was copied by the Prussians, Austrians and Russians and it became the basis of army organisation for all armies up to modern times. Wellington shunned the corps system and retained the older system of divisions and brigades. This was mainly because of his lack of trust of other generals when left to their own devices. Napoleon would allow a corps commander or a commander of several corps to operate independently from the main army in order to carry out a specific function. Wellington kept it all under his own eye and under his own control. When he did leave them on their own the army suffered and as the army was small he could not risk unnecessary losses.

The problem here was that Wellington was an employee of the State whereas Napoleon was in charge of the State. Wellington was bound by what his lords and masters in London dictated to him. He had to deal with the civil service at Horseguards, now the Ministry of Defence.

The relationship between the army and its Government was a bizarre one. To get a better understanding of it we need to understand a little about British society, a massive subject in its own right, as the army was in fact a reflection of that society. It was a class society that was in the main accepted by each class in its turn. At the top was a King whose power was limited. Beneath the King was Parliament but not everyone was represented here, only land owners and only male landowners at that. Below them were the professional classes, doctors, lawyers and so on, and below them were the workers. Now this was before the industrial revolution and Britain was in the main an agricultural society. People accepted their place and in general those of the upper class were respected and they, in turn, treated those of the lower class reasonably fairly. Remember in 1649 Parliament had cut the head off a King who got above his station. In more recent times the 'London Mob' had threatened violence but a more typical and lesser known incident goes further to explain the system than these mighty events.

Some time ago BBC Radio Four told the story about a man who lived near my hometown. The story as I remember it was as follows:

In Quainton in Buckinghamshire an ex-soldier and farm hand got into a row with his employer over a matter of pay, something like sixpence a month was the amount in question. The farmer lost his temper with the farm hand and dismissed him. The farm hand walked from Quainton to Aldbury in Hertfordshire to appeal to the local Squire. He arrived late in the evening and the Squire told him it was too late to do anything about it now so he had better sleep in the barn and they would sort it out in the morning. Next day Squire and farm hand went back to Quainton, a distance of some twelve miles, the Squire riding and the farm hand walking. They arrived and discussed the matter. The farmer had by now calmed down and realised that perhaps the farm hand was in the right. The farm hand was reinstated and paid the sixpence due to him.

And this in the main was how things worked. People were in the main far more reasonable to one another than one would expect or are led to believe. If they were not then there was a remedy. Of course there were exceptions; there were cheats, thieves, liars and scoundrels at each and every level of society but each level seemed to accept its place and behaved accordingly.

The same was true in the army. In the first place officers purchased their commission. You had to be wealthy enough to pay for the rank you wanted. It did not matter that you might be totally incompetent at being an officer so long as you had the money to buy your way up the ladder. That meant that you came from the upper or wealthier class and you were therefore accepted by each level of the army society.

Proof of this can be seen from the hard time those from the ranks who won a promotion had, not just from above but also from below, from their former colleagues.

On paper and no matter how you examine it the British system of class ruling the army, despite the level of competence each officer had, was weaker than other more efficient systems and in particular the French army system. Evidence of this comes from the fact that after the Crimea War, some forty years after Waterloo, the system was finally abandoned and a system of merit put in its place, or was it? Even in the twentieth century the officer class of the British army came from the wealthier level of society. They had gone to private school, which had to be paid for and was therefore unavailable to the poorer classes of society; then onto military college where at least they were taught their trade before being sent into the army regiments to serve as before.

The great fear of the British ruling class was violent revolution. They had seen the effects of such disturbances in America and then in France. Britain had its revolution in 1642 with a civil war as bitterly fought as any of the time. Britain hated the thought of it. The army hated the thought of it and so the system of class ruling the army was tolerated by each level of class in it, even down to the flogging imposed on the rank and file to ensure their obedience. Oddly enough the letters and books written by rank and file soldiers hardly mention the issue of flogging and when they do it is mostly regarded as being justly meted out. And here is probably why it was accepted. Providing it was just the officers could punish offenders, for by doing so the army as a whole benefited, as did all of

those in it. When punishment was unjust it was frowned upon as it was likely to cause unrest at all levels. Providing the system was accepted or at least tolerated by the rank and file then the officers could rely on them not to run away at the first opportunity. That meant that the army could deploy in a two deep line and defeat the French system.

On paper the system was poor but in the reality of battle it worked. It won almost every major battle it fought and defeated bigger and better organised armies time and again. Something unusual, something odd, something secret about the British Army in the Napoleonic Wars contributed towards the success it had and everyone has at some time laid claim to it.

"The battle of Waterloo was won on the playing fields of Eton."

Here is the claim of the officer class for the success. They learnt how to play fair and win at cricket. It was this that was our secret weapon that defeated the enemy whose officers were of course made up of a mixture of all sorts of people.

"It was our diet of Beef and Beer that made us warlike and won all the battles."

Even the food and drinks industry was getting in on the act.

"They are the scum of the earth" words attributed to Wellington himself when describing the rank and file; *no chance of the lower classes getting a claim in then.*

Well in fact Wellington did not say these

words or rather they were not said in this way. What Wellington actually said was;

"They come from the scum of the earth and it is remarkable what fine fellows we make of them."

Now this is a totally different set of words from those attributed to Wellington and in these words is the truth of the matter. Just before the campaign in Belgium in 1815 Wellington was in a park in Brussels with his friend Creevy when Creevy asked him whether he thought that he could do the business of beating Napoleon. "It all depends upon that article there" he said pointing to a British infantryman gawping at the many statues in the park. "Give me enough of it and I am sure of it."

The British army had many things going for it, its infantry, its system and its commander in chief. Wellington had to trust his men not to run away when during the battle they might not, due to smoke, even be able to see an officer or sergeant.

Wellington could only rely on his officers to do the simplest things. There were exceptions, many exceptions. But in the main Wellington did not trust his officers to act on their own initiative but only under his direct orders. The men had to rely on Wellington to do the right thing. Fortunately for Britain his orders were usually right. Because of this Wellington could rely on his British trained infantry to stand in a two deep line and deliver three, or even four, aimed shots from their muskets per minute. Given enough of this infantry Wellington was certain that he could win, deny him these troops, either because of Whitehall or enemy action and the outcome was in doubt.

Perversely Whitehall more than the French denuded Wellington of the very tool he needed to do the job. Until General Lambert arrived at Waterloo on the morning of the battle Wellington had only 27,000 British trained infantry to hand, at Vittoria he had 72,000.

Chapter Ten

The French Army

The French army was very different from the British army in its organisation, formation, size and fighting ability. The French army of the revolutionary and Napoleonic wars was born on 20th April 1792 when in response to threats from Prussia and Austria to restore the monarchy in France, the French Assembly declared war on Austria. The remarkable thing was that the three armies that came from this decree were made up of those regular forces that survived the revolution, and a mass of volunteers. The French public was enthusiastic in its desire to defend its newfound freedom. The French aristocracy had, unlike its British cousins, not been just and fair. It had not been witness to a civil war culminating in the public beheading of a King.

France had helped the American Colonists throw out their British masters and the troops had seen the wonder of civil liberty. Then they returned to France into something close to serfdom. No wonder they revolted and kept on revolting, despite Waterloo, until they finally won their freedom from Monarchy in the 1830s. The military volunteers, however, were little more than an enthusiastic mob apt to run away from the enemy just as much as towards him. After the victory at Valmy, where the cannon did most of the fighting and defeated a combined Austrian and Prussian army of 70,000 men, the French formed a National Convention that took over the Government of France. The Monarchy was initially abolished and King Louis XVI was executed on 21st January 1793.

The French army had enthusiasm but no control. The guillotine had decimated the officer class. Officers of quality were hard to find but unlike any other European army the officers could come from anywhere, within the army or without, from the lowest rank to the highest. But no sooner had an officer risen to the highest rank than he became a threat to Robespierre and the young, nervous French republican government. In his turn a successful officer might be sent to the guillotine.

In 1794, Robespierre finally went to the guillotine himself. This brought about the end of the terror. Now generals could command without the fear of madam guillotine looking over their shoulder.

Step forward one Napoleon Bonaparte, a junior gunnery officer just out of training school and in charge of a battery in Paris. In the confusion and riot of the Paris mob he let off a whiff of grapeshot and restored order. The French government was grateful to him but nervous of his popularity. They decided to send him off to Italy where the army was in ruins and facing defeat. They hoped that they could let him and his reputation die there in the fertile plains of the river Po.

In March 1796, Napoleon arrived in Northern Italy and found an army demoralised, unfit for action, ill equipped and hungry. Napoleon was shorter, thinner, younger than the other generals in the army, but he commanded them and he commanded them to attack. He spoke to the troops themselves. "Soldiers, I will lead you to the richest cities and wealthiest provinces of Italy and you can help yourself to whatever you want, all you have to do is what I tell you to do and you will defeat the enemy and all the riches of the world will be yours". No wonder they loved him. He led them from hunger and defeat to victory, glory and riches beyond their wildest dreams. They marched south, Montenotte, Mondovi, Lodi, Milan captured, Lonato, Castiglione, Bassano, Rivoli, victory after victory after victory. Until in April 1797, just over one year since he took over command, the Austrians asked for a truce which eventually led to the Treaty of Campo Formio.

In October 1797, France was victorious. By now Bonaparte was famous not only within the army of Italy but in Paris and beyond. Who was he? This general who fought through the snow and ice of winter and kept on fighting until the enemy was crushed, who was he?

We could fill a volume on the man himself. Here was a man, not even from France itself but rather an Italian born in Corsica, sent to a military school to be a gunner officer not a general, a commoner, a man of the people, the worst nightmare of every Monarchy in Europe. In November 1799 Napoleon became First Consul of France. Napoleon, a superstar hero, stepping forward at the behest of the army to take over command of the country to end the turmoil of amateur Government and to install an efficient military style administration that would restore order to France and its quite remarkable little army. This remarkable little army fought and won yet more battles with Marengo being regarded by Napoleon as his finest triumph.

The order and success Napoleon brought to both nation and army was hailed by the people as a miracle. Napoleon was the saviour of France. Peace arrived in March 1802; even the hated English signed the treaty. The war was over but just over one year later, in May 1803, war broke out again. The only solution to a long lasting peace was the defeat of England, by invasion if necessary. To invade he needed an army of excellence and so was born what came to be known as 'La Grande Armee'. This army was created by Napoleon, forged on new principles of war, designed to conquer, designed to win.

It was a new army concept created by Napoleon himself, his army his soldiers. Many historians have said that in fact the embryo army already existed. Griebville had reorganised the artillery decades before. The cavalry was as always excellent. The revolutionary army had formed the concept of the column of infantry as a fighting technique. All Napoleon did was to bring these disparate sections together into a fighting force. That is rather like saying that Enzo Ferrari did nothing for the sports car as the wheel had been invented long before he came on the scene.

Napoleon created in La Grande Armee a new fighting force that was unlike anything seen in Europe since the invasion of the Mongol Horde five centuries before. The army could march forty kilometres a day, faster than any other army of the period, and it was mobilised faster than any nation would have believed possible. When war was again declared in May 1803 the army needed to be organised and supplied. By September 1803 the Grande Armee reported that it was ready to set sail to invade England. It could embark 114,000 men, 7,100 horses, 32,000 reserve muskets, 14 million cartridges, 1,300,000 musket flints, 1,500,000 rations of biscuit, 240,000 pints of brandy, 5,000 live sheep, 7,000 rations of bran and 7,000 rations of oats, 432 cannon with 90,000 cannonballs and shells. No wonder those in Britain felt under threat.

The Royal Navy, however, kept Britain safe for the army could not cross the channel until they had command of the seas; something they never achieved. Austria and Russia had joined Britain in a coalition against France and as Napoleon could not invade Britain he turned east to deal with the Austro Russian army. Nelson crushed the French threat against England at Trafalgar off the Spanish coast near Cadiz in October. But in August, Napoleon realising that his army was powerless without control of the sea had turned his gaze towards Austria. On 23rd August, some seven weeks before Trafalgar, he marched the army eastward to deal with the Austro Russian threat.

The French army was excellently organised into corps each of which contained troops of each arm of the services, infantry, cavalry, artillery, engineers, medical staff, supplies; a small army in its own right. The corps could act independently or together as an army. They could march in lines behind one another or by different routes to the same place. Napoleon had created an officer corps from all ranks of society based upon merit and ability. Their names are legend, Lannes, Murat, Victor, Soult, Ney, Besseries, MacDonald, Poniatowski, Junot, Jordan, Kellerman, Massena, Bernadotte, Marmot. Their names are emblazoned on the Arc de Triomphe in Paris. They were the Generals of their age, fierce rivals but loyal, whilst he was successful, to Napoleon himself.

The Ulm campaign demonstrates better than any other the effectiveness of this new force. Sweeping north through the neutral Prussian territory of Ansbach whilst demonstrating against the Austrians in the west, where the Austrians expected the attack to come from, Napoleon fell on the flank and rear of the Austrian forces before they realised that he had left Boulogne. Napoleon captured 50,000 Austrians in the Ulm campaign, virtually without firing a shot or sustaining a casualty. 50,000 men put out of the war in a four week campaign which included a march half way across Europe and ended up with Napoleon marching in triumph into Vienna, the capital of his arch enemy. Following Ulm came Austerlitz where he routed 90,000 Russians and Austrians and brought the war to an end.

The following year, 1806, it was Prussia's turn to taste defeat at Jena and Auerstadt. Pursued relentlessly after the battle by Napoleon's corps the Prussian army ceased to exist as a fighting force, crushed by the new army. The world was shocked.

Peace, better to come to terms with a man such as Napoleon rather than be defeated by him. At Tilsit in 1807 two Emperors met on a raft in the middle of the River Niemen and a deal was struck. But it would not last. Only England, fighting against Napoleon's restriction on her trade fought on by supporting the uprising in Spain, which would soon turn into the Spanish ulcer.

In Spain and Portugal a new type of fighting soon developed. Regular Spanish armies were no match for the professional experienced French corps nor their expert commanders. But their people fighting a guerrilla war sapped the strength of the invaders and gnawed away at their morale. In Portugal a small British army, less than the size of one French corps, landed and fought a larger French corps to a standstill at Vimiero causing it to withdraw and then surrender. Remarkably the British victors then had the good manners but poor strategic sense to transport the defeated French army, together with the booty they had stolen, all the way back to France.

The British commanders were recalled home and a new British commander was sent in their place. He was Sir John Moore and he, with astounding audacity, launched an invasion of French held Spain from Portugal. In doing so he upset the careful plans laid down by Napoleon for the occupation of the whole of the Peninsular. Napoleon turned on this tiny British force and chased it away into the mountains and back via La Coruna to Britain.

War again with Austria in 1809, more victories culminating at Wagram, a massive battle involving armies of three hundred thousand men fighting over two days with dreadful losses all round. Then more trouble in Spain; Wellesley was back, defeating Napoleon's marshals at Talavera, Busaco, Torres Vedras, Feuntes de Onoro and then Salamanca. Defeats certainly but not against an army led by Napoleon whose eyes were focused even further eastwards, towards Moscow.

The campaign of 1812 saw the pinnacle and nadir of the Grande Armee. It had swelled in size to 430,000 men and comprised the nations of France, Bavaria, Poland, Austria, Italy, Spain, Switzerland, Saxony, Westphalia, Dalmatia, Croatia and Prussia. Organised on the corps system it was the most formidable army of the age of gunpowder. Nothing like it had been seen since ancient times, a massive force. Russia also had a massive force at her disposal but only half the size of the Grande Armee. No one relished the thought of facing an army commanded by Napoleon even with a larger force at their disposal. Facing Napoleon when he had numerical superiority was unthinkable. The Russians avoided battle and in doing so discovered almost by accident the way to defeat La Grande Armee. Don't fight it, let it starve.

It is not widely understood that the Grande Armee lost more troops in the summer heat on their way to Moscow than they did on their way back through the bitter snow. The Russian commander Kutuzov retreated before the invading French until goaded by his own side into accepting battle in front of Moscow he stood and fought at Borodino, nearly losing his army in the process. The battle caused massive casualties on the French as well as the Russians. Napoleon occupied Moscow but the Russians let him have it then set it on fire. Stranded and facing an implacable foe Napoleon retreated and in the process lost the better part of the remains of his army to cold, Cossacks and desertions.

The remnants of his army limped back into Poland at the end of 1812 and then fought and were defeated at the largest of the Napoleonic battles at Leipzig. 1813 and 1814 saw the French thrown back to France's borders on all fronts, The allies in the east had learnt how to defeat the French. The French might win the battles but the allies, Russian, Prussian, Austrian and Swedish, simply withdrew away from Napoleon and advanced elsewhere. In Spain Wellington continued his run of victories using his method of fighting whilst in the east the allies continued to be defeated on the battlefield but were strategically victorious along the front as a whole.

Exhausted, betrayed and defeated Napoleon tried to take his life but the poison was beyond its sell by date and did not work. He surrendered and was sent to the Isle of Elba just off the coast of Italy in the Mediterranean. That should have been the end but for the stupidity of the restored Bourbons who acted as though the previous twenty years had not happened and attempted to put back the clock to before the revolution. France would have none of it.

In March 1815 with a thousand men, Napoleon landed at Cannes in the south of France and marched on Paris. He re-took the country in twenty days without losing a man or firing a shot in anger. He was back. In a very short time he had his army back, a fine army, an experienced army. I have read that some say the French army was only a shadow of its former self but the Armee Du Nord was a fine instrument of war. Organised on the corps system, well equipped and with good officers and men it was a formidable fighting machine. Some authors seek the answer on why the army failed to win at Waterloo in its soldiers. They were not to blame, nor as some say were the Marshals, nor was Napoleon as we shall see.

French casualties at Waterloo

French casualties at Waterloo are not known. They have been variously estimated at between 19,000 and 42,000. I have made my own analysis of the French casualties. These are my estimates and are not based upon historical documents or returns and should not be relied upon as such. They are however based upon other known casualties from other Napoleonic battles, namely Borodino and Leipzig.

They are also compared with the British losses suffered at the Somme on 1st July 1916, just over 101 years later.

At Borodino just outside Moscow on 7th September 1812 a French army of 103,000 men attacked a Russian army of 120,000 men. The battle was extremely bloody and lasted from 6.00am until nightfall, at around 8.00pm. The battle lasted therefore fourteen hours although the last two hours were in the main just an artillery duel. French losses in this battle were 28,000 (approximately) 6,600 killed and 21,400 wounded. This represented 27% of the troops engaged with a ratio of 23% killed and 77% wounded.

At Leipzig on the three days of 16th 18th and 19th October 1813 a French army of 203,133 fought a Russian, Austrian, Prussian and Swedish army of 361,942 men. During this, the largest and longest battle of the Napoleonic wars, the French suffered 46,064 casualties, 9,212 killed and 36,851 wounded. This ratio is 80% wounded and 20% killed. The overall percentage of casualties to troops engaged was 23%.

At the Somme on 1st July 1916 the British suffered the worst casualties in their military history for a single day. 57,470 casualties of which 19,240 were killed and 35,493 were wounded. These ratios are 62% wounded and 38% killed with overall casualties being 31% of the 186,000 troops engaged. The Somme is widely regarded as the epitome of high casualties in a short time span; troops were mowed down by machine gun and rifle fire.

These ratios are repeated in many battles of the Napoleonic and other wars. However if we compare the estimates for the French casualties for the battle of Waterloo in killed and wounded then the ratios are very different. 40,000 casualties, 55% of troops engaged, is totally out of proportion to real casualties in any battle of the period and even up to the First World War.

25,000 killed and wounded out of 72,000 troops engaged is 35%. This still seems too high as it would mean that the French suffered a higher casualty rate at Waterloo than the British did at the Somme. 19,500 killed and wounded represents 27% of the troops engaged and seems to be a more reasonable number. It is also the French number reputedly quoted by Napoleon himself.

This seems to me to be a more reasonable figure for killed and wounded and if we apply the ratio of 80% wounded 20% killed, then we get a casualty rate of 15,795 wounded and 3,900 killed.

How we apportion these casualties is yet another matter. Casualties were suffered right up until the French army broke and routed at about nine in the evening, and it is the casualties suffered up until that point that are of interest. After the rout the French may have suffered further casualties but these casualties did not impact on who won or lost the battle. The battle was already won and lost at that time.

Most corps were engaged for most of the day and were involved in heavy fighting at one or more times. Therefore I have attributed the casualties on the basis of hours engaged and heavy fighting experienced shown below:

1st Corps	six hours	twice heavily engaged
2nd Corps	seven hours	generally engaged all day
6th Corps	four hours	twice heavily engaged
3rd Cavalry Div	four hours	lightly engaged
5th Cavalry Div.	four hours	lightly engaged
3rd Cavalry Corps	three hours	heavily engaged
4th Cavalry Corps	three hours	heavily engaged
Guard cavalry	three hours	heavily engaged
Guard infantry	four hours	very heavily engaged
Artillery	eight hours	once heavily engaged

If we therefore attribute casualties at a percentage rate for hours engaged and the severity of the action then we can calculate killed and wounded as follows;

1st Corps	suffered	15%	of all French casualties.
2nd Corps	suffered	26%	of all French casualties.
6th Corps	suffered	6%	of all French casualties.
3rd Cavalry Division	suffered	2%	of all French casualties.
5th Cavalry Division	suffered	2%	of all French casualties.
3rd Cavalry Corps	suffered	9%	of all French casualties.
4th Cavalry Corps	suffered	8%	of all French casualties.
Guard Cavalry	suffered	10%	of all French casualties.
Guard infantry	suffered	22%	of all French casualties.

Once again this is only my estimate, which is needed to evaluate the strength of each corps at the point in the battle when the French army broke and was routed. These figures do not include those troops captured. During the day this amounted to about another 4,000 troops. I have distributed the casualties among the corps regiments as shown in the army list opposite.

In the French army at the end of the battle it could be argued that 90% of all troops went missing in the rout. What we need to determine is the probable number of troops that went missing during the battle, up until the rout. It seems to me that this should be the same for the French army as it was for the British army, particularly in respect of the Guard units. In the British army there were 580 missing, 1,251 killed and 4,639 wounded. The ratio of missing to killed and wounded therefore was 1 in ten or 10%.

Therefore if the first corps suffered 15% of all of the French casualties which in my estimate is 19,500 they lost 2,925 plus 10%, 292 who would have gone missing. Of the 2,925, 80%, 2,340 were wounded and 20%, 585 were killed. They also had 3,000 troops captured during the British cavalry charge. Their total losses up to the end of the battle were therefore in the region of 6,217, almost all infantryman, out of 16,931 infantry, 37%. This seems to me to be about right and is compatible with other losses in both the Anglo Netherlands and Prussian armies.

The French Armee Du Nord.

Commander in Chief The Emperor Napoleon Bonaparte

NOTE:

Figures in RED are author's estimates and are not based upon any casualty returns.

K = Killed   W = Wounded   M = Missing   C = Captured

The Imperial Guard

Headquarters.

	Troops	Figures on model	Casualties (in men) K	W	M	C
Engineers	219	6	1	4	0	0
Artillery reserve	24 guns	3	20	55	0	0
Marines	219	6	1	4	0	0

The Division of the Grenadiers a' Pied   Lieut. Gen. Count Friant

1st Grenadiers   Baron J.M. Petit

1st Battalion	640	18	34	116	0	0
2nd Battalion	640	18	30	125	0	0

2nd Grenadiers   Baron J. Christiani

1st Battalion	545	15	38	110	0	0
2nd Battalion	545	15	30	116	0	0
6 Pounder battery	8 guns	1 model	3	10	0	0

3rd Grenadiers Baron Poret de Morvan

1st Battalion	582	16	46	155	0	0
2nd Battalion	582	16	40	150	0	0

4th Grenadiers   Baron L. de Harlet

1st Battalion	520	14	40	160	0	0
6 Pounder battery	8 guns	1 model	0	10	0	0

The Division of the Chasseurs a' Pied   Liet. Gen. Count Morand

1st Chasseurs   General Cambronne

1st Battalion	653	18	35	194	0	50
2nd Battalion	654	18	50	245	0	75

2nd Chasseurs   General Pelet

1st Battalion	581	16	34	125	0	0
2nd Battalion	582	16	30	140	0	0
6 Pounder battery	8 guns	1 model	5	10	0	0

3rd Chasseurs   Colonel Malet

1st Battalion	531	15	30	160	0	0
2nd Battalion	531	15	40	100	0	0

	Troops	Figures on model	Casualties (in men)			
			K	W	M	C
4th Chasseurs General M de Henrion						
1st Battalion	545	15	40	100	0	0
2nd Battalion	545	15	45	175	0	0
6 Pounder battery	8 guns	1 model	5	10	0	0
The Division of the Young Guard Lieut. Gen. Count Duhemse						
1st Brigade General C. Chartrand						
1st Tirailleurs,						
1st Battalion	560	16	50	100	46	25
2nd Battalion	549	15	50	100	45	20
1st Voltigeurs						
1st Battalion	615	17	40	190	50	20
2nd Battalion	607	17	45	185	40	30
6 Pounder battery	8 guns	1 model	8	15	0	0
2nd Brigade Baron Guye						
3rd Tirailleurs,						
1st Battalion	500	14	40	110	65	30
2nd Battalion	488	14	55	180	75	20
3rd Voltigeurs						
1st Battalion	480	13	40	188	46	20
2nd Battalion	487	13	45	170	35	25
6 Pounder battery	8 guns	1 model	5	30	0	0
The Imperial Guard Light Cavalry Division						
Count Lefebvre-Desnouttes						
Chasseur a' Cheval,	1,197	33	40	156	25	20
2nd Chevaux-Legers	880	24	125	300	80	64
6 Pounder Horse Battery	6 guns	1 model	5	10	0	0
6 Pounder Horse Battery	6 guns	1 model	5	10	0	0

	Troops	Figures on model	Casualties (in men)			
			K	W	M	C
Imperial Guard Heavy Cavalry Division						
Count Charles Etienne Guyot						
Grenadiers a' Cheval	796	22	160	440	102	82
The Empress Dragoons	816	23	61	250	40	32
Gendarmerie d' elite	106	3	4	16	3	2
6 Pounder Horse Battery	6 guns	1	5	10	0	0
6 Pounder Horse Battery	6 guns	1	5	10	0	0
Imperial Guard totals;						
Infantry	14,024	470	927	3394	402	190
Cavalry	3,795	42	390	1146	250	200
Guns	80	12	0	0	0	0
Artillerymen	1,440	40	66	180	0	0
Total casualties		6755				
Total losses		7145				

The estimated casualties in red are the casualties suffered up until the great rout that occurred around 8.30pm to 9.00pm on the evening of 18th June. After 9.00pm the routing French were pursued and harried by the British and German cavalry off the battlefield. Then the Prussians took over the pursuit as far south as Charleroi. We do not know how many casualties were suffered during this phase of the battle but it was considerable, especially in 'missing'.

We do however have the muster roll figures for 26th June for the Imperial Guard infantry. These show that eight days after the battle the corps, which had 13,250 troops in it on 18th June was reduced to 3,289, losing some 75%.

The main 'casualties' were in the Young Guard who lost 90% of their strength. It is concluded by Mark Adkin in his book that these were all casualties but I would suggest that this is not correct. The majority of the losses would be in my view 'missing'. By missing I believe that these troops left the army and did not muster on 26th June. If the Guard's strength was reduced by battle from 13,250 to 3,289 they would have lost 9,963 on 18th June. The Guard infantry represented 17% of the total French forces engaged.

If the rest of the army lost a similar proportion of its fighting strength, remembering that the rest of the army was more constantly engaged in the

1st Army Corps   Count Drouet d'Erlon

	Troops	Figures on model	Casualties (in men) K	W	M	C
Reserve artillery;						
12 Pounder battery.	8 guns	1 model	0	14	0	0
2nd Battalion 1st Engineers	351	10				

1st Infantry Division   Baron Quiot

	Troops	Figures on model	K	W	M	C
54th Line.	962	27	30	140	20	200
55th Line	1,149	32	35	135	10	250
28th Line	898	25	25	140	10	200
105th Line	983	27	25	140	20	250
6 Pounder Foot battery	8 guns	1 model	5	20	0	0

2nd Infantry Division   Baron Donzelot

	Troops	Figures on model	K	W	M	C
13th Light Infantry	1,875	52	35	140	20	200
17th Line	1,002	28	30	135	10	250
19th Line	1,032	29	30	130	10	200
51st Line	1,168	32	20	130	20	200
6 Pounder Foot battery	8 guns	1 model	5	15	0	0

3rd Infantry Division   Baron Marcognet

	Troops	Figures on model	K	W	M	C
21st Line	1,137	32	40	150	10	200
46th Line	888	25	30	145	15	200
25th Line	974	27	40	150	10	200
45th Line	1,003	28	50	170	40	250
6 Pounder Foot battery	8 guns	1 model	5	15	0	0

4th Infantry Division   Count Durutte

	Troops	Figures on model	K	W	M	C
8th Line	983	27	21	100	22	100
29th Line	1,146	32	30	110	10	100
85th Line	631	18	25	110	22	100
95th Line	1,100	31	30	100	20	100
6 Pounder Foot battery	8 guns	1 model	5	20	0	0

1st Cavalry Division   Baron Jacquinot

	Troops	Figures on model	K	W	M	C
7th Hussars	439	12	12	35	5	0
3rd Chasseur a' Cheval	365	10	20	30	8	0
3rd Lancers	406	11	15	35	5	0
4th Lancers	296	8	12	25	5	0
6 Pounder Horse Battery	6 guns	1 model	5	20	0	0

1st Corps totals;

	Troops	Figures on model	Casualties (in men) K	W	M	C
Infantry	16,931	470	580	2454	269	3000
Cavalry	1,506	42	50	85	23	0
Artillerymen	828	23	0	92	0	0
Guns	46	6	0	0	0	0

Total casualties	**3,217**
Total losses	**6,217**

2nd Army Corps   Count Reille

Reserve artillery

			K	W	M	C
12 Pounder Foot battery	8 guns	1 model	5	10	1	0
1st battalion 1st engineers	431	12	2	20	1	0

5th Infantry Division   Baron Bachelu

			K	W	M	C
3rd Line	1,114	31	40	95	20	10
61st Line	830	23	50	95	10	15
72nd Line	970	27	40	95	20	10
108th Line	1,072	30	30	90	10	15
6 Pounder battery	8 guns	1 model	5	20	5	0

6th Infantry Division   Prince Jerome Bonaparte

			K	W	M	C
1st Light Infantry	1,852	50	100	430	55	25
2nd Light Infantry	1,461	40	150	400	65	25
100th Line	1,093	30	140	380	60	20
4th Light Infantry	1,604	45	165	520	75	30
6 Pounder battery	8 guns	1 model	10	40	3	0

9th Infantry Division   Count Foy

			K	W	M	C
92nd Line	1,018	28	85	320	40	15
93rd Line	1,461	40	85	400	40	10
100th Line	1,093	30	95	320	50	15
4th Light Infantry	1,604	45	85	520	60	10
6 Pounder battery	8 guns	1 model	5	30	5	0

2ⁿᵈ Cavalry Division Count Pire

Troops		Figures on model	Casualties (in men)			
			K	W	M	C
1ˢᵗ Chasseur a' Cheval	485	13	15	40	8	0
6ᵗʰ Chasseur a' Cheval	560	16	15	35	5	0
5ᵗʰ Lancers	412	11	25	40	5	0
6ᵗʰ Lancers	405	11	30	45	8	0
6 Pounder horse battery 6 guns		1 model	5	15	0	0

2ⁿᵈ Corps totals;

Infantry	15,603	431	1065	3665	505	300
Cavalry	1,862	51	85	160	26	0
Artillerymen	828	23	32	135	15	0
Guns	46	6 models				

Total casualties 5,688
Total losses 5,988

6ᵗʰ Army Corps Count Lobau

19ᵗʰ Infantry Division Baron Simmer

Troops		Figures on model	K	W	M	C
5ᵗʰ Line	952	26	30	120	14	7
11ᵗʰ Line	1,176	33	25	120	16	7
27ᵗʰ Line	821	23	30	115	12	7
84ᵗʰ Line	929	26	25	125	14	7
6 Pounder battery	8 guns	1 model	5	10	2	1

20ᵗʰ Infantry Division Baron Jeanin

Troops		Figures on model	K	W	M	C
5ᵗʰ Light Infantry	886	25	30	122	17	7
10ᵗʰ Line	1,431	40	35	130	15	7
107ᵗʰ Line	735	20	30	120	10	7
6 Pounder battery	8 guns	1 model	10	10	2	7

6ᵗʰ Corps totals;

Infantry	6.930	470	205	852	98	49
Artillerymen	288	8	15	20	4	8
Guns	16	6 models				

Total casualties 1,194
Total losses 1,251

3rd Cavalry Division   **Baron Domon**

Troops		Figures on model	Casualties (in men)			
			K	W	M	C
4th Chasseur a' Cheval	337	9	25	100	10	5
9th Chasseur a' Cheval	362	10	20	95	10	5
12th Chasseur a' Cheval	318	9	25	110	10	5
6 Pounder Horse Battery	6 guns	1 model	5	10	0	0

5th Cavalry Division   **Baron Subervie**

1st Lancers	415	12	25	100	10	5
2nd Lancers	420	12	30	97	8	5
11th Chasseur a' Cheval	485	13	25	110	6	5
6 Pounder horse battery	6 guns	1 model	5	10	1	0

Total casualties	**852**
Total losses	**882**

3rd Reserve Cavalry Corps   **Count Kellerman**

11th Cavalry Division   **Baron L'Heritier**

2nd Dragoons	593	16	40	160	20	22
7th Dragoons	517	14	45	165	15	20
8th Cuirassiers	300	8	35	165	10	20
11th Cuirassiers	241	7	40	165	20	20
6 Pounder horse Battery	6 guns	1 model	5	30	0	0

12th Cavalry Division   **Baron Roussel d'Hurbal**

1st Carabineers a' Cheval	434	12	45	165	20	20
2nd Carabineers a' Cheval	413	11	40	160	30	15
2nd Cuirassiers	311	9	46	165	20	18
3rd Cuirassiers	480	13	45	185	20	15
6 Pounder horse Battery	6 guns	1 model	2	13	1	0

Total casualties	**1,875**
Total losses	**2,025**

4th Reserve Cavalry Corps — Count Milhaud

13th Cavalry Division — Count Watier

	Troops	Figures on model	Casualties (in men)			
			K	W	M	C
1st Cuirassiers	465	13	40	160	18	22
4th Cuirassiers	314	9	38	150	22	25
7th Cuirassiers	180	5	36	155	20	30
12th Cuirassiers	258	7	40	140	16	30
6 Pounder horse Battery	6 guns	1 model	6	13	2	0

14th Cavalry Division — Baron Delort

	Troops	Figures on model	K	W	M	C
5th Cuirassiers	518	14	40	165	18	25
10th Cuirassiers	359	10	30	155	20	20
6th Cuirassiers	285	8	40	150	18	30
9th Cuirassiers	412	11	35	140	20	25
6 Pounder horse Battery	6 guns	1 model	7	20	2	0

Total casualties 1,721
Total losses 1,928

fighting than the Guard was, then the French would have lost a staggering 58,605 troops during the battle. Clearly this was not the case. Nor was it the case that the Guard suffered unusually high casualties compared with the rest of the army. The most probable reality is that between the 18th and 26th June a vast number of French troops deserted the army, including Napoleon himself it must be said, and dispersed into the general population of France and its surrounding countries.

The French army knew that after such a defeat as Waterloo the monarchy would be restored and a 'white terror' would soon follow. It did indeed soon follow. They knew that to be found in the uniform of the Empire would risk arrest and execution so naturally they deserted the lost cause and tried to escape. Many succeeded and many failed but they did not fall at Waterloo as the muster records suggest.

The fear of treason was probably the greatest weakness in the French Grande Armee. Politics were ingrained in the culture of the army. They had after all come from the revolution that had swept away the ruling class. They had then been subjected to a terror by the new revolutionary government and, finally, after the defeat of Napoleon, had seen the monarchy restored and witnessed the former Marshals of the army bend the knee and pledge obedience to the new

King. Even Marshal Ney had promised to bring Napoleon back in an iron cage and yet here he was in charge of half the army, the half that was at Waterloo. Once the army fell apart who could they trust? Only their closest friends and their trusty legs. They made good use of both.

What the estimated casualties show is that at the time of the rout or just before it occurred, the French army was still a powerful force in numbers of troops in action. They still had over 47,000 troops under arms and prepared to fight. The sudden break-down of morale turned this mighty force into a vulnerable rabble without direction or control. What caused that breakdown will become apparent as we progress through the battle itself.

Chapter Eleven

The Prussian Army of the Lower Rhine

If one word was required to describe the Prussian army of the Napoleonic wars it would be resilient.

In 1806 the Prussian army was still organised on the lines set down by Frederick the Great some fifty years before. This system was one of rigid discipline with lines of infantry drilled to march in close formation and to fire three rounds per minute until the incessant volleys crushed the enemy. However when it came up against

Napoleon's French system it found that it was cut to pieces by artillery and skirmish fire to which it had no effective reply. Then with its lines fractured and its officers dead the awesome spectacle of massive columns marching over it was enough to drive it into ruin. Following its crushing defeat at Jena and Auerstadt and the pursuit that followed the battle, the country and the army were in ruins. In 1808 the Treaty of Paris was signed which limited the size of the Prussian army to 36,000 men. The Prussian King, Frederich William, became a puppet of France, their army a force hardly large enough to police their own territories.

To counter this the 'Krumper' system was introduced whereby soldiers were brought into the army, trained, and then sent back into civilian life with some rudimentary military training. This system of rotating civilians into soldiers increased the number of partly trained troops by an extra 37,000 men.

When Napoleon invaded Russia in 1812 a Prussian contingent of 20,842 men under the command of General Hans Yorck was ordered to become part of the Grande Armee. Yorck was a fiery character who hated the French and who was loyal to his country rather than his King or Government. He took little part in the campaign and when disaster struck the French he negotiated the convention of Tauroggen in which the Prussians became first neutral and then hostile to the French, joining forces with the Russians. This act caused outrage in Prussia. Both King and Parliament repudiated the treaty and publicly declared support for Napoleon on 10th January 1813. But Yorck held firm, ignoring both King and Government. This was in effect treason, a revolution of sorts, almost a civil war.

Clausewitz under Yorck's direction drew up the plans to raise a conscript army of every able bodied man between the ages of 18 and 45. Initially it was planned that 20,000 would be raised with more later on. In response to this and a request from Napoleon, King Frederick William and his government ordered the mobilization of the reserves created by the Krumper system. They raised the 37,000 partly trained reservists by the middle of February 1813. These opposing acts of mobilisation caused others in Prussia to form 'Friewilligen Jaeger' units. In the East the 'Landtag' or local Government approved the Clausewitz plan for the raising of the 'Landwehr' militia who would fight on the side of the Russians under Prussian command.

The King and the Berlin Government were out of touch with reality. Napoleon was a spent force, his army destroyed in Russia. Yorck knew full well that Prussia was better served on the allied than on the French side. By March it was clear that the Russians would win the contest and the Prussian Government and its King fell into line with reality and approved Yorck's actions. Civil war avoided, Prussia was revitalised.

The actions of the King and those of Yorck had the effect of rapidly raising the size of the Prussian army from 36,000 to 127,394 supported by 269 cannon. This rapid growth brought with it its own problems. Firstly they did not have enough muskets to arm all of these troops. The British Government supplied

113,000 muskets whilst other weapons were obtained from Russia and Austria. Uniforms were also a problem and, despite the efforts of the cotton mills of Lancashire supplying thousands of uniforms many soldiers were still in civilian clothes when the war ended.

The major problem was, however, the lack of officers. The Landwehr numbered 120,000 men by July 1813 whilst the regular army had risen to 150,000. The regular army took the best of the officer class but still needed more. They had to fall back on the old and disgraced officers who had fought the 1806 campaign. They were all they had. These officers, who had to learn a new way of fighting rapidly on the march, commanded almost all of the Landwehr units.

Throughout 1813 and into 1814 the Prussian army fought in ten battles and twenty-one smaller actions. In most instances they were part of a larger army commanded by either a Russian or Austrian General. Of all of the Prussian Generals of 1806 only one, Blucher, was exonerated of any blame. When Yorck raised his army of resistance in 1813 he naturally recruited Blucher and gave him the army of Silesia with the technical support of Gneisenau without whom even Blucher would admit he could not function properly. Nevertheless it was officer experience that was sadly lacking in the Prussian Army especially at the higher command level.

Blucher commanded the Prussian Army of the Lower Rhine that fought at Waterloo. He had only twice before been in overall command of an army at the battle of Katzbach on 26th August 1813 and at La Rotherie on 1st February 1814.

At La Rotherie he did in fact defeat Napoleon in the field, a notable achievement, despite the fact that by then Napoleon's army was but a shadow of its former self. Blucher also commanded at the smaller clash at Vauchamps but in all the other battles and actions he fought in he was a subordinate commander. Von Bulow was the only other Prussian General with any experience of higher command and in fact had also been in command in two battles and four smaller actions. No other Prussian General had any independent tactical or strategic experience although most generals had been present at two or more actions.

Therefore the army that assembled to fight at Ligny, at which Von Bulow was not present, was very inexperienced. Indeed this was only the third time Blucher had been in overall strategic command at anything like a battle. It is no wonder therefore that Wellington commented that if they fought where they were deployed they would be 'damnably mauled'. Nor is it surprising that they were defeated by Napoleon but in defeat they were not destroyed. The generals, whilst not greatly experienced in battle, were experienced in keeping order among the troops and the troops themselves had learnt that death comes to a disordered group much quicker than it does to a formed body of men.

During the 1813/14 campaign the units that formed the Prussian army at Waterloo had fought eight battles and eight smaller actions. They were on the winning side in five of the battles and lost three of them. In the smaller actions they lost only once. The army was both confident in its abilities and pragmatic about its weaknesses. The army was organised along French corps lines and those elements that fought at Waterloo were organised as follows.

The Prussian Army of the Lower Rhine

Commander in Chief Field Marshall Gebhard von Blucher
Chief of Staff Lieutenant General Count August Gneisenau

1st Army Corps   General Count Hans von Ziethen

	Troops	Figures on model	Casualties (in men) K	W	M
Maj. Gen Steinmetz					
1st Brigade			31	158	111
12th Line Reg.	1,460	41			
24th Line Reg.	1,460	41			
Maj. Gen. Von Treskow					
1st Cavalry Brigade			2	11	0
2nd Dragoons	290	8			
5th Dragoons	340	9			
4th Hussars	270	8			
3rd Uhlans	280	8			
Artillery			1	4	0
7th Foot Battery	8 guns	1 model			
7th Horse Battery	8 guns	1 model			
2nd Horse Battery	8 guns	1 model			
1st Corps total Casualties			34	173	111

2nd Army Corps   Maj. Gen. von Pirch

	Troops	Figures on model	K	W	M
Maj. Gen. Von Tippleskirch					
5th Infantry Brigade					
2nd Line Reg.	1,630	45	0	0	0
25th Line Reg.	1,580	43	0	8	0
5th West Landwehr	1,630	45	2	8	7
Maj. Gen. Von Kraft					
6th Infantry Brigade					
9th Line reg.	1,650	46	0	0	0
26th Line reg.	1,008	27	0	0	0
1st Elbe Landwehr	1,530	42	0	0	0
Maj. Gen. Von Brause					
7th Infantry Brigade					
2nd Elbe Landwehr	1,650	46	1	4	0

	Troops	Figures on model	Casualties (in men)		
			K	W	M
8th Brigade					
21st Line Reg	825	23	0	15	4
23rd Line Reg.	825	23	7	36	9
3rd Elbe Landwehr	825	23	21	68	50
Maj. Gen. Von Sohr					
2nd Cavalry Brigade					
3rd Hussars	537	15	0	1	8
5th Hussars	523	15	1	3	1
Artillery					
10th Foot Battery	8 guns	1 model	0	3	0
5th Foot Battery	8 guns	1 model	0	0	0
34th Foot Battery	8 guns	1 model	0	0	0
6th Horse Battery	8 guns	1 model	0	3	0
The 4th Army Corps					
General Count Frederich Bulow von Dennewitz					
Lt. Gen. Von Hake					
13th Brigade					
10th Line Reg.	2,393	66	0	3	45
2nd Nmrk. Landwehr	2,074	57	10	105	109
3rd Nmrk. Landwehr	2,366	66	27	133	134
21st Foot Battery	8 guns	1 model			
Maj. Gen. Von Ryssel					
14th Brigade					
11th Line Reg.	1,438	40	44	314	52
1st Pom. Landwehr	1,640	46	115	258	0
2nd Pom. Landwehr	2,415	66	287	178	2
13th Foot Battery	8 guns	1 model			
Maj. Gen. Von Losthin					
15th Brigade					
18th Line Reg	2,400	66	132	595	88
3rd Sil. Landwehr	1,930	54	143	452	57
4th Sil. Landwehr	1,775	48	38	217	101
14th Foot Battery	8 guns	1 model			

	Troops	Figures on model	Casualties (in men) K	W	M
Col. Hiller von Gartringen (Hiller)					
16th Brigade					
15th Line Reg	2,445	66	63	569	25
1st Sil. Landwehr	1,800	51	156	417	55
2nd Sil. Landwehr	1,710	48	37	192	308
2nd Foot Battery	8 guns	1 model			
The Reserve Cavalry					
Col. Von Schwerin					
1st Reserve Cavalry Brigade					
6th Hussars	575	16	7	146	45
1st West Prus. Uhlan	640	18	1	20	0
10th Hussars	575	16	1	15	15
Lt. Col. Von Watzdorf					
2nd Reserve Cavalry Brigade					
8th Hussars	450	13	8	58	2
Maj. Gen. Von Sydow					
3rd Reserve Cavalry Brigade					
1st Neu. Landwehr	346	10	1	0	0
2nd Neu. Landwehr	426	12	7	105	10
1st Pom. Landwehr	304	8	0	3	0
1st Sil. Landwehr	426	12	1	1	3
2nd Sil. Landwehr	316	9	1	15	4
3rd Sil. Landwehr	316	9	12	42	6
Artillery Reserve			15	66	10
1st Horse Battery	8 guns	1 model			
2nd Horse Battery	8 guns	1 model			
12th Horse Battery	8 guns	1 model			
3rd Foot battery of 12 pndrs.	8 guns	1 model			
5th Foot Battery of 12 pndrs.	8 guns	1 model			
11th Foot Battery of 12 pndrs.	8 guns	1 model			
13th Foot Battery of 12 pndrs.	8 guns	1 model			
11th Horse Battery of 12 pndrs.	8 guns	1 model			

Totals for the Prussian Army at Waterloo

	Troops	Figures on model
Line Infantry	19,114	576
Landwehr Infantry	21,345	616
Line Cavalry	4,480	124
Landwehr Cavalry	2,134	59
Foot Batteries	12	12
Horse Batteries	7	7
Total number of Guns	152	

Total troops	48,000 reaching the battlefield of Waterloo.

The Mysterious 8th Brigade

In all of the accounts I have read of the Prussian involvement in Waterloo the 8th Brigade of von Pirch's second Corps did not arrive in time to take part in the fighting around Plancenoit. General Bose commanded the 8th Brigade. At sometime during the battle of Ligny Bose went missing either wounded or absent. At Ligny the 8th Brigade was involved in the defence of the town of Ligny itself. There was a bitter struggle for the town, which changed hands several times. At the end the Imperial Guard attacked and sent the Prussians out of the town in rout. After this command fell to Colonel Langen but he was wounded during the retreat from Ligny to Wavre. Whilst he lay by the roadside awaiting treatment he was run over by a gun carriage and put completely out of action. So command fell to another colonel, Colonel Reckow.

Colonel Reckow led the brigade back to Wavre. On 18th June the brigade was deployed to the south east of Wavre and marched north of the town crossing the river Dyle at Wavre. Oberstlieutenant von Ledebur commanded the rearguard of the army retreating away from Marshall Grouchy and towards Waterloo. He was commanding officer of the 10th Hussars who formed part of the rearguard. They were slowly driven back until they crossed the river at the mill at Bierges. Here they met up with the 8th Brigade and Colonel Reckow detached two battalions of infantry to assist von Ledebur in holding the crossing. The remaining seven battalions marched onto Waterloo behind the 7th Infantry Brigade. And that is the last we hear of them except that in the casualty returns they suffered 200 casualties.

Where did they get these from? The casualties are noted as being caused at Waterloo, not Wavre, which was a separate battle. The action of the rearguard at Bierges was according to von Ledebur minor and in any event it was the 10th Hussars who came under most of the fire and they suffered 31 casualties, only one of whom was killed. Also the two battalions of the 8th Brigade left Bierges one hour before the Corps of Vandamme reached the Dyle and was long gone before the battle of Wavre began. So if they did not get the casualties at Wavre, and 200 casualties at Bierges would have elevated this action to more than a skirmish, then they must have suffered them at Waterloo. The casualties they suffered were greater than the rest of the 2nd Corps put together.

Clearly the 8th Brigade was involved in some fighting somewhere during the day and at Waterloo not at Wavre. The most probable reason for the error is the loss of General Bose at Ligny. The 8th Brigade was under the command of a Colonel. Von Pirch had placed all of the rear guard under the command of General Von Brause of the 7th Brigade. It seems logical that the 8th Brigade remained under his command for the rest of the day and marched with the 7th Brigade to Waterloo. It was here at the attack on Plancenoit that they suffered their 200 casualties.

I have therefore attached the 8th Brigade to the 7th Brigade, under General Von Brause, and marched them to Waterloo accordingly.

Section Three

The Evidence from the Battle Re-creation

Chapter Twelve

The Battle of Waterloo – The Initial Deployment

The map below shows the deployment of each army at the commencement of the battle. How this might have looked can be seen from the photos of the model on pages 118 to 126. In the first array it will be seen that

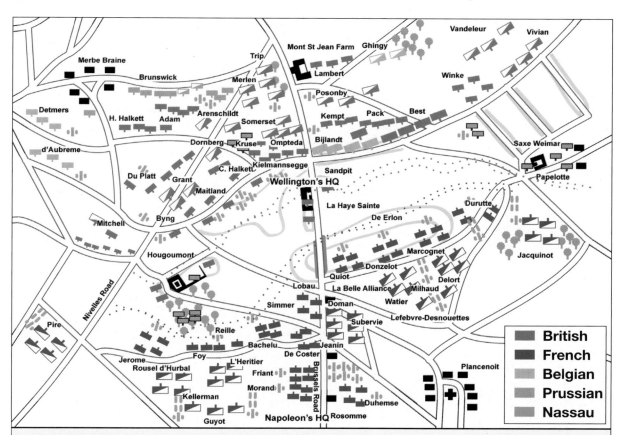

The initial deployment at 11.30am, just about the time when the first three gunshots were fired to signal the commencement of the action.

Bijlandt's Brigade has withdrawn to a position behind the hedge on top of the ridge and behind the Ohain road. This is in my view the correct position for these troops.

All other deployments seem to make sense and should not be contentious. Much of what happened during the battle is also not contentious but the whole crux of the argument against Siborne comes down to two very different versions of what happened at the end of the battle.

As we scan from West to East across the battlefield we can see the strength of Wellington's position. Clearly he expected an attack on the right flank of his army and deployed the bulk of his

troops on that flank in readiness for it. Equally he must have felt that the Prussians would arrive early in the day otherwise he would not have left the left flank so short of troops.

It is also clear that he expected the French to attack earlier than they actually did. The best explanation I have read of why they did not comes from Jac Weller in his book *Wellington at Waterloo*. In this book he argues that the French did not decide to delay the attack due to the rain-soaked ground, but rather they were not able to attack earlier because the troops had not yet arrived from their overnight deployment further down the Brussels/Charleroi road. This makes perfect sense to me. On the 17th

The French centre facing the allied front line between La Haye Sainte and Papelotte.

Wellington began his withdrawal late in the morning because the Prussians failed to let him know that they had withdrawn in the night. The infantry and all but the rearguard got away unmolested by the French. It was only later on in the afternoon that Napoleon himself led some French cavalry to reconnoitre the British position.

He at once saw that Wellington had escaped northward and it was only at this late hour that the French began their advance towards the Waterloo position. No sooner had they started when a downpour of tropical proportions turned the roads into mush. By evening when the Allies stopped their retreat at the Waterloo position and Napoleon, with his advanced guard, caught up with them, the rest of the French army would have been stretched out for more than ten miles, soaked and in darkness. They halted where they were and did not stir until dawn. It was not until late morning that the last of the French troops, the Imperial Guard Infantry, arrived in position on the field of battle. Only then could battle commence.

Talk of waiting for the ground to dry out does not really stack up. Firstly it was still raining, albeit lightly, when the battle started at 11.30am. Secondly ground does not dry out in a few hours, it takes days. Thirdly it was reported that during

La Haye Sainte early in the morning with the first rays of the eastern sun breaking through the rain clouds.

the French first attack the ground was so sticky that it sucked off the boots of the advancing French infantry. By the time of that attack the French Grand Battery had already advanced and deployed on the ridge, which meant it had been dragged through up to one thousand yards of mud without much being made of it. The delay was not the weather. It was the slow start on 17th June caused by the dilatory state of the French commander's mind after the battle of Ligny on the 16th.

Wellington's initial deployment is excellent. The rolling ground has gentle slopes not high ridges and steep slopes. The variation in height generally across

the battlefield is less than one hundred feet. In most cases within cannon shot range the difference in height rarely gets beyond twenty-five feet. It took a practiced eye to notice these subtle variations and to see that here was indeed a battlefield that could serve Wellington's purpose. Just what was that purpose?

To understand the battle and the battlefield we need to understand the purpose each army had during the day. Without a clear purpose no battle would have been fought. If Wellington had thought that the Prussians would not arrive then he would have abandoned the

The centre of the French position with Lobau's Corps and Domon's and Subervie's cavalry either side of the Brussels road. La Belle Alliance is shown in front of Domon's cavalry with Plancenoit at the top of the picture.

The view of the battlefield from the French centre where the Guard infantry have deployed.

battlefield and retreated westward towards Ostend or northward towards Antwerp.

Wellington was confident that Blucher would arrive on the field sometime during the morning. He expected Napoleon to attack but he expected him to manoeuvre around his right flank to attack his line of communication with Ostend and to threaten his line of communication with Antwerp and Brussels. That is why Wellington's right or western flank is so strong. Wellington had to keep Napoleon at the Waterloo position long enough for the Prussians to arrive in order to bring a numerical superiority to bear on the French and thereby defeat

them. As we know Wellington thought that he faced two more French corps than he did in fact face. What if Wellington had known that he faced fewer troops than he thought he faced? Would he have attacked Napoleon without waiting for Blucher?

Certainly not!

Wellington had no intention of taking any risk with his army for an early victory. Time was not of the essence for Wellington. Once Blucher arrived victory was certain. For Wellington the only issue was whether he would be able to hold off Napoleon's attack for long enough for Blucher to arrive and secure the victory. That was it, nothing more, nothing less.

Wellington's deployment makes this clear. It is a wholly defensive deployment, capable of defending the right flank from any out manoeuvring tactics employed by the French. The deployment forced the French into a frontal assault. There was no way round it. It would be a matter of French bravery against English musketry or rather Irish, Welsh, Scottish, German, Dutch, Belgian and English musketry, swords, cannon and bayonets.

Wellington was rightly confident on the morning of the battle, as his deployment, choice of battlefield and tactical position was more than adequate to achieve the strategic aim of defeating Napoleon. The only doubt he could have had was the time of arrival of Blucher's army and the time of the inevitable attack of the French. When would those times be?

Wellington was prepared for the French to attack earlier than they in fact did. He was up at first light and the army was deployed ready for battle probably by 7.00am. He could have reasonably expected the attack to be launched by 9.00am and for Blucher to arrive by midday or 1.00pm at the latest. He therefore expected to have to fight for about three to four hours alone against a

The view looking north from behind the French position. Kellerman's cavalry is in the foreground with the Hougoumont enclosure to the left. The allied line can be seen at the top of the picture with the village of Mere Braine Allude behind it.

French force of 90,000 men, which outnumbered his force by nearly one and a half to one. In fact he ended up fighting alone from 11.30am to 4.30pm, for five hours, but against 72,000 men rather than 90,000.

Looking at the southern side of the battlefield we see the French deployment. The French initial deployment also tells us what was in the mind of the Emperor on the morning of the battle. The deployment is symmetrical. Each wing has roughly equal numbers of troops deployed upon it. The Brussels road neatly intersects the battlefield giving it a left/right division with the road itself acting as a divisional boundary. On the left, towards the west, is Reille's Corps, which although only three infantry and one cavalry division strong has nearly as many troops in it as de Erlon's Corps of four infantry and one cavalry division. Behind Reille is the heavy cavalry of Kellerman's Corps and behind them is the heavy cavalry of the Guard. On the right, on the eastern side of the Brussels road is deployed de Erlon's Corps of four infantry divisions and one cavalry division. Behind de Erlon is Milhaud's cuirassier Corps and behind him is the light cavalry of the Guard.

The centre is equally as strong as each wing, stronger in fact as it also contains the artillery reserve. So the French deployment is a two wing and strong centre position, which means that Napoleon accepted the challenge thrown down by Wellington to attack him frontally and not to manoeuvre either to left or right. The key is the strong centre of Napoleon's position. Had he intended to outflank Wellington then Reille and de Erlon could have pinned Wellington's front whilst the Guard infantry and Lobau's 6th Corps, supported by the cavalry of Domon and Subervie, manoeuvred either left or right around Wellington's flank. Why did Napoleon not do this?

The answer lies in the confidence he had in his troops. In the book written after the battle and purported to have been dictated by Napoleon himself he estimates the power of the French troops as being equal in infantry to the British but twice as powerful as German, Dutch or Belgian troops. On this basis he would have calculated that Wellington had 33,000 British troops and 34,000 German, Dutch and Belgian troops. He would by this calculation estimated Wellington's army at 50,000 troops of equal strength to his Frenchmen. He therefore estimated that his force was one and a half times as strong as Wellington's and he did not therefore need to risk an outflanking manoeuvre. He could easily succeed with a frontal assault by delivering a local numerical superiority at the decisive point, breaking the line and scattering Wellington's army in all directions.

He is believed to have said as much at breakfast on the morning of the battle. When asked what his plan was he said, "I will crush them with my artillery, shatter them with my cavalry and then march over them with my Old Guard," and that was his plan, pure and simple. He planned to deploy his artillery in a Grand Battery, which would shatter the enemy line. Then he would attack them with his infantry and gain a position on the plateau of Mont St Jean. Once that had been achieved he would bring up his artillery to close quarters so that he could fire canister into the enemy ranks. Then he would charge the shattered enemy with his heavy cavalry and finally, if there was any resistance left, march over them with his Old Guard.

It is a good plan, it is simple, it has been well thought out, calculated for success and should have worked. I have analysed the options open to Napoleon many times over many years and have come to the conclusion that the plan he actually adopted was the best plan he could have employed on the day. A flank attack around Hougoumont does not work and ends in failure. The model makes the reason for this plainly obvious. Hougoumont forms one bastion and Mere Braine Allude forms the other between which is a solid line of British infantry. They would have blasted away any flanking force sent round here to attack Wellington's right.

Had this happened then Napoleon would have had either to withdraw, which would have meant accepting defeat, or to go back to the other plan of a frontal assault but with fewer troops than he would otherwise have had. The same is true for an outflanking attack on the left, eastern, side of Wellington's army. The ground here constricts movement and the villages, farms and chateaux of Papelotte, Le Haye, Frichermont and Smohain break up any attacking force. Add to this the Smohain brook, over which cannon could hardly move, and an attack via this flank is less attractive than the frontal assault he chose.

Napoleon was clear in his objective:-

Pin down Wellington's right flank by a diversionary attack on Hougoumont.

Deploy the Grand Battery to the right of the Brussels road and smash Wellington's line with round shot fire.

March de Erlon's Corps through the shattered enemy line and establish a position on the Mont St Jean plateau with artillery support.

Charge the rest of Wellington's line with the heavy cavalry supported by de Erlon's and Lobau's Corps.

March the Guard over what is left of Wellington's army and scatter it to the four winds.

No matter which way you look at it, it is a good plan. Contrary to popular belief it does not require Wellington to deplete his centre to defend against the attack on Hougoumont. The Hougoumont attack is a diversion aimed at pinning down Wellington's right to prevent it from supporting his centre against the attack from de Erlon's Corps. The plan should have delivered de Erlon's Corps onto the plateau virtually unscathed. From Napoleon's point of view the artillery should have shattered the flimsy line of Hanoverian and Dutch Belgian troops deployed along the Ohain road, leaving de Erlon simply to march into their position.

Equally once they were established on the plateau the battlefield widened out to a longer front than before. The cavalry could now come into their own by attacking frontally and via the flank of the British troops deployed on the western side of the Brussels road. Furthermore they would be supported by the infantry of de Erlon's and possibly Lobau's Corps, together with the guns of the Grand Battery, which would have been of no use in its former position and would have been free to advance in support of de Erlon.

There is no doubt that had this phase of the plan succeeded then Wellington would have been in some difficulty as he was driven further westward from the field of battle. A final attack by the Guard, supported by Reille's Corps, across the ground between Hougoumont and La Haye Sainte would have delivered the *coup de grace* and would certainly have

won the battle for the French. The plan is remarkable for its simplicity and effectiveness. It should have worked. Why it did not we will discover as we progress.

What is however equally remarkable is the fact that Napoleon came to this conclusion on a rain-soaked night in less than half an hour of contemplation. Perhaps fifteen years of war and fifty battles fought and won made such a feat less remarkable then than it seems to be now.

And what of Blucher? As we have already discussed his objective was also simple. He needed to support Wellington to defeat Napoleon on that day at Waterloo so that the war would be over soon afterwards. Prussia could not afford

The view looking southeast from Merbe Braine Allude towards Plancenoit.

The right of the Allied line behind Hougoumont showing the Brigade of Guards under Maitland and Byng and part of Halkett's British brigade to the left of the Guards.

to have Britain abandon the continent, leaving Napoleon in charge of a vast army that would threaten Prussia for ever more. Blucher had to take the risk of marching into the lion's mouth and placing his army at risk of annihilation in order to ensure that both he and Wellington defeated Napoleon together.

He did not need to get there too early only to find that Wellington was not heavily engaged, leaving the Prussians to be swallowed up by the French. Nor did he wish to arrive too late only to find Wellington defeated and Napoleon bearing down upon him in force. Blucher needed to arrive at the precise moment when he judged that Napoleon would be heavily engaged with Wellington so that he could enjoy an overwhelming numerical superiority.

Timing was everything for if the timing was right then victory was assured and in war that is the prime requisite for any commander, certainty of outcome, nothing left to chance.

Chapter Thirteen

Hougoumont

The Battle Commences – 11.30am

Reports of the time of the opening signal shots vary but in general it is accepted that the first three cannon shots fired by one of Reille's batteries to signal the commencement of the action took place at 11.30am. For the first half hour the French cannon opened a dispersed fire aimed at the whole allied front. The allied response was even less impressive as most of the guns were British and they had been told not to engage in counter battery fire. Long range fire, even at a stationary large target such as a column of infantry, was unlikely to be very effective. Tales of remarkably accurate gunnery such as that seen at the siege of Matagora fort in 1810, when the French cut through the flag pole of the garrison not once but four or five times, are so remarkable that they have found their way into the history books.

Generally at ranges over 600 yards cannon balls were unlikely to hit anything the gunners aimed the guns at. That is not to say that if by chance a ball did in fact strike a target that it did not cause casualties, as even at 1000 yards the ball itself would still maim or kill if it hit a living object. Wellington had however specifically ordered that counter battery fire was prohibited for the very reason that it was unlikely to be effective and both wasted ammunition and heated up the gun barrels. If the gun barrels became over-heated then at the crucial moment the guns might not fire and might as well not be there.

It was better to reserve the artillery fire until the French were close to the British line and then to blast them away with ball over canister.

At the same time as the French guns opened up so other guns from the artillery reserve, notably four batteries of twelve pounder's, began to move from

The view of Hougoumont from the west showing the Nassau troops in both the wood and the Chateau enclosure.

the rear up the Brussels road and into the position of the Grand Battery. To the eastern extremity of the battlefield Durutte's Division was still moving into position, whilst in the west Prince Jerome was beginning his diversionary attack on Hougoumont.

Napoleon stands accused that in attacking Hougoumont he used up and wasted Reille's Corps, which was bogged down in a protracted fight with a handful of Wellington's troops, namely the light battalions of the Foot Guards. This is not the case. The Foot Guards were not the only troops defending Hougoumont. There were also the Nassau battalion, the Luneberg battalion, a company of Hanoverian jaegers and a few Brunswick light infantry.

However the model clearly shows better than a map that Jerome's and then Foy's Division actually tied down more troops than they themselves used. It was not just the enclosure of Hougoumont that was affected but also the troops in the rear of Hougoumont who had to stay there in case the French broke through. These troops included Hew Halkett's Hanoverians, the Brunswick Corps, Du Platt's King's German Legion, Adam's Brigade, Chasse's Netherlands Division, Mitchell's infantry Brigade, Maitland's and Byng's Brigades of Foot Guards. The cavalry pinned down by Reille's attack on Hougoumont were the Brunswick Hussars and Uhlans, Dornberg's Brigade, Grant's Brigade and the Cumberland Hussars. In addition to this there were the batteries of the Netherlands divisions plus at least five British batteries, more than 60 guns and of course the troops in the immediate vicinity of the Hougoumont wood, Chateau and enclosure.

Reille pinned down 25,000 infantry, 4,000 cavalry and over 60 allied guns by his diversionary attack on Hougoumont.

At the beginning of the battle the comparative forces were 72,000 French against 67,000 allies. After the attack on Hougoumont had commenced, the French had 56,000 available to use against 35,000 allies. In percentage terms Napoleon had increased his superiority from 7.5% at the start of the battle to 60% after the diversion at Hougoumont. Viewed from this perspective the attack on Hougoumont looks less like an error. It was a good plan well executed and changed the balance of available troops at the critical point very much in favour of the French before the grand attack on Wellington's left and centre began.

Hougoumont was a battle within a battle. From the French point of view it was a diversionary sideshow, from the British a titanic struggle of brave

The model showing the Allied troops pinned down by Jerome's attack on Hougoumont.

defenders overcoming overwhelming odds to retain command of this vital outpost. It was indeed an epic struggle costing 1,669 allied casualties and probably three times as many French. Julian Paget and Derek Saunders in their book 'Hougoumont The key to Victory at Waterloo' estimate that Hougoumont cost the French some 6,500 men in killed or wounded. This represents about 33% of the total French casualties. My estimate is lower at 5,000, or 25% of French casualties. Either way the fighting around Hougoumont was so intense as to represent a battle in its own right.

If it was not Napoleon who made the mistake then was it Jerome who went too far and turned what should have been a mere diversion into a major battle?

Jerome commanded 6,000 crack French light and line troops and had been ordered to attack Hougoumont in order to pin down Wellington's right flank to prevent him from moving troops towards the centre, where the main assault was going to take place. The attack had to be a strong one. It was not enough merely to skirmish with the defenders of Hougoumont, Wellington's attention had to be diverted to this part of the field and he had to be convinced that it was under serious threat. He would have known instantly if the attack was merely a feint and would have

Baudin's Brigade starts the attack on the Hougoumont wood driving out the Nassau and Hanoverian troops deployed there.

ignored it. He did not ignore it but rather he sent in reinforcements from the left flank to make sure that the position was held. Clearly Jerome's attack succeeded in its primary objective.

The attack began with Baudin's division consisting of the 1st Light Infantry and the 3rd line infantry regiments, advancing into the wood south of the Chateau. The 1st battalion of the 2nd Nassau Regiment, consisting of some 800 men, was sent to defend this area but two thirds of the men were inside the Chateau or garden. The troops outside the Chateau were supported by 100 light troops from the 1st Luneberg battalion of Count Von Kielmansegge's 1st Hanoverian Brigade, together with some Hanoverian jaegers. Within half an hour, (David Hamilton-Williams says that it took an hour), the French had driven this force out of the wood and back across the orchard, a distance of some 600 yards. The resistance offered by the Nassau and Hanoverian troops is stated by some as being stiff, whilst Siborne is less enthusiastic.

Either way it hardly stemmed the steady forward movement of Jerome's light troops. They drove back the Germans, killing and wounding over 100 of them, and inducing a further 50 to absent themselves from the battle. Wellington had brought up the artillery

Jerome's troops attack across the meadow towards the orchard where the Nassau troops line the hedge.

batteries of Sandham and Cleeve, comprising a dozen guns that fired on the troops in the wood. At the same time he ordered Bull's howitzer battery to open fire on the wood, a delicate operation due to the proximity of the allied troops. But this cannon fire was so successful that Wellington even mentioned it in his despatch, praise indeed from one who gave so little. The French officer leading the troops in the wood commented that the first salvo from Bull's guns brought down seventeen men, a little less than three casualties per gun, but this was also enough for the officer in charge to recall it sometime later.

Baudin himself was killed in the wood either by the gunfire or from the defenders musketry.

The French probably suffered few casualties in this phase of the assault but they soon came upon the buildings and walls of the Chateau and rushed forwards to seize this valuable prize. The withering fire from the gardener's house and from behind the garden wall met their advance and brought it to a halt.

The light companies of Byng's Foot Guards delivered the coup de gras. Colonel MacDonell was posted to the right, or western, rear of the Chateau. Lord Saltoun had been ordered by

The Nassau troops are driven out of the orchard whilst Saltoun's Guard light infantry charge across the orchard towards the vastly more numerous French Tirailleurs and, incredibly, force them to retire.

Wellington not to withdraw to the main position when the Nassau troops arrived but to stay put on the lower slopes of the forward position. As the French advanced through the wood the Nassau and Hanoverian troops retreated. This is not too surprising as they were heavily outnumbered by French troops, expert in fighting in woods and in loose order. However they did not just retreat but ran hurriedly back beyond the Chateau on the western side and through the orchard on the eastern side.

A Major Bugsen commanded the Nassau troops and he left a detailed account of what happened. The Nassau troops had been ordered from the extreme left of the battlefield to the extreme right at Hougoumont earlier in the day by Wellington. A staff officer guided them to their new position. Major Bugsen had taken command of the battalion as the battalion commander had taken command of the regiment because the regimental commander had been injured. When Bugsen arrived at Hougoumont he found the Chateau to be devoid of troops. However the Guards had earlier occupied it and they had prepared the defences by building firing platforms and making loopholes in the garden wall.

Bugsen placed his Grenadiers in the house and then found that the gardener's

The French come up against the Chateau where Bugsen's Nassau troops and the British Guards open fire bringing the advance to a bloody halt.

house was still occupied by the Coldstream Guards. They had prepared the defences and stored their ammunition in the upper rooms and had barricaded the gateway that faced to the south. Bugsen deployed two companies in the vegetable garden and then sent two companies into the wood and kept a third in reserve a little to the rear. The final company was sent to occupy the hedge of the orchard. Bugsen placed himself in the Chateau and was not therefore able to control the companies he had placed outside the buildings.

Once attacked, the company in the wood and the company in the orchard were thrown back in some disorder, so much so that the Guards under Lord Saltoun positioned behind the orchard called out "The Nassau troops are driven out, advance the light company". MacDonnell to the right and Saltoun to the left now charged forward with their Guardsmen in a bayonet charge well suited to their type of fighting. The French light infantry, not wishing to engage the Guards in a bayonet and hand to hand combat, fled before them.

Part of the wood was retaken but could not be held, as now the Guards were in the fighting territory that best suited the light infantry of Jerome's division. The Guards, outnumbered, fell back to open ground behind the orchard

The charge by the British Guardsmen throws back the French assault causing much loss and great confusion to the attackers.

Some of the 1st Light Infantry manage to get round the back of the Chateau and arrive at the north gate bursting through into the courtyard, causing alarm in the ranks of the Guards defending the Chateau.

hedge where there was a hollow way and to the west back onto the Chateau itself. As MacDonnell fell back he ordered his troops into the Chateau and took command of the building's defence.

So, by noon, the French had attacked Hougoumont and driven off the Nassau troops outside the buildings. But they had then come up sharp against the Chateau and were halted by the fire of the troops defending it from the inside. They were then bayonet charged by MacDonnell's Guardsmen and driven back into the wood. Further east the French had advanced across the orchard in pursuit of

the fleeing Nassau infantry, only to be charged by the light companies of the 1st Foot Guards under Lord Saltoun and driven back into the wood.

In the centre the French reserve artillery was still moving into position to form the Grand Battery but it would be another hour before the guns were ready to begin their bombardment. In the meantime the battle for Hougoumont had to continue if Wellington's attention was to remain focused on this sideshow rather than preparing for the main event.

Jerome now sent in a second attack, still using the 1st Light Infantry, part of which swung round the western side of the farm and attacked the farm from the rear. There is a series of hedges running down the western side of the farm and few windows or lookout points exist on this side of the barns and buildings. There was also a considerable amount of musketry, causing smoke to build up and in the heat of battle much confusion.

Private's Clay and Gann were separated from the rest of the Guards and found themselves probably the last of the light company of the 3rd Foot Guards outside the buildings. They skirmished their way from hedge to haystack and finally arrived at the north gate of the Chateau. No sooner had they passed through than the French suddenly appeared at the gate. A huge man named Lieutenant Legros grabbed an axe and smashed a panel in the door and rushed inside. Reports vary as to whether 40 or 100 soldiers followed him into the farmyard but there were enough to cause alarm and threaten the security of the position.

First to see the danger was Lieutenant Colonel Macdonnell, the commanding officer of the garrison. He called out to three other officers nearby to join him in closing the gate. His urgent call alerted other Guardsmen, ten in total, who rushed to the open gate and drove off the remaining Frenchmen who were still trying to get into the farmyard.

They succeeded and closed the gates, securing it with a strong beam laid as a crossbar across the wooden panels. The names of those who closed the gates have been recorded in history. They were:

Lieutenant Colonel Macdonnell
Lieutenant Colonel Henry Wyndham
Ensign James Hervey
Ensign Henry Gooch
Sergeant Ralph Fraser
Sergeant Bruce McGregor
Sergeant Joseph Aston
Corporal James Graham
Corporal Joseph Graham
Private Joseph Lester

The Grahams were brothers and one of them, James, was promoted to sergeant after the battle and had the honour of saving Colonel Wyndham's life. After the gates had just been closed Wyndham noticed a French Grenadier who, standing on the shoulders of a comrade, was leaning over the wall and was about to take aim at Wyndham with his musket. Wyndam called to Graham by name and threw him a musket which was doubly fortunate to be both leaning up against the gate and being loaded. Graham was quick enough to aim and fire at the same time as the French grenadier. Fortunately Graham's aim was better than the Frenchman's for it was he who fell backwards shot through the head whilst Wyndham remained unharmed.

Wellington himself had said that the success of the battle of Waterloo depended upon the closing of the gates at Hougoumont. Sadly, whilst he may have said it, this is not true. The closing of the gates was important but they were not the reason why the French lost the battle.

Legros and his companions were wrong to rush into the farmyard, as they would have been better served by staying

MacDonnell and nine other Guardsmen force the French back and close the gates.

at the gates in order to keep them open whilst reinforcements arrived. Whether there were forty or a hundred does not matter at this stage for it is certain that forty would have held the gate from nine Guardsmen. The rest of the attacking force would have then been able to build up around the gate until they were able to attack the farm in force.

However immediately after Macdonnell had closed the gates three companies of Coldstream Guards arrived outside in counter-attack. Major General Byng, commander of the 2nd Brigade of Guards, saw the commotion at the north gate and ordered the rest of the Coldstream Guards to attack. These three companies numbered nearly 400 men and they arrived just after the gates closed and forced the rest of the attacking Frenchmen back down the track towards the French lines.

The First Light Infantry regiment of Baudin's Brigade comprised 1,852 men. Some of these had been fighting in the orchard and others in the wood. The attack on the rear of the farmyard was conducted by no more than a few hundred French light infantry. Even if all of these had gathered around the open north gate ready to attack the Chateau they would have been attacked themselves by 400 screaming Guardsmen from their rear, whilst further

Photo showing that the more numerous Allied troops in the rear of Hougoumont were able to get to the chateau before the less numerous French troops could.

troops from within the Chateau attacked their front. No matter what the French did they would have been driven off by this counter attack and if not, then Byng would have sent down further reinforcements until the farm was once again in British hands. The danger to the farm from this attack is somewhat exaggerated, as ultimately the British could get more men there faster than the French could and must, therefore, have driven off any attack that seriously threatened the farm.

As it was, ten men closed the gate, brave men, strong men and incredibly only ten of them. Legros and those who dared to venture inside the farmyard all died, save for a drummer boy who surrendered and was not killed for his trouble by his captors.

In the centre the Grand Battery was still being formed. Guns were being dragged across muddy fields into position. In all 80 guns and their caissons together with all of the other accoutrements of war needed to man these monsters had to be dragged across six hundred yards of boggy field and then up a hill to their final position. Wellington still had to be kept occupied at the extreme right of his position at Hougoumont. It was now 12.45 pm; The

The French guns moving up the Brussels road to form the Grand Battery in front of de Erlon's corps.

battery was nearly ready but not quite. Another attack had to go in if Wellington's attention was to be kept focused away from the centre.

Jerome's Division was exhausted and totally committed; he had no reserves left to carry out another assault on the Chateau. Foy's Division would have to lend a hand. Some say that it was Jerome that ordered Foy to support him but this is not the case. Jerome, although he was the Emperor's brother, did not command General Foy. It was the corps commander Count Reille who ordered Foy to support Jerome in the third attack on the Hougoumont position.

Foy's Division marched down from the heights towards the orchard heading for the light companies of the Guards positioned in the hollow way. As the French approached through the orchard they came under a withering fire from behind the garden wall, as well as a well-directed fire from the Guards in the hollow way. The French stopped their advance and hurried back to their position higher up the hill. The third attack on Hougoumont had once again been driven off by the Guards - or maybe not.

The third attack started about 12.45pm and lasted only until 1.00pm or shortly after. It was a diversionary attack not an attempt to take the Chateau or to

Foy's attack advancing on the Chateau from the east. You can see from the scale of the attack that it would not be driven off in fifteen minutes because of fire even from the Guards light infantry.

assault the main position. It was only intended to keep Wellington focused on his right flank whilst the Grand Battery moved into position ready for the main assault on the Allied line. Foy advanced, came under heavy fire, and then withdrew. The actual cause of his withdrawal was not the fire from the Guards and the troops in Hougoumont, including part of the Nassau battalion, but a sudden and massive sound of the Grand Battery opening up at around 1.00pm. It was a sound so loud that it was heard over one hundred miles away in Kent, and was reported on in the next day's local paper.

Once the Grand Battery opened up Reille's task of keeping Wellington focused on his right flank was completed. The noise of the Grand Battery was bound to divert the Allies' attention towards the centre left of their position. Hougoumont was not under threat, nor had it ever been throughout the first phase of the battle. Reille had achieved his objective but at a higher cost than he would have hoped for; 4,000 casualties of whom 900 were probably dead, with another 400 missing for the moment even though they may have returned later in the day. Jerome's Division was shattered, Foy's damaged, only Bachelu's and Pire's Divisions remained virtually unharmed.

Nevertheless the diversion had been a success. Not a single soldier was transferred from the right to the left during this phase of the operation. On the contrary two batteries of guns and a battalion of infantry had been moved from the left to the right. The Grand Battery would now fire for half an hour before the divisions of de Erlon's Corps marched forward across the field to occupy the Mont St. Jean Plateau.

Wellington could not ignore the attack on the Hougoumont position for he did not know where Gerard's Corps of infantry and Exelmans' Corps of cavalry were. They could still be lurking somewhere behind the French front line. They could quite possibly be positioned down the Nivelles road, just waiting for Hougoumont to fall so that they could attack on a front extending from La Haye Sainte to Mere Braine Allude, a distance of nearly one mile.

But what of Siborne? What did Siborne make of all of this? Did he embellish the role of the British Guards at the expense of the Nassau, Brunswick and Hanoverian troops?

The analysis

Siborne makes little mention of the Nassau troops in his history of the battle. He does say that they were sent into Hougoumont and that Saltoun was told to retire to the main position, as it was Wellington's order that they be relieved by the Nassau infantry. Wellington himself then came across the Guards retiring and stopped them, ordering them to stay where they were until they heard from him directly. When the French attacked the Nassau troops retired but Siborne says that they put up a stiff fight. But when they retired the shout went up "the Nassau's troops are driven out". This is the last we hear of them in Siborne's account, so from his point of view they took some part in the defence of Hougoumont but ran away when the French attacked.

Peter Hofschröer in his account of the battle claims that they were both in the wood, the orchard and in the Hougoumont enclosure at the beginning of the first attack. This is perfectly true. This comes from the eyewitness account of Major Bugsen. Bugsen's report appears to me to be honest and true. It does not embellish the Nassau role in the fighting nor does it cover up the fact that the troops outside the Chateau ran away from the French onslaught. Hofschroer's account, however, does give the impression that in this first attack it was only German troops who were engaged and that it was they who saved Hougoumont.

David Hamilton-Williams in his account goes further by saying that the Nassau troops held on to the wood for an hour before any British troops got engaged.

Neither of these views are correct.

The contribution from the Nassau, Hanoverian and Brunswick troops in this phase of the battle depends upon the length of time they resisted the French attack on the wood and their part in the defence of the Chateau.

It is clear that, as Bugsen had placed himself inside the Chateau, he was unable to control those companies deployed outside. These troops were then pushed back and retired in the face of the French assault, Bugsen could only watch as his soldiers ran from the French onslaught.

The resistance in the wood lasted only half an hour, not an hour. If it had lasted longer then there would not have been any need for Foy to make the third attack

before the guns of the Grand Battery opened up at 1.00pm.

Both Siborne and Bugsen say that the murderous fire from the buildings and garden wall brought the French attack to a halt. Siborne says that this fire came from the Coldstream Guards.

Bugsen does not claim that it was his troops who fired the murderous volley. We know that the Grenadier Company was deployed inside the Chateau complex but did not occupy the gardener's house. They must therefore have occupied other buildings inside the Hougoumont complex. These troops could not have effectively fired on the French attacking from the south through the woods as the gardener's house and the garden wall would have blocked their aim. The only troops who could have fired the volley were the Coldstream Guards, who were in the gardener's house, and the troops behind the garden wall. These could have been both Coldstream Guards and the two companies of Nassau infantry Bugsen deployed in the vegetable garden and along the hedge in the orchard. From here they did contribute towards the volley. Bugsen does, however, go on to say that the troops behind the orchard hedge fired a volley, which brought the French to a halt. This is patently untrue. The Nassau troops broke and ran away from the French. They might have fired a volley but it did not stop the French attack, for the French drove them out and pursued them across the orchard only to be driven back themselves by Saltoun's Guardsmen.

Both left and right the French were thrown back when the British Guards deployed outside the buildings charged them. The French were driven off in a state of flight and with great loss. Clearly what happened was this.

The conclusion

The Nassau, Brunswick and Hanoverian troops deployed in the wood gave way against a numerically and tactically superior French force. They hardly impeded the advance of the French who covered some six hundred yards in thirty minutes through a wooded area under shellfire. The shellfire from Bolton's guns was reported as effective.

The French arrived at the Chateau and were met by a murderous fire from both the British Guards inside the Chateau and Bugsen's Nassau fusiliers whom he had positioned in the garden behind the wall.

At the same time as the volley from the Chateau, or very soon after it, other Guardsmen under Macdonnell, stationed to the western rear of the Chateau, charged the French with fixed bayonets. The French ran away from the attack "in a state of flight and with much loss" as Bugsen states.

On the left or eastern side of the Chateau the Nassau Company placed there by Bugsen ran away and the Guards under Lord Saltoun charged forward and drove the French back across the orchard and into the wood.

When the Guards entered the wood, however, the boot was on the other foot. Now the French were in their element, hiding behind trees and skirmishing with the British. The outnumbered British drew back and a temporary stalemate ensued until a fresh attack, the second attack, forced the British back into the Chateau and Saltoun back to the hollow way.

The fight at the north gate and the repulse of the French by the reinforcement of the rest of the Coldstream Guards ended this phase of the attack on Hougoumont.

Further east on the other side of the Chateau a third attack by Foy's division received fire from the garden wall, which was manned by Coldstream Guards and Nassau infantry. But this time the French withdrew because the Grand Battery opened fire and the diversionary attack was no longer required.

Siborne did not mention the assistance of the Nassau troops inside the Chateau or the garden. The overall impression Siborne gave was that it was the Guards who threw back the French. Bugsen confirms that this is right and the modern claims that in fact it was a wholly or mainly German effort that defeated the first attack cannot be true. Just because they were there does not mean that they were effective. Bugsen himself makes that perfectly clear.

I cannot therefore find much justification in this part of the action to accuse Siborne of being unjust to the Nassau troops or any of Wellington's allies. He does give the credit to the Guards but they did drive off the attacks and did prevent the French from getting into the North Gate. That is simply a matter of fact. The Nassau contribution was made but it was only the supporting fire from behind the garden wall that assisted in stopping the French attack.

What is also a fact to be borne in mind

is that over 5,000 French casualties were suffered in and around Hougoumont during the day. The Coldstream, 3rd Guards and the light companies of the 2nd and 3rd Battalions of the First Foot Guards conducted the greater part of the defence of Hougoumont. It was these regiments who were chiefly responsible for causing the French casualties suffered throughout the day in and around Hougoumont.

After the gates have been closed the wary defenders look out to see if it is safe. Seconds later the remainder of the Coldstream Guards arrived at the gate.

The Grand Battery opened fire at one o'clock with 80 guns firing 2-3 rounds per minute for a short burst of 30 minutes intensive fire.

These 2,500 Guardsmen, it should be remembered, probably caused more French casualties than the entire Prussian army did in the battle.

I would ask you therefore to consider these facts and comment on the website on whether Siborne's description or the more recent versions of the Hougoumont action is the most accurate.

The guns of the French Grand Battery made it clear to Wellington that his attention was required elsewhere. He rode eastward towards La Haye Sainte and we shall now go with him.

Chapter Fourteen

de Erlon's Grand Attack

At 1.00pm the guns of the Grand Battery opened up in a resounding crash that was heard everywhere from Kent to Grouchy's Corps south of Wavre. Wellington heard it and soon moved off from the Hougoumont area to the centre at the crossroads behind La Haye Sainte. On the southwest corner of this crossroads stood an elm tree, which Wellington chose as his local command post. This is not to say that he set up a HQ here but rather that, if he was going to be in this area, then this is where he would be. Furthermore when he went off to other areas word would be left here on which direction he had gone. At the end of the battle Alexander Gordon, an aide to Wellington, died of his wounds and was buried near to where the elm tree grew. A monument was erected by his family on the spot and it is still there today. This monument and Gordon's body saved this section of the field from being dug away to form the Lion Mound, erected later to commemorate the Prince of Orange and the Netherlands' forces part in the battle.

It is therefore at the same height as it was on the day of the battle. From here you can get a good look at the battlefield and it is easy to see why Wellington chose it as his command post. Wellington liked to see for himself what was going on, to see what was on the other side of the hill. It would have taken Wellington about fifteen minutes to detach himself and ride from the Hougoumont area to the crossroads. Jerome's diversion had worked well, for by the time Wellington arrived at the crossroads it was too late for him to order reserves from the right to re-deploy to the left. He would have to fight off the French attack with what troops were already available to him in this area.

A quick scan of the horizon by his experienced eye determined that he was probably going to be alright, a close run thing, but alright none the less. From the crossroads running east along the Ohain road were the following troop formations. In the front line was Bijlandt's Netherland Brigade of infantry. Next to him was Best's and Winke's Hanoverian Brigades

The allied position just after the Grand Battery opened fire. Wellington had formed his army in two lines of infantry with cavalry in the third line. Adam's Brigade forms a strong reserve on the right flank whilst on the French side you can see a gap is opening up between Bachelu's and Foy's Divisions to the east of Hougoumont.

and further east at Papelotte were the Nassau troops under the command of Saxe Weimar. Behind them in the second line were the British Brigades of Kempt and Pack. Further back Lambert's British Brigade stood in reserve. At La Haye Sainte itself and in its rear were the King's German Legion troops of Ompteda's Brigade.

Therefore in the area under the artillery bombardment Wellington had available 20,000 infantry. In cavalry he had Somerset's and Ponsonby's heavy Brigade supported by Ghingy's Dutch Belgian light cavalry and the British light

cavalry Brigades of Vandeleur and Vivian. In total 6,556 cavalry. Supporting these were five batteries of guns and an extraordinary unit armed with rockets, Whinyates' rocket troop.

Across the valley Wellington could see an infantry corps deployed behind the Grand Battery and another in the centre by the Brussels road. These were the Corps of de Erlon and Lobau. Supporting them were the cavalry of Milhaud's cuirassier's and Lefebvre's Guard light cavalry. Further east the cavalry of de Erlon's Corps under the command of Baron Jacquinot protected the infantry's

Wellington arrives at the crossroads some fifteen minutes after the Grand Battery opened fire. Uxbridge is to his left and the ill fated Luneberg Battalion is in line behind him.

flank. The cavalry divisions of Domon and Subervie supported the infantry of Lobau's Corps.

In all the French troops available for the attack on Wellington's left centre were 25,096 infantry and 9,887 cavalry supported by 80 guns. Napoleon was therefore going to commit some of the numerical superiority he had created with the Hougoumont diversion bringing to bear a local superiority of 5,000 infantry, 3,300 cavalry and fifty guns.

At this stage there are two points of controversy. Firstly was Bijlandt's Brigade deployed on the forward slope in full view of the Grand Battery or were they pulled back earlier to a position behind the Ohain road? As we have seen Bijlandt was certainly behind the double hedge that ran along the Ohain road and was not deployed on the forward slope as Siborne said he was.

The second point of controversy is whether Napoleon intended to use Lobau's Corps in the attack on Wellington's centre left or whether de Erlon was to attack alone. The clue here is the use of Bachelu's Division. When de Erlon moved off to assault the allied line Bachelu moved his division forward and deployed it on the rising ground between La Belle Alliance and La Haye Sainte. This

The allied line as seen from Wellington's position with Bijlandt's Brigade behind the double hedged Ohain road.

division was there as a reserve ready to advance once de Erlon had positioned himself on the Mont St Jean Plateau.

The same was true for Lobau's Corps. Napoleon did plan for Lobau to be part of the overall plan but not the initial assault on the allied line. The reason for this is one of space. There was simply not enough room to deploy Lobau's Corps alongside de Erlon's in the first assault. Lobau would certainly have been used to support the position on the Mont St Jean Plateau once de Erlon had established himself on it and would have deployed his Corps nearly in line with Bachelu but slightly further back in order not to mask

the guns of the Grand Battery. See photograph on page 150.

Why are these matters controversial?

Let us deal with the issue of Lobau's Corps first as this is less complicated than the matter of Bijlandt's Brigade.

Lobau's 6th Corps

The importance of Lobau's Sixth Corps was that just before Napoleon ordered de Erlon forward to attack with his 1st Corps he spotted dark shapes moving on the horizon in the east. Could these be

Prussians? The question was soon answered by a captured Prussian Hussar, brought to Napoleon in person, who told him that the whole of Bulow's Corps was marching to Waterloo to link up with Wellington. This should have been devastating news. Suddenly Napoleon faced another thirty thousand enemy troops advancing on his flank. In fact it was forty eight thousand troops, as both Von Ziethen and Von Pirch were also advancing from Wavre to Waterloo. To delay this advance Napoleon ordered Lobau, supported by both Domon's and Subervie's cavalry Divisions, to march east and find a suitable location from where they could defend the right flank and hold off the Prussians until Napoleon had defeated Wellington.

The appearance of Bulow's Corps took away much of the numerical advantage Napoleon had gained by his attack on Hougoumont.

Napoleon, it seems, was not unduly concerned about the appearance of the Prussians at this stage. They were still some way off and he still expected to defeat Wellington with his first attack. If this did prove successful then it would take no more than another hour or two to

Bachelu's division has moved forward to the edge of the Grand Battery in support of de Erlon's attack. Quiot's Division has Charlet's Brigade attacking La Haye Sainte whilst Bourgeois's Brigade advances upon the allied main position. Lobau would have deployed next to Bachelu's position behind the Grand Battery ready to advance once de Erlon had taken the Ohain road had he not been diverted to face the Prussians.

Domon's and Subervie's cavalry together with Marbot's 7th Hussars form a line facing east to protect the flank. Lobau's 6th Corps advances into position facing east toward the Prussian advance, whilst de Erlon has launched his attack on Wellington's left and centre.

drive Wellington into the woods or westward towards his ships. This would then mean that Napoleon could turn on the Prussians with his Guard, and crush them utterly.

What is true however is the fact that Lobau would not be available to support de Erlon if the attack failed. This was wholly due to the appearance of the Prussians at this crucial moment. The question is would this have made any difference to the outcome of the 1st Corps attack or not? We will discover the answer to this question once we have re-created the 1st Corps attack on Wellington's line.

Bijlandt's Brigade

The matter of the location of Bijlandt's Brigade is important because Siborne reported this whole Brigade as having run away and having taken no further part in the battle. The Dutch/Belgians at the time disputed this and claimed that whilst they did break and run it was only after the French had reached the Ohain road that Bijlandt's troops fired a volley. Then some of them ran away but not all. Many historians come down on the side of the Dutch Belgians.

Siborne says that they suffered so

many casualties that they broke and ran away as de Erlon approached and in such a manner as to appear that it resulted from a word of command.

The more modern versions tend to argue that Bijlandt's Brigade stayed long enough in position to fire a volley at the French column, which then returned fire and devastated the two militia battalions. This caused massive casualties resulting in them fleeing.

The arguments are based upon testimonies and the interpretation of those testimonies from all sides.

Neither side of the argument is actually correct.

Both arguments blame the cause of Bijlandt's flight on the 'massive' casualties the Brigade suffered. According to Siborne this was due to the artillery fire aimed at them because they were deployed on the forward slope. According to others it was due to the volley from the French column, delivered fifty metres from the Ohain road behind which Bijlandt's Brigade was deployed.

The actual casualties recorded in the muster rolls from the 18th June included those casualties suffered on 16th, 17th and 18th June. On 16th June at Quatre Bras the Brigade fought well and suffered 685 casualties of whom the largest number, 303 were from the 5th Militia who held firm and did not run. On 18th June the 5th Militia suffered only 18 casualties and did run away. The 7th militia did not suffer any casualties on the 16th but on the 18th they lost 285 men. However 201 of these went missing and only 20 were killed and 64 wounded, hardly massive casualties.

Bijlandt's Brigade was some 3,000 men strong. In total throughout the campaign they lost 146 killed and 626 wounded with a further 621 missing. Most of the missing would have occurred after they ran from the French attack at Waterloo. Therefore they suffered 26% killed and wounded, of which the majority were caused at Quatre Bras. If it was not the casualties, however caused, that made them run away then it must have been something else.

Equally the issue of their being either on the forward slope or behind the hedges on the Ohain road is of importance and can be easily resolved by the model. Here Siborne is wrong in his version. Bijlandt's Brigade was behind the Ohain road as the letter from Captain Charles Gore (an Aide de Camp to Sir James Kempt) points out in both text and sketch. Other letters that place them on the forward slope seem to come from those positioned on the reverse slope, who could not then have seen what the Belgians were doing on the forward slope if they had been there at all.

Hamilton-Williams is correct in that Bijlandt was behind the hedges that ran along the Ohain road. But he is wrong when he takes the testimony of Colonel Van Zuylen that the Brigade stayed at the hedge until the enemy column was within fifty yards of them and then gave them a volley before retiring. Bijlandt's Brigade could not have stayed at the hedged road until the French were within fifty yards of them before they ran away, because if they had been then the French would have occupied the road position and would have been able to defend it against the counter-attack from the British Cavalry. Failing this, if they had advanced, which they would not have done, then they would have engaged Kempt's Brigade as it was deploying from column into line on the north side of the Ohain road position some 100 to 150 yards further into the allied position.

What the model shows is this

Bijlandt's Brigade was posted behind the Ohain road and suffered some casualties from the French artillery and skirmish fire. At some time they turned and ran away back past Kempt's and Pack's Brigades. Kempt and Pack were positioned some 150 yards behind Bijlandt. Bijlandt's men therefore had to run back 150 yards to the front of the British columns, and then a further fifty yards to clear the rear of the British columns before Kempt and Pack could advance. Kempt and Pack then had to deploy the columns into line and advance the 150 yards to the hedge on the Ohain road. The flight of the Belgians would have been quicker than the advance of the British, probably twice as fast. The British line would have advanced at a rate of 100 yards per minute and it would have taken them one and a half minutes to reach the hedge plus the time it took to form line from column which is surprisingly quick, taking only 30 seconds to achieve. So from this we can see that it would have taken the British two minutes to reach the hedge once Bijlandt's Brigade cleared the rear of their columns. At twice the speed it would have taken Bijlandt's men at least one minute to clear the British columns, which means that the French must have been three minutes from the Ohain road when Bijlandt's Brigade broke.

The French were advancing in column at a rate of 150 yards per minute, which means that they must have been at least 450 yards from the Ohain road when the Belgians fled. Any volley fired by them could only have been, at best, at the French skirmish line but most probably it was at nothing at all. Just a reflex volley into the mist of gun-smoke not unlike that fired by the Spanish at the battle of Talavera after which they broke and ran away.

450 yards from the Ohain road places the French column at the edge of the La Haye Sainte orchard or in line with it, too far away to be of much threat to the Belgians but close enough to threaten the 95th Rifles in the sandpit and behind the Knoll. The calculation may be wrong by as much as a hundred yards either way, but no more. What is clear is that Bijlandt's Brigade did break and run away long before the French column reached the Ohain road. It is also likely that the 7th Line battalion of Bijlandt's Brigade did not in fact run but held firm.

So what was it that made Bijlandt's Brigade run away?

At that moment in time there was much going on all around the vicinity of Bijlandt's Brigade. The French were advancing, there was gunfire and skirmish fire, the French cavalry were also advancing, La Haye Sainte was under attack and there was a lot of smoke around.

Events on the other side of the Brussels road were to impact on

Bijlandt's Brigade without him even knowing about it. So let us join the French columns as they advance upon the British line in order to see from their perspective what actually occurred.

The French View
The attack of the 1st Corps against Picton and Uxbridge

The guns of the Grand Battery had been firing for over half an hour and had fired some 5,000 cannon balls at the enemy line. Even if they are only two deep and if only 10% of the shots fired hit them, there must be at least one thousand dead and mangled bodies in the enemy ranks,

or so the French commanders thought. Suddenly the guns fell silent as the infantry divisions of Quoit, Marcognet, Donzelot and Durutte marched forward to the attack. The formation chosen was an old one, but it had not been selected in error. In the morning the generals gathered together to discuss how best to attack Wellington's line. Many had faced him in Spain and knew of the power of his infantry volleys delivered from a two deep line on a massed column of infantry, which was unable to reply because of their tight formation. They chose to advance in *Battalion Carré*, that is to say a column composed of battalions in line one behind the other.

de Erlon's massive columns march through the Grand Battery to assault the allied line at the Ohain road. At the bottom of the picture a brigade of Durutte's Division advances on Papelotte.

The advantage of this is to deliver at the critical moment a battalion in line with the added advantage of a column in depth. Also the front line cannot easily run away as they have another battalion in line behind it, and so on. Quiot's column had only Bourgeois' Brigade in it as Charlet was diverted to attack La Haye Sainte. It is therefore only four battalions in line deep. Donzelot's and Marcognet's columns are eight battalions deep whilst Durutte has a column of four battalions comprising Pegot's Brigade, as Brue had been sent to attack Papelotte.

They marched on through the guns of the Grand Battery and down the slope into the valley between the two armies.

As the French columns advanced their left flank was protected by cuirassiers from Traver's Brigade, which formed part of Milhaud's Corps.

La Haye Sainte came under attack and from the main allied position a battalion of infantry was seen by the French, advancing to reinforce the Germans in the farmhouse. As they advanced in line they were suddenly charged by the 1st Cuirassiers who cut them to pieces. A cheer went up from Bourgeois' column as the enemy were cut down and routed. No sooner had this happened when, as the infantry columns reached the edge of the La Haye Sainte

Wellington orders the Luneberg Battalion forward to help in the defence of La Haye Sainte. He is unaware of the French cavalry deployed to the south west of the farm just waiting for such an opportunity.

The Luenberg Battalion is decimated by Colonel Ordener's Cuirassiers. The 95th Rifles on the other side of La Haye Sainte witnessed their fate and panicked.

orchard, the 95th Riflemen, deployed behind a knoll just in front of the French column, began to run back towards the main position. This was most welcome, as their rifle fire had just begun to take effect on the packed French ranks. Further fire came at them from the farm buildings and the column inclined to its right to avoid both this fire and the Knoll.

The French troops in the column could not see too clearly but it appeared to them that not only did the light troops withdraw, which was only to be expected, but the whole line of enemy troops behind the Ohain road suddenly turned and ran away. Another cheer went

up from the ranks of the column. The enemy was defeated, crushed by the power of the cannonade and the mighty appearance of a full infantry corps of sixteen thousand men, advancing in massive unstoppable blocks of men.

Onward came the columns marching up the slope towards the Ohain road, drums beating, the men in high spirits and cheering loudly despite the cannon balls carving lanes through their ranks. Some officers later complained that there was too much cheering and noise. They found it hard to make their orders heard over the din but they marched on, the double hedged road only fifty yards away. Their objective was easily within their grasp.

La Haye Sainte was under attack from Charlet's Brigade who had virtually surrounded the farm. In the east Brue's Brigade was pushing the Nassau troops out of Papelotte. The right flank was secure and the left flank almost so; everything was going according to plan. From his vantage point at Rossomme Napoleon could see the progress of the attack. He could see that the columns were almost at the Ohain road. The farm of La Haye Sainte was almost surrounded and the reinforcements sent in by Wellington to bolster the farm's defence scattered by Dubois' cuirassiers. He

would then have seen the rout of the 95th Rifles and Bijlandt's Brigade. On the right the Nassau troops of Saxe Weimar's Brigade were scurrying back up the hill away from Papelotte.

Napoleon's plan was working exactly as he would have wished. The diversionary attack on Hougoumont had not only pinned down Wellington's best troops on the western side of the battlefield but had induced Wellington to send two batteries of cannon from the intended point of attack to counter the diversion in the west. Then the guns of the Grand Battery opened up and smashed the centre of Wellington's line, so much so that when de Erlon marched forward the enemy ran

Unnerved by the decimation of the Luneberg battalion, the 95th Rifles rout right into the face of Bijlandt's Brigade. The peculiar guns in the lower left are Whinyates rocket troop.

from his impressive columns. The appearance of Bulow's Corps in the east was a blow, but never mind, victory was at hand.

Many Waterloo histories imagine that de Erlon's plan was to march over the Ohain road and attack whatever was on the other side of the hill. What is more likely is that he intended to capture the farms of La Haye Sainte and Papelotte and the double hedged Ohain road, so that he could then advance the Grand Battery and place it on the south side of the road in order to fire onto the plateau beyond. If he had been able to do this

then no counter-attack by Wellington would have dislodged him for they would have had to close on the muzzles of eighty guns firing canister from behind a double hedged position. Furthermore, if de Erlon had captured and held the Ohain road then the farm of La Haye Sainte would have fallen, as its position would have been untenable.

At this point Lobau's Sixth Corps would have been most useful, but in the absence of the Sixth Corps Napoleon would have been able to use Bachelu's Division or the Young Guard Division and even part of the Old Guard infantry if

Suddenly the whole of Bijlandt's Brigade panics and joins the rout of the 95th Rifles, leaving the Ohain road completely undefended for a distance of 900 yards from the Brussels road running eastwards. Only Picton, trying to rally some of the riflemen, stands by the road where in a few minutes he will be shot dead by a French Tiralleur.

Sir James Kempt and Sir Dennis Pack address their brigades before marching them in line towards the approaching French columns. Behind them Ponsonby's Brigade of heavy cavalry have formed into line ready to charge. The British gunners fire their last salvo before retiring.

necessary. The model shows this up quite clearly. It would have been folly to have advanced blindly across the Ohain road when its capture would have ensured that whatever was on the other side of the hill would have been blasted away by the Grand Battery, once it had advanced to the hedged road. All they had to do was take the road from which the enemy had already fled and hold it; it was only fifty yards away, a few seconds march.

Then suddenly a line of redcoats appeared from behind the hedge, some had feather bonnets, others shakos but all of them levelled their guns in one swift movement.

The Allied View
Of
de Erlon's attack

When the Grand Battery ceased its cannonade, those on the Allied side who were in a position to see saw four huge columns of infantry emerge from behind the battery and march forward in perfect order. On their left came the French cuirassiers protecting the column's left flank. On their right rear in the far distance were the lancers of Jacquinot's Division. In all, over twenty thousand men were advancing on a slender line, which had been weakened by the transfer of two batteries from the left to help defend Hougoumont against Jerome's diversionary attack. No time to bring them back now, the French would be among us within fifteen minutes. La Haye Sainte looked very vulnerable and isolated in the face of such an attack and clearly a whole Brigade was deployed to attack this position. It needed reinforcing, or so someone of very high rank on the Allied side thought. Some histories have placed the blame of this decision onto the shoulders of the Prince of Orange, but it was Wellington himself who ordered Lieutenant Colonel Von Klencke of the Hanoverian Luneberg Battalion to advance in order to reinforce La Haye Sainte.

Down the hill they marched unaware that Dubois was advancing with 780 cuirassiers in the high corn and at that moment in dead ground, out of sight. As the Luneberg Battalion advanced down towards the Farm, Dubois caught sight of them through the smoke. What a gift, a line of infantry, clearly unaware of his presence, marching towards him. Colonel Ordener ordered the charge and the 1st Cuirassiers moved from the walk to the trot. Within seconds and with the allied skirmishers falling back, the line of Hanoverians were hit end on and scattered by the cuirassiers who captured their colours and cut the battalion to pieces. From across the road the elite riflemen of the 95th Rifles watched in horror as the Hanoverian battalion was decimated. They panicked.

Who says they panicked? Their own Colonel, Lieutenant Colonel Andrew Barnard, said so in a letter to Major Cameron of the 95th Rifles, which says;

"I regret to say that a great number of our men went to the rear without cause after the appearance of the cuirassiers. There were no less than 100 absentees after the fight and this vexes me very much as it is the first time such a thing has ever happened in the regiment. Kincaid says that very few if any quitted the corps after the charge of the cavalry. Many of those that went to the rear were men that I had little expected to have heard of in that situation."

The sight of the Luneberg battalion being cut down by the cuirassiers was a shock to the elite riflemen in the sandpit across the Brussels road. They had never fought against cuirassiers before and had not witnessed the devastating effect of such a charge. The Rifles were regarded as the second most elite troops in the army, second only to the Guards. Nevertheless it was the Rifles who panicked and ran back. Maybe only a few hundred of them but enough to unnerve the Belgians behind the Ohain road and cause them to panic, fire a volley into the air and run.

When they ran back Kempt, Pack, Picton, Wellington, and everyone else could see what was going to happen. The French had an open route to the heart of the allied position. All they had to do was march up and take the double-hedged road and then hold it whilst the Grand Battery moved forward and blasted Wellington's army into ruin.

Kempt and Pack had to advance their brigades to plug the gap created by the flight of Bijlandt's Dutch Belgians. The 7th line infantry of Bijlandt's Brigade did not run but held their position. On their left, however, Best's Hanoverian Brigade fell back in good order to line up with Winke's Brigade posted some 100 yards in the rear. Kempt and Pack could have done the same, formed a new line in the rear of the Ohain road and awaited the further advance of de Erlon's Corps, but they knew that the double hedged road was vital to both armies. Just as de Erlon needed to hold it so that reinforcements could be brought up, so Wellington needed to hold it in order to drive away any French advance on the Mont St Jean Plateau. The question was could Kempt and Pack advance their brigades in time to get to the hedged road before de Erlon?

There was just enough time if the decision was taken now, not in ten seconds time but now. Without any orders from Wellington, Picton ordered his division forward. The situation was best summed up by Sir Denis Pack when he said to the 92nd Highlanders "92nd, everything has given way on your right and left and you must charge this column."

Kempt arrived at the hedge moments before both Pack and the French and fired a volley into Bourgeois column at forty yards distance. The column, staggered by the firepower and the shock of the sudden appearance of Kempt's Brigade, hesitated for a moment before firing back and then it surged forward.

Pack's Brigade arrived at the hedged road seconds after Marcognet's column but nevertheless they fired first bringing confusion into the French ranks. Donzelot's Division came up and was faced by the 7th Belgian Line of Bijlandt's Brigade, the sole surviving battalion of the Netherlands Brigade. They fired an effective volley at the French and then went forward with the bayonet. But the odds were stacked heavily against the allies.

Kempt's Brigade numbered 1,923 of which 418 were the Rifles who had either run away or were in the process of being rallied by Picton himself. Pack's Brigade numbered 1,697 and the 7th Belgian Line had 700 men, less some casualties and losses suffered when the rest of the brigade broke. In total the Allied line composed of no more than 3,800 men. Against this the French were bringing the divisions of Donzelot and Marcognet and the Brigades of Bourgeois and Pegot. On paper these troops numbered 13,453 but they must have lost some troops on their way across the valley.

Sir Thomas Picton was killed by a musket shot to the head as he tried to rally the fleeing riflemen.

Nevertheless they must have had over 12,000 men against less than 4,000 men, a superiority of at least three to one. It was only a matter of time before the French overwhelmed the Allies and drove them back from the double-hedged road. Reinforcements were not easily available. The Netherlands Brigade had broken and run away. Best and Winke's Hanoverian militia had withdrawn and showed no enthusiasm for the fight. Saxe Weimar's Nassau Brigade was retiring from Papelotte.

Across the main road the King's German Legion, formed square to defend themselves against Dubois cuirassiers. Kielmansegge's Hanoverians were still in shock at the loss of the Luneberg Battalion. Only Lambert's Brigade, 2,289 strong but positioned further back at Mont St Jean, could be used to support Kempt and Pack, but they were too far away to be of immediate help. At this moment another disaster struck the allied cause. Picton himself was hit in the head by a musket ball and fell dead from his horse. The issue was in doubt. The French looked likely to drive the British off the road.

Now another character from the British side stepped up to the mark and came to the army's rescue.

Kempt and Pack arrive seconds before the French at the hedged road. They appear from behind the hedge and fire their volley into the massed ranks of the French columns at forty yards distance.

Despite the sudden appearance of the British line and their deadly close range volley the French column surges forward and engages them in hand to hand combat, where their numerical superiority should eventually win the fight.

Chapter Fifteen

Uxbridge's Cavalry Charge

Henry William Paget, The Earl of Uxbridge

Henry William Paget, The Earl of Uxbridge, was an English Aristocrat of the first order. He was also one of the finest cavalry commanders of the period. It was Uxbridge, then known as Lord Paget, who won the battles of Benevente and Sahagun in the Peninsular whilst serving under General Moore in the Corunna campaign. However when he returned to England, after the evacuation of Spain in 1808, he fell in love and eloped with Charlotte Wellesley, the wife of Sir Henry Wellesley, Wellington's brother.

Consequently he did not serve again in the Peninsular under Wellington.

Although Wellington requested Stapleton Cotton to command the cavalry in Belgium he was given Uxbridge by the Horse Guards. He appears to have accepted him without any animosity, placing him in command of all of the Allied Cavalry on the morning of 18th June.

For once the Horse Guards seem to have got it right for Uxbridge had not been tainted by years of service under Wellington in Spain and Portugal. Wellington was the premier General of the age but his style was a double-edged weapon. The army was bedevilled by Wellington's insistence on being everywhere and making every decision.

On the plus side Wellington's genius meant that the decisions he made were generally militarily sound, whereas those made by less able officers were often disastrous. On the other hand, the fear of the wrath of the Commander in Chief inhibited other officers in the field and prevented them from using their initiative at the crucial moments.

One such figure was Norman Ramsay who commanded 'H' troop Royal Horse Artillery at Waterloo. At the battle of Vittoria he had disobeyed a direct order from Wellington to stay put and went into action on his own initiative. In doing so he contributed towards the victory but nevertheless he was arrested and the promotion he expected for his bravery was denied to him. You could be brave

The King's Dragoon Guards appear on the flank of Colonel Ordener's Cuirassiers who barely have time to deploy into line before the British heavy cavalry charge.

The King's Dragoon Guards and the 1st Life Guards charge the French cuirassiers shattering them and driving them off in rout.

certainly, but only under the direct orders of the Commander in Chief, not on your own initiative. Uxbridge had seen none of this, for whilst Wellington was winning the war in Spain, Uxbridge was serving in Parliament and after his father's death in 1810 in the House of Lords.

Such a man did not think twice about whether Wellington would approve of his actions or not. He judged the situation and took what action he thought best served the army at that moment. And the moment was on a knife's edge. Uxbridge rode at speed to Somerset's Household Brigade of heavy cavalry and ordered it to form into line ready to charge. Then he galloped over to Ponsonby's Union Brigade and ordered it to form line and charge the French infantry, who were approaching the crest of the position. Then he galloped back again to the Household Brigade and put the whole force in motion.

Uxbridge led the charge himself, a mistake he often lamented in later life as he was unable to command the rest of the cavalry if things went wrong. They did go wrong, but not yet, for now they went very well indeed, beyond all expectations.

The timing of the charge was seconds perfect. It caught the French off guard at every point and utterly destroyed their attack.

The 1st Cuirassiers, having slaughtered the Luneberg Battalion came up sharp against the sunken road, which at that point is some fifteen feet deep. On the other side of the ravine the King's German Legion line Battalions were drawn up in square. There was no way through. To their right was the garden of La Haye Sainte beyond which was another steep embankment held in place by a brick wall. No way through there either. In the few seconds between slaughtering the Luneberg Battalion and deciding upon what to do next Uxbridge struck with the Household Brigade.

About three hundred yards further west the ravine flattened out and presented no obstacle to men on foot or horse. The Household Brigade commanded by Lord Somerset comprised the 1st and 2nd Life Guards, the 1st Kings Dragoon Guards and the Blues and Royals. In total 991 men. Three regiments charged the 700 French cuirassiers of Dubois Brigade and one, the 2nd Life Guards, veered to the left and attacked further to the east. The clash of cuirassiers against 1st Life Guards and 1st Dragoon Guards when it happened was, according to one eyewitness, like two walls coming together in the most perfect lines he ever saw.

The British Heavy Guards cavalry had the better of the elite French cuirassiers and shattered their line, driving most of them back down the slope and some of them over the brick walled embankment on the Brussels road behind the garden

The 2nd Lifeguards drive into the flank of the French column whilst the 1st Royal Dragoons hit their front. The Infantry have wheeled back, as best they could, to allow the cavalry through without causing too much confusion in their own ranks.

of La Haye Sainte Farm. Behind the 1ˢᵗ Cuirassiers stood the 4ᵗʰ Cuirassiers who numbered 314 troopers. These cuirassiers were overwhelmed and driven off by the 1ˢᵗ Life Guards, the Blues and the 1ˢᵗ Dragoon Guards (King's Dragoons).

The 2ⁿᵈ Lifeguards took a different route and funnelled themselves through the narrow gap at the high-banked crossroads of the Brussels and Ohain roads. Here they came upon the open flank of Bourgeois' Brigade, which dissolved into panic at the sudden appearance of the British heavy cavalry on its flank, whilst the 1ˢᵗ Royal Dragoons of Ponsonby's Brigade were attacking its front. Both cavalry regiments literally walked through the column slashing left and right cutting it into ruin and capturing the eagle of the 105ᵗʰ Line regiment.

Further east the rest of Ponsonby's Brigade comprising the Irish 6ᵗʰ Inniskilling Dragoons and the 2ⁿᵈ North British Dragoons, the Scots Greys, which were brigaded together with the English 1ˢᵗ Royal Dragoons, hence the 'Union Brigade', arrived at the hedged road just as the French were in disorder, having been fired at by the British Infantry who were now engaged in a hand to hand struggle at bayonet point.

The French thought that they were winning the fight at this stage, but once the cavalry arrived they knew the fighting

The rest of the Union brigade charge through their own infantry to get at the French. Most battalions wheeled back to allow them through, all that is except the 92ⁿᵈ Foot who grabbed the stirrups of the Scots Greys and dashed into the fight with them. "Scotland Forever."

The Charge of the Scots Greys

It was as well the British cavalry charge succeeded as there was very little behind them that could have stopped the French advance. Only Lambert's Brigade posted besides Mont St Jean farm was available and they could not have pushed de Erlon back on their own.

was over and the slaughtering was about to begin. Panicked by the certainty of defeat, they turned and ran back across the field towards the French lines and the protection of the Grand Battery.

The Allied line was safe, the French driven away, but now the British Cavalry, over-excited by their success went out of control, because Uxbridge, and other senior officers, were too involved in the charge to control the aftermath of their success.

The victorious British heavy cavalry dashed onwards in pursuit of the beaten foe. Two to three thousand French infantry were taken prisoner and another eagle was taken from the 45th Line regiment by Sergeant Charles Ewart of the Scots Greys, whilst it was Captain Clarke Kennedy and Corporal Stiles of

Corporal Stiles displays the captured Eagle of the 105th Line. There was quite some controversy about who actually took the eagle, as Captain Clarke Kennedy claimed that he captured it. Both have been credited with the honour.

Ponsonby's Brigade herd the French infantry back across the field like sheep cutting them down as they go. The blood lust drives the cavalry out of control and they pursue too far. The rocket troop has moved forward to support the charge whilst the infantry, carried forward by the charge, re-group and retire.

the 1st Royal Dragoons who had taken the other eagle from the 105th Line Regiment.

Onward dashed the Scots Greys into the teeth of the Grand Battery, slashing at the gunners with their long sabres, putting up to forty guns temporarily out of action.

Disordered and exhausted on tired-out horses the cream of the British heavy cavalry was now further into the French main position than their own. They were at the mercy of any fresh French cavalry that could be brought into play in a counter-attack.

Napoleon himself sent the order to the remainder of Milhaud's Cuirassiers to charge the British heavies. Further east

Jacquinot's Lancers wheeled left and moved in to cut off the retreat of the disordered British cavalry. Everyone could see what was about to happen but nothing could be done.

The lancers have been credited with most of the casualties caused to the British heavy cavalry during this phase, but the cuirassiers also cut down many of the Scots Greys. It was the lancers, however, with the tactical advantage of their weapon that stuck in the minds of the British as they saw their comrades cut down without mercy and unable to defend themselves.

As the Scots Greys reach the battery Jacquinot's Lancers manoeuvre to cut off their retreat whilst Milhaud's Cuirassiers advance against their front. Everyone could see what was about to happen but no one could do anything about it, as the senior officers had charged with the men and could not direct the reserves.

As the Scots Greys fall back they run straight into the lancers who decimate them.

The remainder of Ponsonby's Brigade and the 2nd Lifeguards fall back in disorder followed by the cuirassiers. La Haye Sainte is the red brick building in the top right hand corner.

The Dutch light cavalry of Ghingy's Brigade did move forward to cover the retreat and assisted in the rounding up of prisoners. But the Brigades of Vivian and Vandeleur hesitated, knowing of Wellington's disapproval of acting without his orders, despite the fact that Uxbridge had told them that he expected them to act on their own initiative and to support any charge being made by him.

Eventually, when the slaughter of the British heavy cavalry became too much to bear, they did advance and cover the retreat, charging the remains of Durutte's column putting it to flight. By then it was too late. Jacquinot had reached the stranded British Dragoons and had cut them to pieces. In this position the lance is superior to the sword in that it has a longer reach. The French lancers were able to catch up with the fleeing dragoons and spear them in the back, causing them to fall to the ground whereupon they would be spitted several times by nine-foot razor-sharp lances.

Uxbridge returned to his position, where he met the Duke of Wellington and the *Corps Diplomatique Militaire* who had witnessed the whole affair. Uxbridge had never seen such a joyous group; they thought the battle was over.

Across the valley Napoleon looked on in disbelief. All his plans had dissolved in these few minutes into ruin. Now he was in a different situation entirely. A few moments ago all was going well. His plan

Bachelu's Division had time to form squares and a defensive line in depth that enabled the routing troops to pass through to safety. The Household brigade suffered the same number of casualties as did the Union brigade and many must have been caused by their fight with the French heavy cavalry and the squares of Bachelu's infantry.

to divert Wellington from the left centre had worked better than he expected. The fire from the Grand Battery had been effective, or so he thought, for the enemy had run away when de Erlon approached. de Erlon had arrived at the critical point with over 12,000 men and, although they were counter attacked by two brigades of red-coated infantry, they were certain to win that fight by virtue of their numerical superiority. But then came the cavalry. It was the arrival of the cavalry at just the right time that turned the battle around and ensured that this attack was defeated. The allied infantry had played their part but unsupported they would have been driven back and

the Ohain road would have fallen into French hands.

The timing was most fortuitous. The French were fifty yards from the Ohain road when Kempt's Brigade arrived at the hedge. It would have taken the French a mere twenty seconds to cover that distance. At the run, had they known, they could have got there in ten seconds. It was that close, a near run thing indeed. The hedge was not a particular obstacle to either to infantry or cavalry, nor was the sunken lane along this portion of the battlefield except near the crossroads. The hedge, however, was a perfect rallying point, a place to fix the defence line on and a specific location to bring the guns forward to. Several reports state that the French crossed the hedged road and fought on its northern side. This might be the case but this does not mean that the plan was to cross the road blindly and keep going until either victorious or defeated.

Wellington cannot take much of the credit for the defeat of de Erlon's first attack, except for the very important point of the initial deployment and the battlefield selection itself. The reverse slope tactics he perfected in the Peninsular were the foundation on which the victory was based. The French could not see the Allies on the reverse slope and did not know that the cavalry were about to charge until they were upon them. Had they known the distance both Kempt's and Pack's Brigades were from the Ohain road, they would have doubled their speed and got to the hedge first. Had they got their first then they could have driven off the British infantry and cavalry attacks with musketry and battalion squares. La Haye Sainte would have fallen.

Bachelu and the Grand Battery would have been able to advance and deploy on the crest of the ridge. The Allied troops on the reverse slope would then have had to face the full force of eighty guns firing canister at them. We will see later on how a mere eight guns deployed further down the slope wiped out the 27th Foot with canister. Just imagine what ten

The remains of the Household Brigade fall back to the main position. Uxbridge is seen in the bottom left hand corner, having already returned to the 'Troupe Doree' where he laments the loss of his finest cavalrymen.

times that number of guns would have done to any troops exposed to its firepower.

Ten to twenty seconds between victory and defeat, ten to twenty seconds in which two generals, Picton and Uxbridge, made the decisions without Wellington's permission and saved the day. Picton rode forward to rally the retreating 95th Rifles and was shot in the head at this crucial moment. Uxbridge fought on through the day and was injured by almost the last shot fired by the French late in the evening. To these two men must go the honour of the victory over de Erlon's attack and the destruction of Napoleon's great plan. Wellington often referred to the French plans as a beautiful bridle, which whilst attractive and functional whilst working was utterly useless once it was broken. His strategy was a knotted rope, if broken he could tie it together and fight on. Napoleon's grand tactical plan was a beautiful bridle but it was also a knotted rope. It had been broken against all the odds by Picton and Uxbridge but Napoleon would fix it and attack again. The plan was foiled but the battle was not lost.

But what of Siborne, how did Siborne report on these events?

The crucial matter of the rout of the 95th Rifle regiment was known to Colonel Barnard, Major Cameron, Captain Leach and Lieutenant Kincaid, all of whom wrote to Siborne to assist him in his history and his model. But they did not tell Siborne the whole truth. They did not tell him about the rout of the 95th Rifles

and he could not connect their flight to the rout of the Belgians. In every other respect his history is accurate. He says that it was Wellington who ordered the Luneberg Battalion forward to its death. It was Uxbridge who ordered the cavalry forward and it was Picton who led the infantry forward. Wellington does not come across as being in control of the battle at this stage and appears relieved that Picton and Uxbridge acted as they did.

Siborne's account of this stage of the battle is an honest and thorough piece of work. He did not know about the Rifles routing. He could have deduced it if he had used the model as a research tool with the figures moving, but not if it was a static work of art depicting a single event in time, and a time later in the day than the attack of de Erlon's Corps. Siborne did make another model depicting the very scene when the cavalry charged but again this was a static model of the moment of the British Cavalry charge, not the flight of the Belgians. Siborne, in a footnote, does in fact excuse the flight of the Belgians and blames the event on their losses because of their exposed position and the fire of the Grand Battery.

With the knowledge he had at the time that would be a perfectly reasonable assumption to make, except that he did have the casualty returns. He could have seen that they did not in fact suffer that many losses from the Grand Battery fire. The matter of the rout of the 95th Rifles did not come to light until Mark Urban had his book 'Rifles' published in 2003 and even then he did not connect the rout of the Rifles with the rout of the

Belgian Brigade. I had calculated from the model that it was the withdrawal of the Rifles, which is perfectly normal for skirmishers to do when a column approaches, that caused the Belgians to rout.

What I did not know was that the 95th Rifles, the second most elite troops in the British army, had panicked and run with as many as 100, 25% of their number, leaving the field and not returning for the rest of the day. I did not know it and nor did Siborne. It is not true to say that he deliberately suppressed evidence of the rout of the Belgians in order to make it look better for the British troops who stayed and fought. He did not mention the 7th Belgian Line Battalian staying in line and fighting, even though some letters do make references to Belgian troops advancing to the attack of de Erlon's column.

Overall the impression Siborne gives that this was an exclusively British event, or at least an overwhelmingly British event, is true. The fact is that the Belgians did run away except for some of the 7th Belgian Line Battalion. The Nassau Battalions fled from Papelotte and the Hanoverian Battalions of Best's Brigade also retreated from de Erlon's attack. It would have been wrong in those days to portray this part of the battle as an allied effort, just as much as it is viewed as wrong, in today's terms, to make it a wholly British event.

Siborne was not writing in today's politically correct terms. He was telling it how it was and the impression he gives is an accurate one.

I would ask you therefore to consider whether the charge against Siborne that he deliberately suppressed information in order to enhance the British role to the detriment of the Netherlands army is true for this part of the battle.

He did not suppress the evidence of the 95th Rifles because he did not have the evidence. Siborne did not wish to offend the Belgians and made their excuses for them. He points out that they suffered over the three to four days of the campaign some 25% casualties, enough to make the best troops run. And here is the nub of the matter. All troops will run away if they are placed in circumstances that would make them run, all troops that is without exception. It is the business of the commander of the army to place his troops in a position where they will not run away and to force the enemy to put his troops in a position whereby they will run away.

At Waterloo the 95th Rifles were in a position whereby they were being attacked by a superior number of light infantry skirmishers behind which was an enormous infantry column. On their right flank they witnessed heavy cavalry cutting up a battalion of Hanoverians and it looked to them as though they were next in line for the same treatment. It should be noted that the Luneberg Field Battalion of Hanoverian Light Infantry wore green uniforms somewhat similar to the 95th Rifles.

It was Wellington himself who had put the Luneberg Battalion in its perilous situation. You could connect the decision to send in the Luneberg Battalion with the rout of the Rifles, and the rout of the Belgians, place the whole blame at the doorstep of Wellington himself, but that would be stretching the point too far. The fact is it was Napoleon's excellent plan that placed the Rifles in peril and caused them to run, just as it was his plan that would have eventually forced the Belgians to run away.

It was certainly unfair to blame the Belgians for their rout when it was in fact started by the British Rifles routing, following the disastrous deployment of the Luneberg Battalion by Wellington himself.

All Siborne had to go on was the testimony at the time. That testimony pointed to the fact that so far the Nassau troops had run away from the French in the Hougoumont wood, the Belgians had run away from the Ohain road, the Nassau troops had abandoned Papelotte when attacked by Durutte and the Hanoverians had fallen back from the French columns advancing against them.

Should Barnard have confessed all to Siborne to set the record straight? Certainly not. Barnard was in the business of making armies not histories. It would not serve the army to have it known that the second most elite unit in the army broke and 25% of its men fled the field of Waterloo; better to allow the Belgians to take the blame, better to keep quiet.

It was Napoleon's excellent plan that made the rout of the front line troops inevitable. The fact that they ran earlier than he had expected was not too big a surprise. What was a surprise was Uxbridge's and Picton's counter-attack. This attack shattered his plan to bits.

Now he had to decide what to do next. Now he was in a different battle, an unplanned for circumstance. Would it have been different if Lobau had been available to join in the attack?

The effect of the absence of Lobau from the attack of the 1st Corps

Lobau's Corps consisted of two divisions, the 19th Division under the command of Baron Francois Simmer and the 20th Division under Jean Baptiste Jeanin. Simmer's Division had 4,122 men in four line regiments whilst Jeanin had 3,311 men in two line and one light regiment. Clearly the light regiment of the 20th Division, 952 men strong, would have been very useful in an attack on La Haye Sainte. As it was, because Lobau had been diverted by the appearance of the Prussians, La Haye Sainte was attacked by Charlet's Brigade consisting of the 54th and 55th Line regiments, 2,111 men.

It is difficult to see how any more than 2,000 men could have attacked La Haye Sainte as there was not enough space to fit in even that many. Charlet's attack had to be abandoned once Uxbridge drove away Marcognet, Donzelot, and the rest of Quiot's Divisions. The same must have been true if it had been Lobau attacking instead of Charlet. Charlet, however, would then of course been deployed in the main attack behind Bourgeois. Would that have had any effect on the outcome? Bourgeois was attacked by the 1st Royal Dragoons and the 2nd Lifeguards after being brought to a halt by the firepower of Kempt's Brigade. Donzelot was attacked by the 6th Dragoons after they had received a less effective volley from

Lobau would have been placed near to where Bachelu stood waiting in reserve to exploit de Erlon's success. There was not enough room for him to have attacked at the same time as de Erlon.

the 7th Line of Bijlandt's Brigade, possibly some fire from the 28th Foot of Kempt's Brigade and also from the 1st Foot from Pack's Brigade. Donzelot's Division had its two full brigades in the column and was driven off by the 6th Dragoons. Quoit, even if he had had Charlet's Brigades supporting Bourgeois, would have suffered the same fate.

It was the speed of Uxbridge's charge and the attendant rout of de Erlon that was the decisive factor in this part of the battle. It would not have mattered whether Lobau was there or not. There was simply not enough time for Charlet or Lobau to capture La Haye Sainte before Uxbridge drove away the rest of de Erlon's Corps, leaving whoever was attacking La Haye Sainte in an exposed and untenable position. They would have had to withdraw.

De Erlon defeated and the Prussians approaching fast, what to do, what to do?

Let us now look, as Napoleon did, at the options open to him.

Chapter Sixteen

A New Battle - A New Plan

It is often reported that Napoleon had to fight on after the defeat of de Erlon because he feared political revolution in France if he retreated. This cannot be the case. Napoleon could quite easily have withdrawn all the way back to Paris if he wanted to. If he had arrived at the gates of Paris with an army of one hundred thousand men who would have opposed him?

Is it impossible to conceive of a political spin to the events up to mid afternoon on 18th June that makes Napoleon the victor? Of course it is not. Napoleon could have said, with enough justification to be believed, that he had marched against a foe that outnumbered him two to one and defeated both armies at Ligny and Quatre Bras causing 50,000 losses to the enemy. Over the next two days the Prussians were defeated once again at Wavre and the hated English cowered from his veterans, whilst their allies ran away at Waterloo.

"The enemies of France have been dealt such a blow to ensure that they will not advance into our Northern territory with any hope of success, I now look to my former allies in the east to come to terms and avoid the humiliation of similar defeats at the hands of my new Grand Army which now stands at half a million men"

Who is to say that such a plan would not have worked? Certainly Wellington's army had been dealt a blow, most of the heavy cavalry ruined, the confidence in the allies at least dented. As for Blucher, his army had twice been beaten, once badly at Ligny and once again at Wavre.

Would he not wait for reinforcements before attacking the fortified towns along the Sambre? Would that delay give enough time for peace talks to start? Napoleon may well have lost in the end if peace was not concluded. But it cannot be true to say that at 2.30pm on the afternoon of 18th June he decided to fight on, despite the repulse of de Erlon's Corps and the imminent arrival of the Prussians because he was afraid of what they might think in Paris. He fought on because he thought he could still win, and for no other reason.

Napoleon held his enemies in varying degrees of contempt. He thought that the Prussians, man for man, were only worth in fighting quality one third of his troops. He felt that only the British infantry was equal to his best troops but there were so few of them they did not matter. If you look at things from this point of view, and remember Napoleon's genius for minute calculation and detailed memory of military matters, then you can see where he, in his mind, was coming from. He knew that Wellington's army consisted of some 69,000 men but he also knew that only 33,000 were British. The rest were a mixed bunch of Germans, Dutch and Belgians whom he did not rate any better that one third the value of his troops.

He had just witnessed thousands of these troops fleeing the field, or so he thought. So he would calculate that Wellington's army was only equal to 40,000 Frenchmen. He knew that Von Bulow with 30,000 Prussians, was approaching his right flank but in his estimation these would only account for 10,000 Frenchmen. In his mind therefore he had an army of over 60,000 men facing an enemy worth only 50,000. From his point of view he still held the upper hand. Was this just arrogance, or simple miscalculation? It looks very much like a mixture of both, but to be fair to Napoleon he had, only two days before at Ligny, defeated a Prussian army of 83,000 men, deployed in a defensive position protected by villages and a stream, with a French army of 60,000 men. In this battle he caused 17,000 casualties and suffered only 12,000 himself.

It could be argued that if 60,000 can cause 17,000 casualties when attacking a defended position (a ratio of one casualty to every 3.5 men engaged) whilst 83,000 men caused only 12,000 casualties from a defensive position against an attacking enemy (a ratio of one casualty to every 6.0 men engaged) it does look as though the French are nearly twice as efficient as the Prussians. When one bears in mind that the defender has the advantage and ought to cause more casualties than the attacker, it could be argued that the French were in fact three times as effective as the Prussians.

Napoleon was therefore still confident of victory despite de Erlon's attack being repulsed. So what to do now?

He had already sent Lobau, Domon and Subervie to stop the Prussians. Now he needed to finish off Wellington and turn on Blucher with all his might. A quick glance at the battlefield shows just

de Erlon reorganised his shattered divisions but even after their losses they still presented a formidable force. In the foreground are the four regiments of Bachelu's Division and in the rear of de Erlon's infantry stands the heavy cavalry of Milhaud's Corps and the light cavalry of the Guard.

what troops were available to Napoleon to attack Wellington. On the left Jerome was still engaged at Hougoumont and Foy had been partially sucked into the fight. Bachelu was available, but a single division of 4,000 men could do little against an army of 60,000. On the right de Erlon was re-organising his shattered divisions. Only Durutte was in any shape to fight at the moment, another 4,000 men isolated on the right flank. Napoleon did have his reserve of the Guard.

This comprised a division of Young Guard, one division of Chasseurs of the Guard and one division of the Grenadiers of the Guard. In total there were 23 battalions totalling 14,052 of the finest infantry on the battlefield, simply not enough.

At this moment if Napoleon scraped together all of his available infantry and hurled them at Wellington's line he would have had only 22,000 infantrymen against 40,000 allies. At least 15,000 of these were British and King's German Legion, every bit as good as his troops. It would have been folly to send in the infantry at this stage and especially his Guard, for above all others he did not wish to lose that Corps.

He did however have the finest cavalry on the field available to him and these he could use against Wellington's line.

Napoleon's new plan was quite simply to grind down the resistance of Wellington's army whilst keeping Bulow at bay with Lobau's Corps. Then when the time was right crush Wellington with his Guard, then turn on Bulow and utterly destroy him. The grinding down process

The field of battle after the repulse of de Erlon's attack.

Wellington's left, re-formed after driving off de Erlon, is much thinned with great gaps in the reserve line.

would require the use of his cavalry, artillery, and some of his available infantry. These would be the recovering troops of de Erlon's Divisions and Bachelu's Division. There was no time for any subtle plan. It would have to be a tough grinding battle of attrition, a pounding match, a blood-bath.

For Wellington the situation was equally clear. He was still concerned about the whereabouts of Gerard's and Exelmans' Corps.

Wellington still had no news from Hal or Tubize so it was unlikely that they were there. They must therefore be either down the Genappe or Nivelles roads. Wellington had to act on the basis that these two corps were somewhere in the vicinity and would at some point be deployed against him. He has been criticised by some writers for not bringing the troops from Hal and Tubize to Waterloo. But this would have been impossible if he thought that there was even the remotest chance that Gerard and Exelmans' could outflank his right and cut him off from the sea.

Wellington could also not attack Napoleon, as the French were too strong, despite the defeat of de Erlon's attack. His plan did not alter. He would cling on to his ridge until the full weight of Blucher's Prussians brought the decisive attack on Napoleon's right flank. Wellington would advance when he was certain of victory and not before.

All Blucher had to do was to get his troops into the fight in sufficient strength and as quickly as possible. Here again is yet more controversy. Wellington wanted Blucher to arrive at Waterloo by 1.00pm. He thought that by then the battle would have raged for some three to four hours and he was confident that he could hang on for that amount of time unsupported. Muffling, the Prussian liaison officer, had made Wellington aware that whilst two brigades of Bulow's Corps had reached St Lambert by 11.30am the Army Corps could not be there until 4.00pm. It would at this rate take the Prussians a further two and a half hours to reach the edge of the Waterloo battlefield in sufficient force to deliver the decisive blow on Napoleon's right flank.

The Prussians have come under some criticism for the length of the time it took them to arrive at Waterloo from Wavre. The question is: was it feasible for the Prussians to have sufficient troops at Waterloo by 1.00pm if the march from Wavre had been organised properly? We shall see.

Napoleon, in line with his new plan of grinding down Wellington's army, ordered his batteries to increase their fire.

Chapter Seventeen

The Second Assault on La Haye Sainte and The Third Attack on Hougoumont

As part of Napoleon's plan to grind down Wellington's resistance, the French launched two new attacks on the farms of Hougoumont and La Haye Sainte.

The attack on Hougoumont started

French howitzers prepare to shell Hougoumont with carcass shells designed to set the chateau on fire.

with a barrage of howitzer shells from a howitzer battery brought up for the purpose of setting the Chateau alight. The battery was positioned at the north east corner of the wood and the British and Hanoverian light troops under Lord Saltoun tried to silence the guns, but were beaten back by the more numerous French infantry.

At 2.45pm the howitzers began firing 'carcass' shells into the Hougoumont buildings.

Carcass shells were incendiary devices designed to set buildings alight. Soon the Chateau and barn buildings were on fire sending a black column of smoke high into the air. Wellington saw the fire from his position on the ridge and sent a note down to the garrison, reminding them to keep men in those parts where the fire did not reach. Once the buildings collapsed and the fire died down the Guards were then to occupy the smouldering embers of the burnt out buildings. Hougoumont must be held at all costs. It must not fall into French hands.

It is clear from this that Wellington was still concerned about his right flank and the Hougoumont position, and quite rightly so. If Hougoumont fell and there were two more corps available down the Nivelles road then Wellington was in danger of having his flank turned and being driven east away from the sea.

A little while later, or perhaps at the

Bachelu moves off to attack Hougoumont but is soon turned back either by the fire from Cleeves KGL battery or more likely because of an order from Reille, Ney or Napoleon. It is doubtful that a full division could be so damaged by a single battery of six guns to make them fall back from a planned attack.

same time as the buildings were set on fire, Bachelu's Division moved westwards towards Hougoumont but was driven back, allegedly by cannon fire from Captain Cleeve's KGL battery. This seems unlikely to be the cause of Bachelu withdrawing from his advance on Hougoumont. It seems more likely that it was by order from someone higher up the command chain, perhaps Reille, who did not want to commit any more troops to the fight around Hougoumont.

At La Haye Sainte there was a lull of about half an hour between the repulse of de Erlon's Corps and the renewed attack by Charlet's Brigade from Quiot's Division. During this time the 95th Rifles had rallied and some 250 to 300 of their original number re-occupied the sand pit

and knoll on the eastern side of the farm. Major Baring, the commander of the garrison at La Haye Sainte, sent for reinforcements and these came in the form of two companies from the 1st Light Battalion of the King's German Legion (KGL) and the light company from the 5th Line Battalion KGL.

Charlet's infantry renewed their attack on the farm in the same manner as before. Two columns advanced, one on each side of the farm, and threw themselves against the walls of the farm trying to take the very muskets and rifles from the hands of the defenders. The attack was as before beaten off, but Baring was now concerned about the lack of ammunition and sent back for a re-supply. In all he sent back five requests

The 1st light battalion from the King's German Legion and the light companies from the 5th Line move into La Haye Sainte.

Once again the renewed attack on La Haye Sainte is repulsed by Major Baring's King's German Legion despite the fact that they were rapidly running out of ammunition.

for rifle bullets; all went un-heeded.

There is a stark difference between the defence of Hougoumont and La Haye Sainte. At Hougoumont there were six Lieutenant Colonels inside the Hougoumont complex, supported by three Major Generals on the ridge together with the active attention of Wellington himself.

At La Haye Sainte there was a high proportion of officers to men present but these were all junior officers, the highest rank being that of Major Baring. Equally there does not seem to have been any one person in charge of this part of the position. Picton was dead. The Prince of Orange was there and nominally in charge but he was very young. Although

he had been in the Peninsular War with Wellington, he was somewhat inexperienced. The Prince of Orange has come under some criticism for sending in the Luneberg Battalion, which he did not do, and when the farm did fall, for sending in Ompteda's KGL which he did do. But this criticism does not come from Siborne. He is rather generous towards the young man carrying such a heavy responsibility in such a difficult situation.

No one competent General seemed to be in overall command of the centre. Even Wellington did not seem to be concentrating on this sector very much either. Baring was running out of ammunition. Eventually he did run out of bullets and the farm fell. Just across the road were the 95th Rifles who had the same guns as Baring's men. Could they not have given some bullets to the garrison? No chance! Bullets had to be accounted for.

The Beaurocracy at War

It is worth our while taking a look at two battles later in the century, Isandhlwana and Inkerman. It is said that at Isandhlwana when the Zulus attacked they were being held off by rifle fire until ammunition ran low and the 24th Foot sent runners from each company back to the commissariat to get re-supplied. The officer of the commissariat would only issue bullets to each company from the correct allocation, so if you turned up from number three company at number two ammunition store you would be sent away. If number three ammunition store had a queue waiting for bullets then you had to wait. While you were waiting the Zulus broke through the line, speared both you and the commissariat officer, and helped themselves to both your rifle and the boxes of bullets.

At Inkerman, the senior officers were not present when the Russians attacked the British camp, catching it by surprise. There were some junior officers in attendance but over all it was the Sergeants who organised the defence,

Milhaud and Lefebvre move their cavalry divisions from the east to the western side of the battlefield. This movement is evidence that the cavalry charges were planned and were not a spur of the moment decision based upon the mistaken belief that Wellington was retreating. Had that been the case then the cavalry would have charged across the open space in front of the Grand Battery.

formed the army into line and drove off the Russians with well aimed rifle fire. But here now is a problem, for the Sergeants who ordered the men to fire did not have the authority of a senior officer to use the bullets, and bullets cost money. Believe it or not, the civil service of the day decided that the Sergeants should pay for the bullets themselves, as they did not have permission to use them in the battle. They did not charge them in the end but they did think of it.

Now of course this was the nineteenth century and would not happen today in the twenty first century, Oh really? What about the British Soldier killed in the Gulf War who had been paid up to the end of the month but was killed in action a few days before the month ended? A civil servant actually wrote to his widow asking for a refund of the money overpaid to her hero husband as he did not work the last few days of the month due to him being dead. That actually happened.

Now with this in mind, let us return to poor Major Baring running out of both ammunition and patience whilst under attack from a French infantry brigade. His man has run back for more bullets. He cannot get them. His wagon, the one allocated to his battalion, is nowhere to be found. The 95th Rifles wagon may be nearby but no way will he be given their bullets. Who can he turn to? No one, for no one is in overall command at this point of the position. Now had a General been given the specific responsibility of the crossroads and the defence of the farm he could have ordered the ammunition to be supplied from the Rifles to the KGL. But that person did not exist. Such is war, such was the civil service and commercial mentality of the commissariat.

Nevertheless, despite the shortage of ammunition, Baring and his Germans drove off the French and kept control of the farm for a few more hours at least.

It was now four o'clock and the French cavalry, having formed up in the valley, began their charge against Wellington's line.

Chapter Eighteen

The French Cavalry Charges

Napoleon had reviewed his options and had decided upon a massed cavalry charge against the enemy's centre right, between Hougoumont and La Haye Sainte.

Whilst the cavalry were moving into position at around 2.30pm he had renewed his attacks on both farms with infantry and artillery. At the same time the main batteries along his front line were brought into play, with 76 guns firing at the intended target area for the cavalry charges. All of this preparation took over one hour to complete. From

Napoleon's point of view this was the most logical next step to take in the battle. The battle was neither won nor lost. It could still go either way. His infantry had been used up in the diversionary attack on Hougoumont and the main attack on Wellington's left. This attack by de Erlon's Corps had been bloodily repulsed but not without loss to Wellington's army. At Hougoumont, Jerome and Foy were suffering unnecessary casualties but were still keeping Wellington's eyes firmly on his right flank. Napoleon did not know, of course, that Wellington thought that both Gerard's and Exelmans' Corps were with his army at Waterloo and thought that it was Jerome and Foy alone that made him look to his right. From his point of view it was this diversion that pinned Wellington to his right and, if that cost the lives of some of his men, then that was the price he would have to pay.

Napoleon could either simply bombard Wellington's line and wait until de Erlon's Corps was sufficiently recovered and then try again with this corps, or he could use his heavy cavalry to grind down and break up Wellington's army so that when de Erlon and the Guard renewed their attack they would have a better chance of success.

The French have been much criticised for using their cavalry in this way at this time. The common view is that it was not Napoleon that decided to send in the cavalry but rather it was the impetuous Marshal Ney who gave the order. The theory put forward is that Ney saw, through the smoke, allied troops retreating back behind the ridge, and even further back up the Brussels road,

and assumed that Wellington was in full retreat. He therefore launched the cavalry against what he thought would be a rear-guard and a broken horde, which the cavalry would simply cut to pieces. This view seems to come mainly from the British side, with some testimonial evidence from French cavalry officers who support the view.

But the view does not stand up to any serious scrutiny. In the first place, neither Ney nor Napoleon could see clearly enough through the smoke and across a thousand yards of battlefield whether Wellington was retreating or not. Secondly, why would Wellington be retreating? He had just driven off de Erlon's attack and Bulow was approaching with 30,000 reinforcements. There was no logic to Wellington retreating at this stage of the battle. Furthermore the cavalry attack was preplanned with an attempt on La Haye Sainte and further attacks on Hougoumont.

The final nail in the coffin of the view that it must have been an impetuous mistake made by Marshal Ney comes from the fact that Milhaud and Lefebvre Desnouettes moved their cavalry from the right of the Brussels road to the left and deployed in front of Kellerman's cavalry Corps, which was already deployed on the left. It took nearly an hour to prepare the attack. It was not a sudden impulse driven by an opportunity glimpsed through the smoke of battle. It was a battle plan devised by Napoleon and executed by Ney, with both believing that it was the best thing to do. From their point of view it was.

The allies saw it very differently.

Wellington, on his ridge, had every reason to be pleased with the situation. Hougoumont had held firm. The attack by de Erlon had been driven off in fine style. His cavalry had been subsequently badly cut up but that was only to be expected. British cavalry was the best in attack but the worst in terms of control. Once launched, off they went. Anything in their path was doomed. But once they had done what they were supposed to do they lost control and ran off in all directions and, in this case, to their own destruction. Neither Wellington, nor indeed any British general, would ever attempt to use cavalry alone to drive away formed infantry with artillery support in its front and formed cavalry in their rear. It would be suicide.

All Wellington would have to do was form his infantry into squares, posted in chequer-board formation on the reverse slope of the position, order his gunners to abandon the guns when the French cavalry got close and run back to the protection of the squares. He would then use his own cavalry to drive off the French cavalry once they had been broken up by the infantry squares and blown to bits by the guns.

If it was suicide then it must have been decided upon out of desperation and could not have been planned as a tactical operation by the greatest general of the age. It might, of course, be part of an attack that would be supported by

The French cavalry are deployed and ready to charge up the slope between La Haye Sainte and Hougoumont. Charging with them are the horse batteries of each division.

Wellington formed his infantry into squares on the reverse slope of the ridge, awaiting the French cavalry charge.

infantry coming up the Nivelles road but there was no sign of any movement from that direction. It looked like it was going to be a cavalry attack, supported by horse batteries and main position guns, but without formal infantry support. It was bound to fail. It was madness. It must have been a mistake.

Wellington had not faced Napoleon's heavy cavalry in Spain and had never seen its awesome majesty in full flight on a battlefield. Those who did see it never forgot it. What Wellington and the other British officers did not know was that this tactic had been tried and had been successful before.

At Borodino in 1812, just outside Moscow, the French cavalry, including

Walthier's Cuirassiers who were here at Waterloo, had attacked and captured the Raevsky redoubt. This was a formed gun emplacement positioned on a hill with a gentle forward slope but protected by a stream and light brushwood. The redoubt contained eighteen twelve-pounder cannon and was supported by two cavalry and two infantry corps. These formations were also supported by flanking fire, from Russian batteries in the north and other batteries south of the redoubt. The French massed cavalry was supported by infantry but the cavalry soon overtook them and attacked the redoubt alone, capturing it and driving back the supporting troops. This was a magnificent feat of arms, unimaginable to British troops, who in large measure held their own cavalry in varying degrees of contempt.

Marshal Joachim Murat had become the King of Naples because of his feats of brilliance in bringing the massed cavalry assault to perfection. Although he was Napoleon's brother in law, having married Napoleon's sister Caroline in 1800, he had betrayed Napoleon in 1814 and was not allowed back into favour when Napoleon resumed the throne in 1815. Murat commanded the cavalry at Marengo, Austerlitz, Jena and at Eylau where his massed cavalry charges saved the day.

Now for the first time the British Army was to face the full force of a French massed cavalry charge. It was just as well that Wellington had perfected the reverse slope technique, for most of the army was spared the awesome spectacle gathering in the valley below.

Napoleon had ordered his cuirassiers from the right wing of his army to move to the left and assemble in the valley between Hougoumont and La Haye Sainte. This was Milhaud's Corps of two divisions commanded by Watier and Delort. The Guard light cavalry division commanded by Lefebvre Desnouettes supported these 3,000 heavy cavalrymen. This division was also deployed on the right in front of Plancenoit and was composed of two regiments, the Chasseur a' Cheval and

The whole battlefield just before the French cavalry charge. You can see from this picture just how empty the eastern side of the battlefield is, with only de Erlon's Corps re-forming behind the Grand Battery and at the top of the picture just in front of the woods is Lobau's Corps, facing east awaiting the arrival of the Prussians.

the 2nd Chevaux Lanciers the famous 'Red Lancers'; in all some 2,400 sabres and lances. This move denuded Napoleon's right wing of heavy cavalry and the best two light cavalry regiments in the army. Clearly, Napoleon was not yet overly concerned by the imminent approach of Von Bulow's 30,000 men, but was instead intent on destroying Wellington before the Prussians arrived. If he had been concerned he could quite easily have replaced Milhaud's Corps with Kellerman's, and Lefebvre's with Guyot's Guard heavy cavalry division, both of whom were already deployed on the left just behind the cavalry assembly area. Both Kellerman and Guyot would be used later but the first charge would be made by the massed ranks of Milhaud's and Lefebvre's cavalry regiments.

The Imperial Guard Light Cavalry deployed on the left of the cuirassiers with the lancers nearest the cuirassiers and the Chasseur a' Cheval on the extreme left. This regiment was the finest dressed in the whole army; in fact the finest dressed of any army. Whether they fought as well as they looked is another matter. Whilst the cuirassiers and lancers, grenadiers and dragoons get mentioned, the Chasseur a' Cheval get hardly a mention in any history of the battle. Yet they were also the largest cavalry regiment on the field, numbering nearly 1,200 men. In total the first charge consisted of just over 5,400 men deployed on a frontage of less than 1,000 yards and to a depth of six ranks.

Wellington could see the cavalry move westward and deploy but he could see no infantry moving in support, no Gerard appearing down the Nivelles road nor

behind the massed cavalry. Wellington had plenty of time to organise his infantry into thirty-three squares deployed in chequer-board fashion, with his own cavalry deployed in line to the rear and his guns, seventy-six of them, massed in front. The guns were so positioned that their final discharge of canister would have overlapping arcs of fire that would cover the whole frontage from La Haye Sainte to the Hougoumont enclosure. Nothing moving into this hail of death could possibly avoid being hit by the thousands of iron balls discharged by the guns as the enemy cavalry crested the ridge. The plan was to fire round-shot as the cavalry moved down into the valley and then to load with ball over canister. This would be fired at close range as soon as the cavalry crested the ridge and came into view.

The view from the guns to where the ground dips down into the valley and out of sight varies from 100 to 200 yards. The plan was to fire once the cavalry came into view and then to run back to the protection of the infantry squares leaving the guns abandoned. Once the enemy cavalry had been driven back down the slope by the allied cavalry the gunners were to run back to the guns, re-load and be ready for the next charge. In theory the 76 guns firing canister at 100 yards should have brought down every horseman in the front rank, killing or wounding nearly 1,000 men with every discharge. As the cavalry charged ten to twelve times this would in theory have wiped them out. The fact that it did not means that something went wrong with the fire plan.

As the French cavalry moved off and

cleared the field of fire of their own guns, these batteries opened up a fearful fire on the allied squares.

An infantry square is usually deployed three or four ranks deep, with the front rank kneeling and the second rank standing with their muskets and bayonets presenting a perfect hedge of steel, through which no horse will willingly pass. Behind them the third and fourth rank can fire their muskets at the cavalry until they are driven off. An infantry square was not a new formation. The Roman army had a formation something like it, which they used when faced by enemy cavalry or elephants. The Romans had spears and javelins. Wellington had bayonets and bullets. But the principle was the same; the front rows fended off the enemy whilst the rear ranks fired or shot missiles at them. Squares could be broken, either by the assistance of musketry or cannon fire, or by driving a horse at the square so that when it fell it broke through the hedge of bayonets and created a gap through which the remainder of the cavalry could pass. Once the cavalry were inside, the square was defenceless and was easily cut up and dispersed. But to do this you had to charge recklessly at the square for if the horse shied away then you were lost, as the musketry would bring you down.

Milhaud and Lefebvre were led into the charge by Marshal Ney who was easily recognisable because of his famous red hair. There was a dispute, reported after the battle, between Delort and Ney as to who should order the cavalry forward. Delort claims that he protested against sending in the cavalry against infantry posted on heights who had not been shaken. Ney lost his patience and shouted at him "The salvation of France is at stake". Ney was right. Delort was a subordinate, although Ney should have given the order to the corp's commander, Milhaud, not the divisional commander Delort. Wellington would have been less dramatic in similar circumstances – "do as you are told sir" would have been his response. Reports such as this are supportive of the argument that the cavalry attacks were made in error which, as I stated, I do not think they were.

The cavalry, once in position, moved off at the walk towards the allied ridge, an awesome spectacle well described by Captain Gronow of the 1st Foot Guards.

"Not a man who survived could have forgotten in after life the awful grandeur of that charge. You perceived it at a distance what appeared to be an over-whelming, long moving line, which, ever advancing, glittered like a stormy wave of the sea when it catches the sunlight. On came the mounted host until they got near enough, whilst the very earth seemed to vibrate beneath their thundering tramp. One might suppose that nothing could have resisted the shock of this terrible moving mass. They were the famous cuirassiers, almost all old soldiers, who had distinguished themselves on most of the battlefields of Europe".

These eloquent lines do give a picture of the approach of the first charge. It must have been awesome to see and terrifying to withstand. Most of the allied infantry

The French cavalry crest the ridge into the teeth of the allied guns. At this range they should have been cut down by canister and ball. The fact that they were not is evidence that the fire plan did not work as expected.

could not, however, see it coming which was a blessing. But they could feel the ground tremble at the approach of 20,000 hooves as they cantered up the slope. As they crested the ridge the shouts of the cavalrymen could be clearly heard, not unlike the sound of a modern day Football crowd, similar to the roar of the sea as it nears the shore. As the cavalry advanced between La Haye Sainte and the Hougoumont enclosure they came under fire from both posts. Naturally they edged away from the fire and bunched up in the middle. In doing so, the horses in the centre were lifted off the ground and were carried up the slope with their legs dangling in mid air. As

soon as they came over the ridge, the allied gunners fired their deadly volleys but some, anxious to get to the protection of the squares, fired too soon and both ball and canister went harmlessly over the heads of the oncoming French cavalry.

Onward they came past the abandoned guns and into the squares, thirty-three of them drawn up in chequerboard formation. The British believed, falsely, that the cuirass was bullet proof and they therefore ordered their men to fire at the horses. Whilst the rumour was false, it did serve to bring down more men and horses. It caused more casualties than the musketry would have caused if it had been aimed higher, as most of the shots would have gone over the heads of the riders. The Klingental Sabre used by the French is just under a metre long; the reach of a musket and bayonet just under one and a half metres. Anything beyond a metre and the sword is useless. As the bayonets were longer the infantry was relatively safe from the French cavalry's main weapon, provided that is they remained steady and stayed in the square formation.

It is doubtful that many allied soldiers in square were injured by a sabre cut, but as the cavalry also had pistols and carbines the infantry were not wholly immune to harm from the enemy cavalry dashing around them.

The cavalry swirled around the squares taking and causing casualties until they were charged by the allied cavalry and were driven off the ridge and back across the valley.

As before the pursuing allied cavalry advanced too far and suffered for their pains, but this time they got back to the allied lines in good order.

Many of the gunners ran back to their guns and got ready for the next attack but others had already fled the field.

At the time no one thought it odd, but after the battle people did wonder why the French cavalry had not spiked the allied guns? This could be done by driving a headless nail into the vent hole making it un-fireable. It took but a few seconds to do, perhaps a minute per gun. Thirty-six horse artillerymen could have crippled the guns, and Wellington's army,

The cuirassiers and lancers reach the allied squares.

Viewed from the Allied side, looking south, we can see the French cavalry break up on the allied squares and then driven off by the Allied cavalry.

The French cavalry re-form in the valley behind their horse batteries ready to charge again.

in a couple of minutes work. Unfortunately for the French no one thought of it. It was of course not quite as easy as it may at first glance have seemed to be. The guns were not far from the squares, in some cases almost touching them. Any French gunner dismounting by the guns would have been shot long before he got his hammer and nails out of his pouch.

Between the charges the French guns wrought havoc among the infantry squares. "Our square was a perfect hospital" wrote Guards Captain Gronow. This statement, together with an analysis of the casualties suffered by the defending troops during this phase of the battle, supports the view that neither Napoleon nor Ney had made a mistake in sending in the massed cavalry attacks. But, rather, that this was in fact part of the "New Battle New Plan" which had been implemented once 'plan A', de Erlon's attack, had failed.

After the first three or four charges by Milhaud's and Lefebvre's Divisions had been driven off, Napoleon ordered Kellerman's cavalry Corps forward to replace Milhaud and Lefebvre in the front line. Guyot, in command of the Guard heavy cavalry division, composed of the Empress Dragoons and the Grenadiers a' Cheval, also moved forward alongside Kellerman.

On the other side of the valley, Wellington had ordered up Captain Cavalie Mercer's nine-pounder horse battery into the front line to replace

Kellerman's and Guyot's cavalry take over the charge whilst Milhaud and Lefebvre re-form further back at the top of the picture.

Sinclair's battery that had left the field. These five nine pound guns and one howitzer galloped forward in fine style and deployed behind the track, which runs from the crossroads by La Haye Sainte to Hougoumont and the Nivelles road. Here the ground falls away back to the reverse slope and a low bank is formed, just high enough to allow the muzzles of the guns to clear the embankment. Mercer deployed his battery here in front of two Brunswick squares. Mere boys he thought as he surveyed the black uniformed Brunswick infantry.

He decided, then and there, that he would not obey Wellington's order to run back to the protection of the squares if threatened, but rather would stay with the guns and trust the low bank for cover rather than the shaky Brunswickers. Whether he was right about the Brunswick troops or not we will never know. They did not break but then again Mercer did not retire to the squares either. What followed amply demonstrated what would have happened all along the gun line if the gunners had remained at their guns and had fired as effectively as Mercer's battery did.

Kellerman's Corps of heavy cavalry comprised four cuirassier regiments totalling 1,332 cavalrymen plus two Caribinier regiments of 847 men and two regiments of dragoons with 1,110 men. In total 3,279 heavy cavalrymen. These were supported by the heavy cavalry division of the Guard which comprised the Grenadiers a' Cheval, 796 men, the Empress Dragoons, 816 men, and a

Mercer's battery deploys in front of the Brunswick square.

squadron of the Gendarmerie Elite, 106 men. In total 1,718 first class heavy cavalry. In fact the Caribiniers in Kellerman's Corps were originally from the heavy cavalry of the Guard division and were the elite cuirassiers of the Guard. In total therefore there were some 5,000 cavalrymen about to charge in replacement of the 5,400 who had charged earlier.

It appears that Guyot's Guard Division had joined the fray on its own accord without orders from anyone. This seems a little odd, but as with other testimonies about the cavalry attacks, it must be borne in mind that success has many fathers but failure is an orphan. The cavalry attacks were regarded as a failure by everyone after the battle, so anyone involved was looking for excuses about why they had been involved.

Napoleon stated in the book that he dictated, or is alleged to have dictated, whilst on St Helena that he did not want Guyot to advance, as this left him without any mounted reserve uncommitted to the battle. This does have a ring of truth to it, for once the Guard heavy cavalry had been committed only the infantry of the Guard remained free to act as a reserve. The truth of whoever ordered the Guard heavy cavalry forward, Napoleon, Ney, Kellerman or Guyot will never be known for certain. But whoever it was has left us with one of the two most memorable icons of the massed cavalry charges, one on the field and the other in Les Invalides Museum in Paris.

As Kellerman and Guyot moved forward, supported by the remnants of Milhaud and Lefebvre's Divisions, the Grenadiers a' Cheval were deployed on the left and were heading straight for Mercer's guns. As they crested the ridge Mercer, who had already decided not to retire, held his fire until they were within fifty yards of the muzzles of his guns. Then he let loose a shower of death that scythed down the front rank of the Horse Grenadiers. The guns recoiled and were re-loaded. The French cavalry could not get through the pile of bodies in front of them but had to pick their way through carefully to avoid falling. Mercer's guns fired again bringing down more men and horses. Now their path was completely blocked. But the cavalry could not retreat as the rear ranks were still pushing forward unaware of the carnage in front of them. The guns fired again and again, piling up dead and dying men and horses in front of the battery.

Eventually the rear ranks opened out and the whole retreated back from Mercer's guns and into the protection of the valley. The Grenadiers a' Cheval with incredible bravery then came forward once again but this time at the walk and were once again cut down by Mercer's guns until, reduced in numbers and unable to gain any advantage, they withdrew leaving a great part of their number lying on the ground in front of the guns. The pile of dead was so great that it was clearly visible from across the field.

It is clear that had the other gunners stayed at their guns and had they been as effective as Mercer was, then the whole front between La Haye Sainte and Hougoumont would have been one huge mound of dead and dying men and horses, cut down in the first charge of the French cavalry. This would have created a

French horse batteries deployed on the crest of the ridge blast away at the squares from close range. Wellington ordered his forward squares to retire behind the crest so as to avoid this gunfire. Once again the reverse slope saved the infantry from unnecessary casualties.

physical barrier, which would have been difficult for the cavalry to get through and would have saved the infantry squares from the casualties they suffered during this phase of the battle.

The slaughter of the Grenadiers a' Cheval and their extreme bravery in their charge is a testament to the effectiveness of Mercer and his battery and to the impotence of cavalry held in front of the guns as they were. It also serves to show how miraculous it was that any French cavalry reached the squares, not just once but up to twelve times.

Clearly the effectiveness of most of the British and KGL guns was less than Mercer's battery. This can only be explained in the first charge by the order to leave the guns when threatened and seek the shelter of the squares. 'Threatened' was to be judged by the gunner officers and they must in some instances have fired too soon. In the later charges it was not the case that the gunners ran out to the guns and found them perfectly serviceable; on the contrary rammers and other tools were scattered and broken by the cavalry charging over them.

What most probably happened was that those gunners who did run back to the guns found them in a mess and searched around for rammers and sponges, powder and ball but before they

French skirmishers advance to pepper the squares with musket fire. This was a critical phase for Wellington. The effectiveness of the skirmishers was greater than usual because the proximity of the French cavalry prevented Wellington from using his own skirmishers to deter the French light troops.

could fire the cavalry threat was upon them once again, and once again they retreated to the shelter of the infantry squares. Nevertheless the guns were effective as the other icon of the charges shows us. In Les Invalides in Paris is the Cuirass of Antoine Faveau of the Caribiniers, whose cuirass was struck by a cannonball which passed through both the front and back of the cuirass, and poor Faveau himself, killing him instantly and adding his body to the hundreds dead and dying before the guns.

The French as part of their grinding down process had bought forward their horse artillery batteries and deployed them on the ridge itself. These guns blasted away at both the gun batteries and the infantry squares. Wellington, however, withdrew his forward squares to the protection of the reverse slope, which negated most of the effectiveness of the horse guns.

Adding to the weight of gunfire a mass of skirmishers came forward and began a Tirailleur attack on the allied line. This was also something of a French speciality.

The French used masses of light infantry going forward in loose formation and engaging the enemy line, knocking out officers and NCOs with deadly effect. Normally Wellington countered this with his own light troops. But this time the

French cavalry made it impossible for Wellington to use his light troops as he had done in Spain.

The French also used mounted troops as skirmishers and it was one of these who annoyed Mercer by lowering the morale of his gunners. Mercer mounted his horse on the bank in front of the guns and rode up and down, inviting the skirmishers to fire at him. He soon regretted his foolhardy act of bravery but remained unscathed despite the deliberate aim the mounted French trooper took at him. The French guns, however, were a different story. A little later a battery of French guns opened fire on Mercer's battery from the rising tongue of ground near La Haye Sainte. Mercer thought that these guns were

Prussian, but they were French and they wrecked his battery in short order. He was only saved by the timely intervention of a Dutch battery from Chasse's Division newly brought up into the line to strengthen the battered centre right of Wellington's line.

On the field of Waterloo there is a monument recording the last known position of Mercer's battery at the battle. Further back from the monument, behind the track is the low bank where Mercer's guns were when they cut down the French Grenadiers a' Cheval. It still exists to this very day. The monument is located where the Grenadier a' Cheval's pile of corpses was, and is perhaps a fitting monument to both victor and vanquished in this almost private fight

"Drive those fellows away." The short order from Wellington sent the Guards and Adam's Brigade forward against the French skirmishers forcing them to retire.

between the two.

The Tirailleurs' attack was having such an effect on Wellington's army that he had to take fairly drastic measures to counter it. He ordered the Guards and Adam's Brigade forward to 'drive those fellows away', as he put it. They marched forward four deep in case of cavalry attack and swept the ridge clear of both French guns and light infantry.

It was in this phase that Wellington displayed his great skill and personal bravery as a commander in chief of an army. Wellington was everywhere in the thick of the fighting. He exposed himself to the same dangers his men were facing, making instant decisions and issuing clear and precise orders to deal with any local threat as it arose. His actions as commander in chief did exactly what was needed of him. He gave his men confidence that came from his own bravery and surety, or at least his outward display of confidence, even if he did in fact feel that things were not going quite as well as he had hoped. He held firm. His men held firm, not a single square was broken.

Adam and Du Platt now formed square on the forward slope to prevent the Tirailleurs and horse guns from gaining the ridge once again. However, under fire from the main batteries, the Tirailleurs and the horse batteries, both Adam and Du Platt soon withdrew to the cover of the reverse slope.

The thinned out state of Wellington's right flank after the cavalry charges, horse batteries and skirmishers had done their work. This view is from the west looking east. The cavalry line to the left is all that remains in the front line of the allied cavalry in this sector.

The grinding down phase using massed cavalry charges supported by horse batteries and skirmishers, and one weak column of formed heavy infantry, which was easily driven off by the British cavalry, was now coming to an end. The French were exhausted, having sustained heavy losses in their cavalry to such an extent that their morale was beginning to crack. "The best cavalry in the world is French" said the Duke after the battle "and I know something about it". He knew about it as he had been attacked and surrounded by it and then watched it crushed by his army and yet then leave the field, in many cases in good order rather than rout.

The Allied army had held firm but had also suffered dreadfully. They too were at breaking point and Wellington summed it up himself when he said "A hard pounding gentlemen we shall see who can pound the longest" and later "Both sides were what the boxers called gluttons, neither side giving way".

The two sides had pounded each other into a bloody mess and, like anyone under such pressure, both sides were in varying degrees of shock. Napoleon could not believe that the allied troops could stand up to such a battering. "Will we never see their backs?" he asked.

Wellington had to hold on a little longer as the Prussians were at last driving into the right flank of Napoleon's army. "Just a little longer lads and you shall have at them." he said.

It must have been around this time that Wellington realised that his right flank was secure after all and was not under the threat he thought it would have been. "The man is a mere pounder after all" he said. "Napoleon did not manoeuvre at all but came on in the old style and was driven off in the old style".

These statements reveal Wellington's relief at surviving everything Napoleon had thrown at him. Even though the Prussians were four hours late in arriving, his army was still holding together. Victory would eventually be his as the numerical advantage the Prussians brought with them began to tell. As a finale to the massed cavalry and Tirailleurs' attack, Napoleon sent in the third and ultimately successful attack on La Haye Sainte. But before we examine that part of the battle let us look at the effectiveness of the massed cavalry attacks on Wellington's line and see how Siborne portrayed them, and whether he was unfair to Britain's allies in his history of the battle.

The Analysis
The effectiveness of the French attacks

The table below shows the regiments that defended the ridge from the massed French cavalry attacks. The table also shows the total casualties each regiment suffered in the battle. The percentage figure is my estimate of the amount of those casualties sustained during this phase of the battle. Those with 100% against them are easy to calculate as these battalions and regiments were not engaged in the other phases of the battle. With those who were engaged in the other phases of the battle I have erred on the side of caution and apportioned some casualties to the other phases of the battle.

For example, in the case of the 30th Foot, this regiment was driven off by the attack of the Guard later in the day but ran before the enemy got within range of them. They did not take part in any other major part of the battle other than the French cavalry charges. Therefore I have allocated 10% of the casualties to the retreat from the Guard and 90% to the attack of the cavalry.

Added to this must be the Cumberland Hussars who suffered 18 killed, 33 wounded and 2 missing but had a further 463 leave the field never to return. In

Regiment/Battalion	Total battle casualties			Cavalry attack only	
	Killed	Wounded	Missing	Percent	Total
1st Guards 2nd Btn.	51	101	0	50%	76
1st Guards 3rd Btn.	84	251	0	50%	168
30th Foot	51	165	14	90%	207
33rd Foot	35	102	48	90%	167
69th Foot	18	53	15	90%	77
73rd Foot	52	187	41	90%	252
Bremen Btn.	12	124	35	90%	154
Verden Btn.	63	101	53	90%	195
York Btn.	24	72	45	90%	127
Grubenhagen Btn.	16	78	48	90%	128
52nd Foot	17	182	0	50%	100
71st Foot	25	174	3	50%	101
95th Rifles 2nd Btn	34	193	20	50%	247
95th Rifles 3rd Btn.	3	40	7	50%	25
1st Line KGL	23	75	17	50%	58
2nd Line KGL	19	81	7	50%	54
3rd Line KGL	18	98	31	50%	74
4th Line KGL	14	84	14	50%	56
Bremervorde Btn	18	22	9	90%	44
Osnabruck Btn.	20	68	6	90%	84
Quackenbruck Btn.	2	10	2	90%	13
Salzgitter Btn.	20	62	1	90%	75
14th Foot	7	22	0	100%	29
23rd Foot	15	84	0	100%	99
51st Foot	9	22	0	100%	31
Brunswick Uhlans	0	15	15	100%	30
Brunswick Hussars	28	50	78	100%	156
1st Light Brunswick	4	44	48	100%	96
2nd Light Brunswick	39	75	114	100%	228
3rd Light Brunswick	36	80	50	100%	166

Regiment/Battalion	Total battle casualties			Cavalry attack only	
	Killed	Wounded	Missing	Percent	Total
1st Line Brunswick	9	46	55	100%	110
2nd Line Brunswick	3	7	10	100%	20
3rd Line Brunswick	10	53	3	100%	126
Nassau 1st Line Reg.	254	389	0	100%	643
Chasse's Division	56	316	364	40%	295
1st Light Dr. KGL	33	111	10	90%	139
2nd Light Dr. KGL	20	55	2	90%	69
23rd Light Dr.	14	194	44	90%	227
7th Hussars	56	99	0	90%	140
15th Hussars	23	51	5	90%	71
3rd Hussars KGL	44	86	0	90%	117
1st Dutch Caribiniers	12	75	15	90%	92
2nd Belgium Car.	58	68	30	90%	140
3rd Belgium Car.	37	29	26	90%	83
4th Dutch Light Dr.	54	143	52	90%	224
8th Belgium Hussars	11	151	122	90%	284

Losses during the cavalry attack in killed, wounded and missing = 6,097.

total therefore the number of troops put *hors de combat* were some 6,500 troops.

The total number of Allied troops killed, wounded and missing was reported at 17,589 in the casualty returns. 36% of these were caused by and during the massed cavalry charges on the sector of battlefield between La Haye Sainte and the Hougoumont enclosure. These losses do not include any of those suffered at Hougoumont nor at La Haye Sainte or further east beyond the Brussels road. There were seven major phases of the battle between Napoleon's, Wellington's and Blucher's armies. These were:-

Hougoumont
De Erlon's attack
The Massed Cavalry attacks
The loss of La Haye Sainte and the attack in the centre
The Attack of the Guard infantry.
The Prussian attack on Plancenoit
The rout of the French.

The massed cavalry attack accounts for more than its fair share of the casualties caused during the battle. Clearly it was neither an accident nor a mistake. It was actually a deliberate grinding down of Wellington's line, planned to weaken it before the assault of the Guard and other infantry columns later in the day.

The number of casualties caused during this phase of the battle, this phase alone mind, was greater than Wellington had ever encountered in any of the battles of the Peninsular War.

The casualty returns for the major actions in the Peninsular War in Spain and Portugal were as follows.

Talavera	4,694
Busaco	1,252
Feuntes D' Onoro	1,800
Badajoz	3,636
Salamanca	4,762
Sorauren	4,125
Vittoria	4,927

The massed cavalry attacks and the casualties they caused on that sector of the battlefield shocked Wellington's army. The fact that not a single square was broken, and only the Cumberland Hussars and some individual infantry and gunners fled the field, is a testament to all those troops, Brunswick, Nassau, Hanoverian, Dutch, Belgian, King's German Legion and British who withstood the onslaught.

Siborne's version of events.

Siborne's history does not agree with Mercer's assessment of the Brunswick infantry and goes to some length to praise the steadiness of those troops. He also praises Tripp's Dutch Belgian cavalry for their part in the early stages of the attack. He does then criticise them for not following Uxbridge when ordered to do so in a charge against the French cavalry. In the main Siborne's history is one of praise for the steadiness and bravery of the British, Dutch, Belgian and German troops and the bravery of the French who were sent into attack, not in error, but by the Emperor himself. They were sent according to Siborne into impossible odds against steady infantry in formed squares supported by magnificent cavalry and well-served guns.

Siborne saw the effectiveness of the massed cavalry attacks and the effect they had on Wellington's army. He does not make any suggestion that it was Ney who made the mistake of attacking with cavalry. Rather he states that it was under Napoleon's direct order that the cavalry attacks took place. Siborne points out that it was during this phase that Chasse's Dutch Belgian Divisions were brought into the centre to bolster up the flagging allied line.

There is no evidence from this part of the battle to suggest that Siborne suppressed evidence or made false allegations in order to denigrate the allies and enhance the British part played in the battle. His history is probably over-zealous in his praise for the bravery and steadiness of the troops for today's more cynical reader, but his history was written in 1840 when today's views were not widely held.

Whilst the massed cavalry attack was in progress, Bulow's 4th Corps finally got into action on the eastern flank of the battlefield. The Prussian attack is dealt with in some detail later in the book but before we look at that 'battle within a battle' we shall look at the final phase of the grinding down operation, the last attack on and capture of La Haye Sainte.

Chapter Nineteen

The Fall of La Haye Sainte

The cavalry attack was coming to its end because of the exhaustion of the horses and men of these fine regiments. The Prussians were by now heavily engaging the right wing of the French army but Napoleon was sticking to his plan, crush Wellington and then turn on Blucher. He ordered Ney to send in a new attack on La Haye Sainte. Ney sent his aide de camp, Colonel Heymes, to request more troops from Napoleon. It was at this point, according to Siborne, that the famous comment "Troops? Where do you expect me to get troops from, do you think I can make them?" was uttered by Napoleon. Later historians move this remark to the point just before the attack of the Imperial Guard after the fall of La Haye Sainte. Siborne has it in French as follows:

"Ou voulez-vous que j'en prenne? Voulez-vous que j'en fasse?"

Ney should not have needed more troops at this stage, for he had Bachelu's Division standing to the left of the main Brussels road. It would appear from this that Siborne got the timing wrong and it was later that the request for more troops was made, if it actually happened at all.

Whether it was because Ney was chastised by the quip from the Emperor, or more likely because they were the best troops for the job, he sent in the 13th Light infantry regiment, all three battalions of it, against the small farm. As they marched down the slope from the French position, Captain Dansey, together with Sergeant Daniel Dunnett and his rocket troop, advanced towards the approaching French light infantry, all 1,000 of them.

Dansey was soon wounded and his men wavered, but Sergeant Dunnett calmly told his troops to lay the rockets on the ground and fire them at the advancing column. The effect was stunning! The French column was hit by most if not all of the rockets fired at them. These rockets were little more than larger versions of today's firework display rockets. They whizzed along the ground sparking flames from their rear

The 13th Light Infantry move forward to attack the farm whilst Dunnett's rocket troop deploy on the road between the farm and the mound in front of the sandpit.

and crashed into the packed infantry, singeing coat tails and moustaches as they passed. These new and fearsome weapons would have seriously injured few French troops but they *were* new and fearsome. The French took cover until Dunnett ran out of rockets and retired to the ridge. This incident paints a picture for me of the strength of the British army system. The officer is wounded. The men naturally look to get back to the ridge and safety. "No you don't" says Dunnett, "pick up those rockets you horrible little man!" and the gunners fear Dunnett more than the 1,000 French infantry only a few hundred yards away. Once the ammunition is exhausted they can retire, but not before.

Once Dunnett retired the French resumed their advance on La Haye Sainte. Major Baring was at his wit's end. His ammunition was almost expended. He did have the support of the Nassau musket armed infantry, sent in earlier. They had been particularly useful in putting out the fires started by the French artillery. The firing from the farm noticeably slackened and the French emboldened by the weakening defence stormed forward. They grabbed at the muskets and rifles poking through the loopholes in the walls and stormed

Sergeant Dunnett fires off his rockets at the 13th Light Infantry as they advance on the farm.

through the gates and openings into the courtyard. Once inside, the defence of the farm was finished. The German defenders, who had held out all day under almost constant attack and against great odds, were finally pushed out of the farm with fewer than fifty making it back to the ridge. The rest were either dead, wounded or captured. It was not true that anyone who surrendered was soon bayoneted by the French troops, as the report of the officers present in La Haye Sainte shows. Captain Holtzermann and Lieutenant Tobin were taken prisoner and so were several of the soldiers who failed to get out of the farm in time.

The officers at the crossroads saw the Germans retreat and the farm fall into French hands. They were horrified. General Alten ordered Colonel Ompteda to advance on the farm with the 5th Line Battalion of the King's German Legion. The German Legion were crack troops, as good as any in the army, but to send 500 men against 1,500 men who were defending the farm that Baring, with less than 800, had defended all day against thousands of French infantry, was suicide. Naturally he protested. Then he noticed that there was a regiment of French Cuirassiers in support of the French infantry and pointed this out to Alten. Up rode the Prince of Orange, "what's up, why aren't you re-taking the

Looking north you can see that the farm has fallen to the 13th Light. Just above the farm you can see the remains of Major Baring's troops running back to the ridge. The cavalry and infantry to the left (west) of the farm have moved up in support of the attack and further south the batteries of guns are being moved forward to help secure the position.

farm?" Ompteda pointed out the difficulties but the Prince cut him short and ordered him to attack.

What followed was as predictable as it was when the Luneberg Battalion was sent in by Wellington five hours earlier. The battalion dashed forward with Ompteda leading on horseback way out in front. He got to the farm garden and leapt over the hedge, slashing left and right with his sabre before being shot in the neck and killed. Behind him the 5th Line was hit end on by the cuirassiers and scattered, losing 162 out of 529 of its soldiers. The 3rd Hussars King's German

Legion charged forward and managed to scatter the French cavalry in an attempt to save their comrades, but they were too late. Only 30 of the battalion returned to the sunken road the remaining 500 were routed with their dead and wounded left on the field.

The farm was now firmly in French hands and they began to bring up reinforcements. On the other side of the Brussels road, the 95th Rifles found their position untenable. They retired to the ridge and took position behind the hedge. The French brought up two guns, deployed them in the garden behind the

Prince William of Orange

The Cuirassiers catch the 5th line King's German Legion end on and run them down.

The French gunners deployed in the garden of La Haye Sainte are cut down by the 95th Rifles before they can re-load and fire a second shot.

The French pour forward in a Tiralleur attack using both light and line infantry. Wellington's centre reels from the shock and is further weakened by both musket and cannon fire. But they hold on causing equal casualties to the French and driving them back.

The 27th Regiment of Foot, the Inniskilling, in square behind the crossroads. In the distance on the small mound by La Haye Sainte is the battery of French guns that decimated them with canister shot.

The 27th lying dead in square having suffered dreadful casualties from enemy gunfire. But not a single soldier went missing or ran away, despite the carnage.

hedge and began firing at Kempt's troops deployed behind the Ohain road. The rifles turned and shot down the gunners before they could discharge another round of canister, silencing the guns.

More and more French troops were coming up and they began a Tirailleur attack on the allied line. The British responded like for like. Rifles and light infantry picking off French Tirailleurs, whilst they in turn cut down the redcoats and green jackets. Kincaid of the Rifles had fought throughout the Peninsular war but he had never seen anything like it. He wondered if the battle would only end when everyone on both sides lay dead or injured on the ground. The remains of Ompteda's Brigade began to fall back, as did Kielmansegge's Hanoverians and Kruse's Nassau troops. Kempt was also in difficulty, losing men all around him.

Lambert's Brigade was brought up to bolster the centre and came under heavy artillery fire from another French battery brought up to the knoll by the sandpit. Later Wellington, on seeing the 27th Foot lying down in square thought that they were asleep and ordered them to be got to their feet. But they were dead in square lying where they fell. In all they lost 478 killed and wounded out of 750

officers and men, 64% lost. The 4th Foot and the 40th Foot of Lambert Brigade also suffered severe losses, losing another 44 killed and 281 wounded. The 40th also had 18 men go missing, the only troops out of the whole brigade that could not be accounted for the next day.

The battering of the centre continued, causing yet more casualties. Wellington brought up reinforcements from both the left and the right. The cavalry of Vivian's Brigade had moved from the left to the centre in order to form a wall of sabres, designed to prevent the infantry from running away from the French onslaught. From the right the Brunswick Corps, and Baron Chasse's division of 7,000 Dutch

The Brunswick Corps and Chasse's division is brought up to bolster the crumbling centre of Wellington's line.

As the Brunswickers approach the front line they panic and fall back. Wellington was there to halt the withdrawal with "an electric voice". They held but would not advance to the front line again and had to be deployed a few yards further back down the slope.

and Belgian line infantry and militia, had struggled through the mud to bolster up the centre right of the line. Wellington's reserves were running out.

Wellington was everywhere, plugging the gaps and encouraging the troops. The grinding down process was coming to its climax. Wellington's army was by their own admission in difficulty but the French attacks were petering out. A brief respite was on its way.

Now here is yet another conundrum. The pause.

At this critical point, from the British point of view, the centre was open, crumbled away by the incessant attacks of all arms, infantry, both column and Tirailleur, cavalry and artillery. The artillery in particular had achieved its main objective and had closed with the enemy to canister range and was blasting away at the allied centre. Had it not been for Wellington's deployment on a reverse slope then the whole line would have been swept away in a cloud of grapeshot. As it was the centre was shattered, but the allied troops posted there had brought the French to the verge of exhaustion. They could not go forward anymore. They clung onto their position gained at

Vivian's cavalry brigade is brought from the left to the centre in order to form a wall through which no infantry could pass. His job was to keep the infantry in the line, where death or injury was possible, by making it a certainty for anyone who retreated.

such a cost, in the face of a fusillade from what was left of the Allied line. From Hougoumont to Papelotte the line was aflame. Musket and cannon in almost continuous fire. It was amazing that anyone was left standing on either side.

Siborne is clear in his history that the conversation through Ney's aide about more troops took place before the fall of La Haye Sainte. But it seems more likely that it took place at the moment of crisis when the allied line was almost broken. Either way there was a pause in the fighting, or at least a slackening off of pressure from the French. This enabled Wellington to restore his line.

Viewed from the British side things did look bad. The Brunswick Corps had been put to flight but was stopped by Wellington himself. The line of cavalry in their rear held them in their position between the front line and the cavalry. Then the Nassau regiment of von Kruse wavered. Again Wellington was on the spot holding things together, keeping the fragile line in place. Napoleon's plan to grind down Wellington and then turn on Blucher and crush him utterly was working even if neither the British nor later historians could see that it was.

This photo shows Bachelu's Division behind La Haye Sainte after its capture by the 13th Light Infantry. They may have been slightly further west but they were certainly in the vicinity and could have been used by Ney to break through Wellington's centre if such a breakthrough were possible.

Wellington was in difficulty. That is admitted by several British Officers. They were present at the battle and wrote to Siborne that if the Imperial Guard Infantry had attacked in the centre at that moment then they would have broken through.

Two factors conspired to make an attack by the Guard in the centre at that moment impossible.

Firstly the remains of de Erlon's Corps were in the way. The model makes this abundantly clear. In an attack the last thing you want is confusion and to pass one corps through another is bound to lead to disorder. Do this in front of the enemy and you should expect them to charge at you and turn confusion into a rout. The only place the Guard could attack was in the gap between Foy's and Bachelu's Divisions. This gap was caused by the involvement of Foy's Division in the attack on Hougoumont and the position of Bachelu as a central reserve near the Brussels road. Some reports, including Siborne, have it that Bachelu was further to the left also engaged in the fight at Hougoumont and that it was Donzelot's Division that supported the Guard in their final assault. David Chandler has it in his book that Bachelu was in position near the Brussels road and took part in the final assault of the Guard.

I agree with David Chandler. It seems to me that the Brussels road was the Corps boundary with Reille on the left and de Erlon on the right. There was no reason for de Erlon to move Donzelot's division, 25% of his infantry, across the road to assault the allied line from that side rather than from the eastern side where it had been all day.

The second reason was that von Bulow, attacking at Blucher's insistence, made it imperative that Napoleon dealt with the Prussians first and then finished off Wellington. Had Bulow not attacked at that time or earlier then Napoleon would have been free to launch his Guards' attack earlier in the evening. It would, however, still have been delivered on the centre right of Wellington's line where it would have had to face the musketry of Maitland's Foot Guards.

There may, however, have not been a pause at all. It is once again viewed only from the British side that a pause seems to have occurred after the fall of La Haye Sainte. From their point of view the centre seemed open; a final push and the line would have broken. From the French perspective, however, the situation seemed somewhat different. The troops of de Erlon's Corps had once before been at the point of victory only to be routed from the field by the British cavalry. They had now captured the farm and were well established in the centre.

Elsewhere along the line the columns were in the declivity between the British ridge and the French grand battery ridge. This dip was filled with smoke that hid Napoleon's troops from the enemy's

OPPOSITE: Wellington's line holds firm in the face of the French attacks whilst the Prussians, seen here at the top of the picture, force the French right wing to bend back at right angles to the line facing the allies.

The battlefield viewed from the west, showing Hougoumont at the bottom right and La Haye Sainte near the top left. Plancenoit is in the top right hand corner. Bachelu's Division is positioned behind La Haye Sainte and it is easy to see from here the gap between Bachelu and Foy, who is attacking the southeast corner of the Hougoumont enclosure.

Bulow's Corps advances from the Paris wood and drives Lobau's 6th Corps back towards Plancenoit.

gaze. Gunfire, for the most part, passed over their heads and they were therefore relatively safe. Both French and British reports state that at this time French officers would stand up and urge their men to advance with them into the British lines. Most times a few brave men joined them and advanced out of the smoke but as soon as they were seen by the British infantry coming through the mist they were fired upon and driven back.

This series of uncoordinated attacks continued for about an hour between seven and eight pm. The French brought up more and more guns. Wellington's

line did buckle several times under this pressure. But he held it together with his iron will and the troops stayed and kept up their deadly fire on any who dared to approach too closely to the Ohain road. To the west of the Brussels road the French guns wreaked havoc among the allied squares and gun lines. Mercer's battery was totally wrecked by French horse guns that were in turn driven off by Krahmer and de Binche's Belgium battery.

Siborne's treatment of the fall of La Haye Sainte seems to be generally accepted as accurate, and there is nothing contained in his history that causes much controversy. His treatment of all concerned is fair, except as ever the French whose tactics and strategy still eluded almost everyone on the British side, both military officers and historians. What Siborne missed, in my view, was Napoleon's grinding down strategy of Wellington's line. The capture of La Haye Sainte is seen as a sudden 'good idea' rather than part of an overall plan of attack. Its fall is seen as a consequence of the lack of ammunition rather than a failure in the command structure of Wellington's army. What the fall of La Haye Sainte shows is that despite the position of Wellington's tree, his battlefield command post being just behind the farm, a mere 150 metres from the rear hedge of the garden, Wellington failed to ensure that both troops and officers properly supported the Farm.

The allies had built an abatis across the Brussels road behind the sandpit and another further forward at the edge of the farm buildings. The rearward abatis was more of a barrier to the allies supporting the farm than it was a hindrance to the French attacking it. A safe route for reinforcements and ammunition could have been created down this road, protected as it was by the high walled bank and the knoll. But none of this was done. Everything was left to a mere Major who did more than he should have been able to do under the circumstances. It was not until the farm fell that the higher command realised their error, which they tried to correct by sending in Ompteda's 5th Line KGL. This was slaughtered and scattered by the French cuirassiers, further weakening the centre of the line.

Wellington made the excuse later, when told about the lack of ammunition in La Haye Sainte that he could not be everywhere. But surely he should have ensured the security of this central outpost of his line. To me the fall of La Haye Sainte was the worst failure of Wellington's command structure in the battle. It almost caused a disaster and it did cost the lives of hundreds of his troops. Wellington was brilliant. It was his battle. But even those who see him as the hero of the day should not gloss over the errors he made. He was after all, as he often said, only a man.

We shall now turn the clock back an hour or two and see how the Prussian build up of troops and the eventual attack came at the crucial moment.

Chapter Twenty

The Advance of the Prussians
from Wavre to Frichermont

The Prussian march to Waterloo is also the subject of much controversy because of many factors. But principally it was the late arrival of the Prussians that is most often both criticised and defended.

According to Peter Hofschröer what happened was this.

Von Bulow was selected to lead the Prussian march to Waterloo because, although he was the furthest away and had the furthest to march, his corps was the strongest and had not been engaged in the fight at Ligny. Another factor might have been that he was also the most experienced Corps commander. Bulow set off from Dion le Mont at 5.00am in the direction of Wavre, which was some six kilometres away. At 7.00am the leading column, the 15th Brigade, reached Wavre. Behind them were the 16th Brigade and further down the road were the 13th and then the 14th Brigades. A fire broke out in Wavre, which may have delayed their march, but in any event by 9.00am the leading troops of the 15th Brigade were at Chapelle St Lambert. The rest of 15th Brigade took another hour to arrive and behind them came the 16th Brigade who arrived at Chapelle St Lambert at 2.00pm. The last Brigade of the Corps, the 14th, arrived at 3.00pm.

So by 3.00pm the whole of the 4th Corps was assembled at St Lambert.

1st Corps under von Ziethen was not allowed to march until Bulow's 4th Corps had crossed its path. 1st Corps was at Bierges and they did not get going until 1.00pm when Ziethen, anxious about the delay, managed to slip his 1st Brigade under the command of von Steinmetz into the gap between 4th and 2nd Corps. Steinmetz quickly marched across the road that was on the line of march of both 4th and 2nd Corps marching first along that same road and then branching off north towards Rixensart. The rest of 1st Corps had to wait until Pirch's 2nd Corps cleared Wavre and passed Bierges. It was for this reason that they did not arrive at Waterloo until after the battle was over.

As each successive brigade arrived at Chapelle St Lambert they rested for three and a half hours waiting for the rest of the Corps to catch up. Even the last to arrive enjoyed the same rest period, which was deemed necessary as the troops had had a long march the previous day with little rest or food.

Between 9.00am and 10.00am the first of Bulow's scouts arrived at the western edge of the Paris Wood, which formed the eastern edge of the Waterloo battlefield. They were surprised that it was not occupied and sent back to Bulow to report on this. Bulow sent forward infantry to secure the wood. These arrived safely and without being discovered. At this point the battle had not yet begun and would not do so for another two hours. Communication between Bulow and Wellington set out the three options for Napoleon's battle plan.

An attack on Wellington's right
An attack on Wellington's centre
An attack on Bulow.

Wellington sent a message at about 12.00 noon to say that option one had been adopted by the French and, therefore, Bulow should attack via the heights between the Paris Wood and Plancenoit. Bulow had already confirmed to Wellington that once he knew where the French attack was on Wellington, he would move across the Lasne brook and through the village of Lasne, in order to attack the French right flank between Le Haye and Aywiers. Bulow also sent a message to Wellington to say that by 11.30am two of his brigades had arrived at Chapelle St Lambert, but that the Army Corps could not be there until 4.00pm. By this message Wellington was made aware of the situation of the 4th Corps and he could work out when he could expect effective support. During the morning Bulow had the Lasne valley and village reconnoitred and knew what difficulties lay ahead. To be extra certain about the best route the chief of staff of 4th Corps, General von Valentini, went to look for himself and met a local farmer who showed him a better route via the Frichermont wood.

Whilst Bulow waited at Chapelle St Lambert until just after 2.00pm before moving off, von Pirch's 2nd Corps was marching along the same road down which Bulow's 4th Corps passed earlier. It took Bulow another hour to cross the Lasne valley and for his most forward troops to arrive at the wood between the Lasne and Frichermont. At 3.30pm the 16th Brigade arrived at Frichermont and the reserve cavalry at 4.00pm. Von Hake's 13th Brigade arrived at 4.30pm and the reserve artillery and the 14th Brigade arrived between 5.00pm and 5.30pm. At 4.00pm therefore and no sooner, Bulow's 4th Corps could begin its operation and attack the left flank of Napoleon's army.

Meanwhile Steinmetz's 1st Brigade was still on the northern road between Rixensart and Ohain. It would be another hour before the 1st Silesian Hussars reached Ohain and made contact with Wellington's forces.

At 4.30pm Bulow started his attack from the woods of Frichermont and Paris

The Prussian 15ᵗʰ and 16ᵗʰ Brigades begin their attack on the French right driving Lobau back to his second position nearer to Plancenoit.

with 15ᵗʰ and 16ᵗʰ Brigades. The 13ᵗʰ and 14ᵗʰ Brigades were still coming up from Lasne and would arrive within the hour. Ziethen's 1ˢᵗ Corps was marching on Ohain but would not begin to arrive for another hour and a half and behind Bulow's rearward troops, von Pirch was marching forward with his four Brigades, the 5ᵗʰ, 6ᵗʰ, 7ᵗʰ and 8ᵗʰ.

Siborne, in his history, makes no criticism of the Prussians over their slow progress and late arrival. Siborne elaborates upon the difficulties of the ground, the fire in Wavre, the heroic urging on by Blucher of his troops whose guns sunk up to their axles in the mud.

Siborne cannot be criticised for being unfair to the Prussians over their march to Waterloo; if anything, he is too kind to them.

The question is, could the Prussians marching from Wavre to Waterloo, despite all of the difficulties of terrain weather and house fires, have arrived at the Waterloo battlefield earlier than they actually did?

The Prussian's March – chaos and confusion, deliberate delay

If we look at the maps shown overleaf we can see the whole area, from Braine

This map shows the Prussian march as it actually happened. Bulow's march is shown in yellow, Zeithen in red and Pirch in purple. You can see from this map where the bottle-neck would occur on the single road from Wavre to Froidmont. The halt at the Lasne stream contributed towards the delay in arriving but the overall reason for the late arrival at Waterloo was clearly poor staff work.

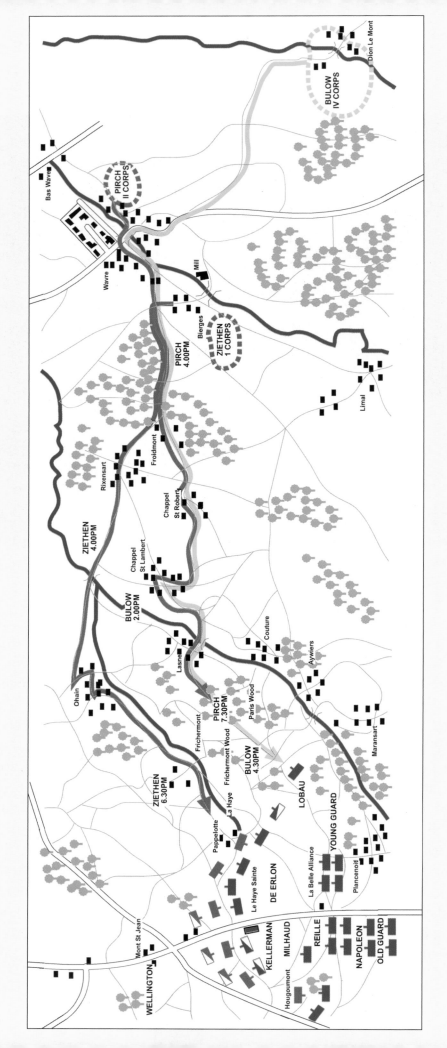

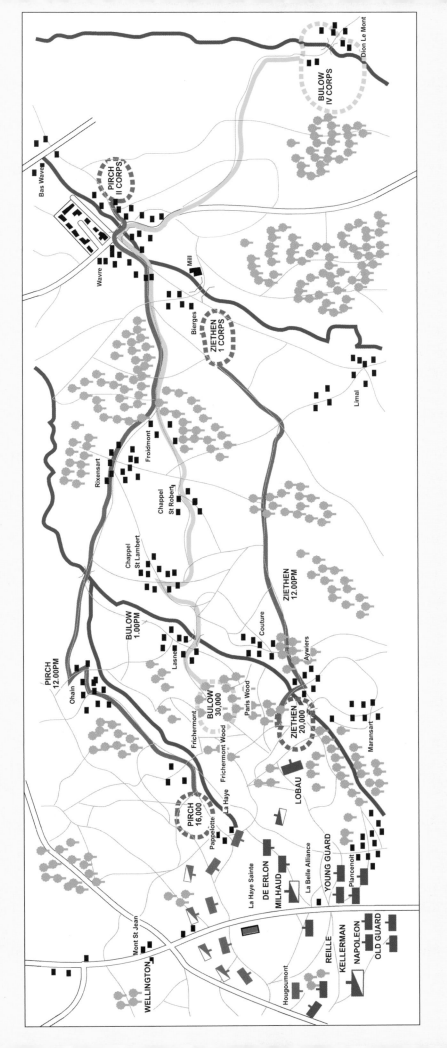

The map below shows how, with proper staff-work the Prussians might have arrived, in force, at Waterloo at 2.00pm. Ziethen could have marched from Bierges at dawn and been at Aywiers with 20,000 men by 2.00pm. Bulow could by this time have had 30,000 men in and around the Paris Wood and Pirch could have been at Papelotte with 16,000 men at the same time. This would have delivered 66,000 Prussians onto the flank of de Erlon's corps as it routed away from Uxbridge's cavalry charge.

Allude in the west to Dion le Mont in the east, a distance of some twenty kilometres. We can also see the positions of the various Corps of each army. Bulow's route of march with timings is shown in yellow, Ziethen's in red and Pirch's in purple. It is easy to see from this plan that the bottleneck would be where the three corps meet on the road from Wavre to Froidmont and in Wavre itself where 4th and 2nd Corps must cross the Dyle by the only bridge. We need to visualise the problem as if there were three traffic jams converging on a single road. A brigade of 5,000 infantry marching four men abreast will take up some 1,500 metres of road allowing for one metre per rank and gaps between battalions and guns etc. A brigade of cavalry, 1,500 strong, marching three abreast will also take up 1,500 metres of road allowing for three metres per rank. Therefore Von Ziethen's 1st Army Corps marching from Bierges with the 1st Infantry Brigade and 1st Cavalry Brigade would take up three kilometres of road.

2nd Army Corps under von Pirch, comprising four infantry and one cavalry brigades, would be seven and a half kilometres long. Bulow's 4th Corps with four infantry brigades, two cavalry brigades and the reserve artillery would stretch for nine kilometres along the road.

The Prussian march falls into five distinct areas:

Bulow's march from Dion le Mont to Wavre, some 6 kilometres.

The march by Bulow and Pirch from Wavre to Chapelle St Lambert, some 8.5 kilometres.

Ziethen's march from Bierges to Rixensart, some 5 kilometres.

Ziethen's march from Rixensart to Papelotte, some 10.5 kilometres.

Bulow's and Pirch's march from Chapelle St Lambert to the edge of the Paris and Frichermont wood from whence they commenced their attack, some 5 kilometres.

Bulow's march from Dion le Mont to Wavre took two hours to cover 6000 metres; a rate of march of 50 metres per minute. The march from Wavre to Chapelle St Lambert took two and a half hours for the leading troops to cover; a speed of 56 metres per minute. Ziethen, marching at the same rate, would have taken one hour and forty minutes to reach Rixensart but Ziethen did not march until 1.00pm and only squeezed two brigades through the gap between 4th and 2nd Corps before the march of von Pirch's troops closed the gap.

The 10.5 kilometres from Rixensart to Papelotte at the same rate of march would have taken three and a half hours to complete. Finally Bulow's leading brigade took one and a half hours to march the 5 kilometres from Chapelle St Lambert across the Lasne valley to the edge of the Paris wood; a rate of march of 55 metres per minute.

These distances covered, in the times stated by Peter Hofschröer, tell us quite a lot about the Prussian march to Waterloo. Firstly the rate of march is broadly the same for each leg of the journey. It is clear that the difficulties claimed for crossing the Lasne valley cannot be true, because the Prussians covered the distance at the same speed as the other legs of the journey. Von Ziethen could have arrived at Papelotte at around 4.30pm. But he did not arrive at Ohain until 6.00pm and that means that it took him from 2.40pm to 6.00pm to cover five and a half kilometres, a rate of march of only 21 metres per minute. It is more likely that Ziethen also stopped marching once he reached the Lasne brook and waited for over an hour.

This can only be because he was ordered to wait by Blucher or Gneisenau. He did not need to allow the rear elements of each column to catch up with the leading brigades, as Ziethen only had Steinmetz's 1st. Brigade and Von Treskow's cavalry across the Froidmont road. The reason he was ordered to wait was because both Blucher and Gneisenau still could not be certain, even at this late stage, that Wellington would hold out against Napoleon's onslaught.

Bulow's column was some nine kilometres long. At a rate of march of fifty metres per minute it would take three hours for the rear regiment to reach the front of the column; that is how long they waited at Lasne.

The deliberate delay at the Lasne brook was one of the causes for the late arrival of the Prussians at Waterloo. The other was simply poor staff work by the Prussian high command.

In any traffic flow plan it is obvious that to try to cross two seven-kilometre columns of troops will cause confusion and delay; add a third column and it will be chaos. It was important that each corps had a clear road down which to march so that they arrived at their allotted place in the least possible time. Had the Prussian staff looked at the situation with a little more care and attention they would have seen that Ziethen could have marched at 5.00am from Bierges to Couture and, at a rate of march of 50 metres per minute, would have covered the 10 kilometres by 8.30am. Equally Pirch leaving at 5.00am and heading via Rixensart for Ohain would have had a clear run. He could have been at Ohain by 9.30am. Bulow's leading brigade also arrived at Chapelle St Lambert at 9.30am but he would have been delayed by the tail of Pirch's 2nd Corps clearing Wavre.

It would have taken another three hours for the rear of each column to close up. But by 1.00pm Bulow could have had all of his forces at the Lasne brook. Pirch could have continued his march and arrived in force at Papelotte by 1.00pm and Ziethen could have marched north to cross the Lasne behind Bulow or crossed at Aywiers and entered the Paris wood from the south before 1.00pm.

I do not blame the Prussians for being cautious. After all if Wellington had been thrown back then the Prussian army would have been in an impossible position. However, I do criticise the excuses made by the Prussians about why they were so slow in getting into battle. It was in truth simply that they needed Wellington to engage the majority of Napoleon's army so that the Prussians would face a numerically inferior French force.

What if they had believed that Wellington would hold out and actually drive back de Erlon's attack and had made every effort to get to Waterloo on time? The leading elements of each corps could have been at the crossings of the Lasne brook at Lasne, Couture, and in the north near Ohain by 9.30am. From the Lasne brook to the right flank of Napoleon's army is about three miles.

By 11.00am the leading elements of each Corps could have been at the edge of the Paris Wood, Aywiers and Smohain. By 2.00pm each corps could have been ready to attack with the following numbers of troops, 1st Corps 20,000, 2nd Corps 16,000, 4th Corps 30,000. In total the proper route of march, as shown in the map on page 233, would have delivered 66,000 Prussians troops onto the flank of the routing elements of de Erlon's force and driven them off the field, together with the surrounding cavalry and possibly the Young Guard as well.

Well maybe yes and maybe no; but the point is it was perfectly feasible for the whole of Blucher's committed force to have engaged Napoleon's right flank effectively at 2.00pm rather than having a mere two brigades attack towards Plancenoit at 4.30pm.

Furthermore, had Napoleon defeated Wellington and turned on Blucher he would have had his army deployed in a battle line from Ohain to Aywiers. The Prussian army would have stood a better chance of defending itself than it would have had being spread out in a column sixteen kilometres long.

Siborne made no criticism of Blucher, Gneisenau, the Prussian organisation or the Prussian army. Perhaps in the interests of truth and accuracy he should have done.

The poor choice of marching order resulted from a lack of experience, fatigue and basic inefficiency. The three hours rest was a tactical decision made by Blucher and Gneisenau to allow them to be certain that Wellington was fully engaged before they got too much into the fight against the Napoleon, the god of war. Who can blame them for that?

Chapter Twenty One

The Prussian Attack on Plancenoit

As Bulow pushes forward, Lobau, Domon and Subervie pull back to form a line at right angles to the front line that is facing Wellington.

At 4.30pm the first cannon shots rang out from the Prussian battery hidden in the Paris wood. Soon more batteries came into action; a welcome sound to Wellington's ears. Soon afterwards von Losthin's 15th Brigade and Hiller's 16th Brigade made their first advance towards Plancenoit. This force comprised eighteen battalions of infantry totalling 12,000 troops. They were supported by the 2nd and 3rd Silesian cavalry, the 6th Hussars and the 1st West Prussian Uhlans totalling 1,847 sabres. The artillery support from the Corps consisted of three six pounder and one twelve pound battery, 32 guns in all.

Facing them were the 5,000 infantry of Lobau's 6th Corps and 2,300 cavalry of the divisions of Domon and Subervie.

Lobau deployed his divisions in line between the two woods flanking the route to Plancenoit. On the outer flanks he deployed the cavalry divisions of Domon, Subervie and Jacquinot who had turned to face east against the Prussian threat.

Bulow detached two battalions from the 18th Infantry and 3rd Silesian Landwehr to link up with the Nassau troops in and around Frichermont. The rest of 15th Brigade deployed to the north of the road to Plancenoit, whilst Hiller

Lobau, having been pushed back to the edge of Plancenoit by the Prussian 15th and 16th Brigades, allowed von Bulow to bring up and deploy his impressive artillery reserve and blast the French line with canister from 86 guns. Note the troops beginning to move through the Vivere wood to outflank the line and enter the village from the south.

brought the 16th Brigade up to deploy south of the road. Hiller detached two battalions from the 15th infantry regiment and the 1st Silesian Landwehr to outflank Lobau's line and to protect Hiller from any attack coming out of the Vivere wood.

The Prussian guns coming into action announced to both Napoleon and Wellington the arrival of Bulow's force onto the battlefield. For half an hour the guns of each side fired at the assembled infantry lines. Then Bulow pushed his force forward, driving Lobau back off the high ground and down the slope into Plancenoit village. By six o'clock Lobau has been driven back to Plancenoit and Losthin and Hiller had received the support of Hake's 13th Brigade, Ryssel's 14th Brigade, the cavalry reserve under Crown Prince William of Prussia and the artillery reserve comprising a further five batteries of 12-pounders. Now the Prussians had an impressive force on the right flank of Napoleon's army - 25,000 infantry, 3,500 cavalry and 86 guns, as many and more than were deployed in the French Grand Battery against Wellington's line earlier in the day.

The village of Plancenoit now came under intense artillery fire from a gun line some 800 metres from the village centre. Hiller moved against the village whilst von Losthin attacked Jeanin's Division formed in a line to the north of the village. The fighting was very bloody.

Hiller's 16th Brigade attacks Plancenoit whilst the supporting batteries open fire on the village.

Canister and musketry cut down both French and Prussian as the two lines came closer together. The nerve of the Prussians was stronger than the French and Lobau fell back allowing Hiller to enter the eastern side of the village. Now the struggle became a house to house contest with hand to hand fighting as each house was attacked and defended to the last.

Napoleon had moved his position of observation to a small knoll to the east of La Belle Alliance. From here he could see Plancenoit and the Prussian threat. It was serious. He ordered the two brigades of the Young Guard Division to move into Plancenoit to redress the balance.

Duhemse led the Young Guard down the road to Plancenoit and entered the fight. Hiller was thrown back and the village was re-taken. Behind Hiller though was the 14th Brigade under von Ryssel. This brigade now joined the fight, as did the 13th Brigade under Hake further to the northeast. Once again Lobau and Duhemse were thrown back as Ryssel's 14th Brigade attacked the village.

The struggle was intense and Napoleon ordered two battalions of the Old Guard to re-take the village. They were the 1st Battalions of the 2nd Grenadiers and the 2nd Chasseur regiment commanded by Marechal de Camp Jean Pelet. He also ordered the

As the Prussians approach the village Napoleon seen here at the top of the picture near La Belle Alliance ordered the Young Guard to support Lobau in Plancenoit.

The fighting in the village became intense especially around the churchyard.

1st Battalion of the 1st Regiment of the Chasseurs of the Guard to march from Le Caillou, where it was guarding the Emperor's baggage, to the wood of Chantelet in order to protect the right flank of the village and prevent it from being turned. The next incident is mentioned in most, if not all, histories of the battle but not much is made of it. Yet it is probably the finest feat of arms by any side throughout the entire campaign.

The first attack by the Imperial Old Guard Infantry.

The Old Guard came down the road from La Belle Alliance with every Guardsman in perfect step despite the quick pace of the march. They came upon Duhemse who had been hit in the head by a musket ball. He died in Genappe two days later despite the best efforts of the Prussian medical staff. No sooner had they reached Duhemse than the Voltigeurs of the Young Guard came running out of the village. Chartrand, commander of the 1st Brigade of Young Guard, told Pelet that all was lost; the Prussians held the village, nothing could be done. The 1st Battalion of the 2nd Chasseurs of the Old Guard were not impressed by these concerns. They marched on, 500 against 5,000.

The Chasseurs charged into the village

The 1ˢᵗ battalion of the 2ⁿᵈ Chasseurs of the Imperial Guard thrust through the retreating Young Guard battalions and advance on the village. Behind them the 2ⁿᵈ Grenadiers are marching in support.

at bayonet point screaming out their war cry as they ran. Behind them the Young Guard had rallied and joined in the fight. Other troops outside the village, seeing the Old Guard attack, returned themselves to the attack and joined in the fight. The Chasseurs broke into the village and headed for the church in the centre. Von Ryssel's 14ᵗʰ Brigade held the village and just outside it was Hiller's 16ᵗʰ Brigade, which had only just recovered from its earlier ejection from the village by the Young Guard. Further north Hake's 13ᵗʰ Brigade and Losthin's 15ᵗʰ Brigade were still advancing against

Lobau's Corps. In all, over 20,000 infantry were in and around the village of Plancenoit when the Old Guard attacked.

The Chasseurs reached the church and engaged in a furious fight, with Pelet himself in the thick of the fighting. Just as it seemed that the vastly more numerous Prussians would throw back the Chasseurs, the 1ˢᵗ Battalion of the 2ⁿᵈ Grenadiers of the Old Guard charged into the melee with bayonet, boot and a mace swung by Drum Major Stubert. This was the final straw for both the 14ᵗʰ and 16ᵗʰ Brigades. They fled in panicked rout from the Old Guard. On went the Guardsmen

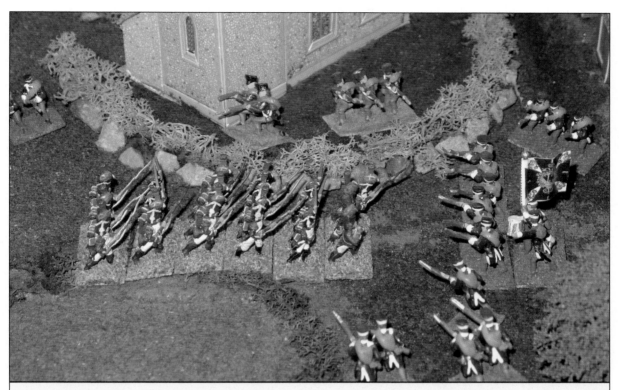

ABOVE: The Guard charge in with the bayonet causing some of the Prussians to withdraw whilst others fight hand to hand with these ferocious warriors.

BELOW: Just as it looked as though the Prussians would beat the Guard back the 1st Battalion of the 2nd Grenadiers burst into the fight and turned the tide.

through the village and out the other side sweeping five thousand Prussians before them. The history of the 2nd Silesian Landwehr reported the matter but glossed over the facts. As Peter Hofschröer says, the record of the 15th Regiment of von Hillers 16th Brigade was a little more frank.

"....we could not hold onto the village this time either. Napoleon sent in two regiments of Old Guard under General Morand from his reserves to Plancenoit. Two of their battalions along with the Young Guard and the remaining troops in the village took control of it again, forcing our men to withdraw."

The Prussian brigades to the north were also forced to retire by the furious charge of the Old Guard. They fell back in good order with Lobau following up cautiously. Onwards ran the Old Guard, up the slope in pursuit of the fleeing Prussian infantry. The Prussians reached the gun line and ran through it taking with them most if not all of the gunners, for we know that when the Old Guard reached the guns they were not fired on by the guns. They had been abandoned. Fortunately behind the gun line were the cavalry of the 2nd Silesian Landwehr, a mere 160 horsemen

Bulow's entire corps is driven back, part of it in panicked rout from the few soldiers of Napoleon's Imperial Guard. There were no more than 1,300 guardsmen supported by Lobau and one brigade of Young Guard against 20,000 or more Prussians.

but they were enough to stem the rout. They swept forward and drove the Old Guardsmen back. The French cavalry, barely able to keep up with the speed of the advance, now charged forward but were beaten back by the 8th Prussian Hussars from von Watzdorff's 2nd Cavalry Brigade. The French withdrew to the village having thrown back Bulow's whole Corps, half of it in rout. They were able to secure the village and the surrounding area and await the next onslaught from Blucher's army.

Bulow's Corps had suffered enormous casualties in the struggle for Plancenoit. In total the Prussians suffered 6,998 casualties including 1,386 who were missing. Of these Bulow's Corps suffered 5,461 casualties including 976 missing. Almost all of these casualties were suffered during the attacks on Plancenoit and the subsequent attack of the Old Guard that threw them back. After this the bulk of the fighting fell onto Pirch's and Ziethen's Corps. Bulow had attacked Lobau's 6th Corps and the Young Guard division with 25,000 infantry and had lost over 5,000 in the fight.

Now Plancenoit was fortified by the remains of Lobau's Corps and the Young Guard division plus the two battalions of the Old Guard. Lobau and the Young Guard had also suffered most of their casualties during Bulow's attacks on

After the Old Guard had driven out the Prussians the Young Guard and part of Lobau's Corps re-occupied the village to bolster its defences.

Plancenoit. I estimate that they lost in the region of 3,300 up to this point. Therefore, if my estimate is accurate, Plancenoit was at this time defended by 10,000 men whereas at the height of the action before the Old Guard attack, it had been defended by 12,000 men. 25,000 Prussians had been unable to hold onto Plancenoit when faced by 12,000 French. Could even fewer Prussians now drive out 10,000 French?

Napoleon was satisfied that they could not. He felt secure enough on his right flank to launch his final assault on Wellington's line with the remainder of his Imperial Guard infantry. But before he did he decided to send his aides galloping along the line announcing that Grouchy had arrived, which Napoleon knew was not true, in order to boost their morale for the final assault. Or did he?

Chapter Twenty Two

'Voila Grouchy'

The story of *Voila Grouchy* has always bothered me, as it makes no sense when you examine the claims made about it. Mark Adkin best describes the story in his book "The Waterloo Companion" as follows:

Colonel Octave Levasseur was an ADC to Ney and was present when one of the Emperor's ADCs, General de Division Dejean, galloped up with the news that Grouchy had arrived with his force. It was a critical moment, just as the Imperial Guard was about to start its attack as part of the general advance all along the line. He described it thus:

'Monsieur le Marechal' he said 'Vive l' Emperor! Voila Grouchy!' The Marshal at once ordered me to go right along the line and announce that Grouchy had arrived. I set off at the gallop, with my hat raised on the point of my sabre, rode down the line shouting 'Vive l' Emperor! Soldats, voila Grouchy!' The sudden shout was taken up by a thousand voices. The exaltation of the troops reached fever pitch and they all shouted 'En avant! En avant! Vive l' Emperor!' I had scarcely reached the end of our line when I heard cannon fire behind us. Enthusiasm gave way to profound silence, to amazement, to anxiety.... The cannonade went on and drew closer. In utter consternation I rode up to the Marshal, who forbade me to go and find out the cause of this panic. I went next to General _____, who said to me 'Voyez Ce sont le Prussiens!' I turned back to look for Marshal Ney, but I could not find him.'

Levasseur was not the only ADC deliberately encouraging false hope. Marechal de Camp de la Bedoyere had been sent on the same mission.

This is all very odd, very odd indeed. In the first place let us look at the practical possibility of actually delivering such an order in the middle of a battle to 50,000 men over a three-mile front. If Levasseur and La Bedoyere were delivering the order at the gallop, it is doubtful whether anyone heard them. On 19th June a Kent newspaper reported gunfire from across the channel. This gunfire came from Waterloo over 100 miles away. Just how noisy was it on the battlefield?

Levasseur then goes on to say that he heard a cannonade behind him. He was surprised to be told that it was the Prussians. Yet the Prussians had first been seen at 1.00pm and had been in action since 4.30pm. Why was he surprised? The 'Voila Grouchy' incident took place at 7.30pm. The whole army knew that the Prussians were attacking the right flank of their army. The best they could have hoped for from Grouchy was that he would attack the rear of the Prussians. If that was the case then the cannonade Levasseur heard could quite easily have come from Grouchy's guns.

But most important of all is the fact that the message is totally out of character for Napoleon. Why would he do it? It is supposed that he gave the order to bolster the morale of the troops. But he could have done this by announcing the attack of the Imperial Guard, which *was* about to happen. The lie, once told, was bound to break the spirit of trust built up between Napoleon and his army over fifteen years and one hundred battles. Napoleon would never had considered this foolhardy military and political act of stupidity.

I then purchased on 'e bay' a book entitled 'The Waterloo Campaign by Napoleon Bonaparte' This book was written by Napoleon himself, or rather it was dictated by him whilst he was a prisoner on the Island of St. Helena. So what did Napoleon himself say about the 'Voila Grouchy' incident? I went straight to the moment when the order was supposed to have been sent and there it was on page 130 and 131 of the book. It

read as follows;

"Some of the regiments drew back. I noticed this. It was of the highest importance to put the cavalry in countenance again; and, realizing that I still needed another quarter of an hour to rally my whole Guard, I put myself at the head of four battalions, and advanced to the left front of la Haie-Sainte (sic), sending aides-de-camp along the line to announce the arrival of Marshal Grouchy, and to say that, with a little determination, the victory was soon to be decided."

So there it was in Napoleon's own words. His betrayal of his own troops; a lie told to get them fighting again; a lie that would eventually be found out either during the battle or soon after it. The army was nervous about treason. Politics was rife throughout the ranks and the officers, or so it is said. And yet despite this, Napoleon took the extraordinary decision to deceive the troops and commit treason against them at this crucial moment. I could not believe it.

Now I looked at the book from the beginning and, at the front, was a forward by Somerset de Chair who translated the book in 1957. Then there was the introduction by Henry Lachouque, the famous French historian. His introduction deals with the authenticity of the original book which was first published in 1820, one year before Napoleon's death. However it was written sometime before 1818 on St Helena. Napoleon's surgeon and the surgeon of HMS Northumberland took care to ensure that it arrived safe and sound in England with the publishers Sir

Richard Phillips & Co, in London.

The publishers said in the preface that the manuscript had been in their possession since October 1818, but they had delayed the publication until 1820 as they wished to get further verification from St Helena that it was genuine and had been dictated by Napoleon himself. The reason for this was that after Waterloo there had been several publications lampooning Napoleon all of which were false, including quoting a speech made by General Bertrand, which he never made. The authenticity of 'The Waterloo Campaign' was assured. The publication was certainly written on St Helena and sent from there to London.

Lachouque then goes on to explain that Napoleon always dictated his orders, memoirs, etc because his writing was so illegible. Then there is the a short sentence quoting the publisher of a work written in 1850, which included the 'Waterloo Campaign' in the work and commented:

"the Comte de Montholon wrote the major part of the notes (dictated by the Emperor)"

And suddenly it all became quite clear.

In 1961 a Swedish dentist named Dr. Sten Forshufvud completed a wonderful piece of forensic detective work on the death of Napoleon on St Helena. He concluded that he had been poisoned with arsenic, which had been administered over a period of some years. Proof came from examination of hair samples by Dr. Hamilton Smith in the Department of Forensic Medicine at the University of Glasgow. It was later claimed that perhaps Napoleon had accidentally been poisoned by the arsenic used in the wallpaper in Longwood House at St Helena. This of course is nonsense. If it were the case then why did not all of the other occupants of Longwood die as well? The quantity of arsenic in Napoleon's hair was such that it could only have got there from deliberate action. Someone murdered the Emperor. Sten Forshufvud looked at all of the possible suspects in his murder enquiry. Was it the British? Was it the French Monarchy? Who was it?

Suspicion eventually fell on the Bourbon Monarchy who had every reason to kill both the man and the myth. The Bourbons were suppressors of the revolution. They regained power in 1815

The Emperor dictating his memoirs to the Comte de Montholon in St Helena.

and held on until they were eventually thrown out by the second revolution in 1830. At that time, 1830, the King of France was the brother of the late Louis Bourbon, Charles X. Charles X was formerly in, 1815, the Comte de Artois. The Comte de Artois was a wonderful conspirer, a French Machiavelli. In 1815 he had looked for and found a person who was vulnerable, in debt, and had committed a crime against the Government by embezzling money from the army. He found the Comte de Montholon, a former minor aristocrat. Montholon had one other attribute of interest, a pretty young wife.

Montholon was a loathsome character, a thief, a liar; an intriguer who used his wife to gain Napoleon's trust by using her in Napoleon's bed. Artois could have had Montholon court-marshalled and imprisoned for theft following the embezzlement of nearly 8,000 francs from army funds, but he did not. He did however keep the threat of it hanging over Montholon's head. One must ask why the brother of the King, the next in line of succession, was the least bit interested in a petty crime committed by a minor aristocrat? The reason was that Napoleon was due to be sent to St. Helena and was allowed to take with him an approved group of companions. Artois saw to it that Montholon was put forward as a likely candidate.

Montholon and his pretty wife were accepted by all sides to accompany Napoleon into exile on St Helena. Once there he was despised by Napoleon's true friends, in particular the Comte de Las Cases and General Gourgaud, who hated him. Montholon, on the order of the Comte de Artois, poisoned Napoleon during the period 1816 to 1821 when the Emperor finally died in agony on 5th May. Montholon lived on, but not in the luxury he had hoped for when he dictated Napoleon's will leaving himself two million francs. He died in August 1853 at the age of 71. Montholon's wife became pregnant on St Helena and left the island to give birth to a girl upon her return to France. It is possible that this little girl was fathered by Napoleon.

This was the man who wrote down the notes 'dictated' by Napoleon that became the book 'The Waterloo Campaign by Napoleon Bonaparte'. This was the man who first mentions the 'Voila Grouchy' order to be sent along the line at Waterloo. This is where it all began.

But what of General Dejean who brought the order from the Emperor, and Colonel Levasseur and le Bedoyere who carried the message along the line with hats on swords, shouting out the false news that Grouchy had arrived? What of them?

Le Bedoyere was tried for treason and was, at the behest of the Bourbon Monarchy, shot by firing squad in August 1815; a victim of the white terror. Ney went the same way. Dejean escaped and went into exile until 1818 and was later allowed to inherit his father's title by Charles X.

I do not know what happened to Levasseur. However he described the event and must therefore have survived the white terror in order to have made the statement, if in fact he ever did make the statement at all.

The issue of testimony about the 'Voila Grouchy' order must be a cause for doubt. The statements were made during the restoration of the monarchy. Those then in power would do anything, including murder, to protect the monarchy from another revolution. If that meant the character assassination of Napoleon then so be it. I think that they would not have hesitated for a moment.

In my view Napoleon never gave any order to anyone to ride along the line to announce the arrival of Grouchy's forces. It simply did not happen. It was a lie concocted by the Comte de Artois and carried out by Montholon. It was so cleverly done that it has been widely believed ever since. Interestingly Siborne makes no mention of it at all!

The matter of Napoleon's death is still debated today, with both sides offering evidence to back up their case. Some say that the amount of arsenic in Napoleon's body had been seen before in 1805 and 1814. Napoleon may have suffered an attempted assassination in 1805. In 1814 we know that he did take poison himself but that it was old and not strong enough to kill him.

It was Winston Churchill who said that the truth should be escorted by a bodyguard of lies. Well the same is true in reverse; a lie is best told amid a bundle of truths. Some of what is written in the 'Waterloo Campaign' does sound as though it is genuine. Much else is clearly not true. The task is to sift the truth from the lies and that is not easy.

I leave it to you to ponder on whether the word of the man who probably murdered Napoleon is worth anything at all. Whether in the face of all of the logic that stands against it the 'Voila Grouchy' order was ever sent at all.

Chapter Twenty Three

7.30 – 8.30pm

The Last Attack of the Imperial Guard
(British and Prussian Versions)

No-one knows for certain what happened in detail during the final moments of the Battle of Waterloo. We only know for certain a few true facts. The rest is supposition. It is this supposition that causes the great controversy about the battle - who did what and when? Let us firstly deal with what we know to be the facts.

Napoleon sent in the remaining battalions of his Grenadiers and Chasseurs of the Imperial Guard to lead the final attack on the Anglo-Netherlands line, in order to break it once and for all. They advanced to the attack. They were beaten off and ran back from the Anglo-Netherlands line in disorder. After this the whole army broke into panicked rout and both the Prussians and the Anglo-Netherlands armies advanced against the fleeing French army. Blucher and Wellington met somewhere on the Brussels road south of La Belle Alliance

and the Prussians then took over the pursuit and drove the French army back into France.

That is as much as we know for certain. But there is such a story to be told at this point, with so much drama and controversy, that we must examine it in close detail in order to get at what is most probably the truth of what really happened.

Basically there are two versions of what happened. One is Siborne's version with several variations from other historians, including me, of Siborne's work. The other is the modern 'Prussian' version as promoted by Peter Hofschröer and David Hamilton-Williams and others. These two versions differ on the cause of the French rout. Both acknowledge the known facts above as being true. But in each case they then tell a widely different story as to what happened in detail, to arrive at their conclusion on the main cause of the rout of the French army. What did actually cause it?

Siborne has it that it was the defeat of the Imperial Guard by the British Guards and the 52nd Foot that caused the rout to spread out from the centre to the wings of the French army, and for the whole French army to run down the Brussels road pursued by the British and King's German Legion cavalry.

The 'Prussian' view is expressed in two ways;

> That it was the final attack on Plancenoit by Pirch and Bulow that drove in the right flank of the French army that caused the rout. This happened at the same time as the attack of the Old Guard on the Anglo-Netherlands line.

> That General Steinmetz (of von Ziethen's Corps) broke through at the junction of the French lines, driving back Durutte's Division. He thereby outflanked the French lines facing both the Anglo-Netherlands and the Prussian armies. It was this break-through that occurred either at the same time or before the repulse of the Old Guard that caused the rout of the French army.

We will examine both versions in some detail before putting forward what I think most probably happened at this critical time in the battle - the moment chosen by Siborne for his model; the moment he described as the crisis of the Battle of Waterloo.

Siborne's version of events.

Siborne made a very detailed study of the moment in time which he wished to represent on his model. From this study he described in great detail what took place all over the field at that moment. Whether he was right or wrong in his conclusions we shall see. But, of all of the subsequent versions of what happened, his stands out as the most comprehensive. What Siborne says is that the centre of Wellington's line was under tremendous pressure, on the verge of breaking. Wellington ordered troops from the left and right to move to the centre to shore up the fragile line. The Brunswickers, Dutch and Belgians were sent from the right, Vivian and Vandeleur from the left. Then he reports that a French cavalry officer deserted and told Adam's Brigade that Napoleon was about to attack with his Guard and that it would be Adam who would bear the brunt of the attack.

Wellington positioned himself in the rear of the British Foot Guards and awaited the onslaught. Siborne has it that there were two columns of Guards attacking Wellington's line. The first met and drove off Halkett's British Brigade in some confusion. But then they came up against the British Guards head-on, who stood up as if rising up out of the ground and blasted the column with deadly fire. The Foot Guards then charged the Imperial Guard and drove them away in confusion. The Foot Guards advanced. But on seeing another column on their right they halted. Because of some confusion over whether to form square or wheel right. The whole of the second battalion ran back to the crest in some disorder.

According to Siborne, two battalions of the Old Guard advanced so far ahead of the rest of the corps that they could be defeated by the British Foot Guards, who still had time to retire in confusion and yet be ready to defeat the second attacking Old Guard column.

ABOVE: The first French Guard column arrives at the British line, right in front of the 2ⁿᵈ and 3ʳᵈ Battalions of the 1st Foot Guards.

BELOW: "Now Maitland now's your time" Wellington orders the guards to stand up and pour a volley into the packed ranks of the Imperial Guard at forty yards distance.

ABOVE: The British Foot Guards pursue the beaten French Guard but suddenly come across the second attacking column advancing out of the mist.

BELOW: The British Foot Guards are thrown into confusion and run back. Moments before the 30th and 73rd Foot collide and also run back in disorder from the advance of the Imperial Guard.

ABOVE: The British Foot Guards manage to recover from their disorder and form up in time to defeat the second column, which is also attacked at the same time by the 52nd Foot. That column also breaks and the whole French army dissolves into rout.

BELOW: The 52nd Foot swing round and deploy on the flank of the Imperial Guard column whilst the British Foot Guards engage their front.

The third battalion withdrew in better order. Once they reached the crest of the ridge, order was restored and they prepared for the second attacking column. The second column was then attacked in the flank by the 52nd Foot and the rest of Adam's Brigade, and frontally by the Foot Guards and the 69th Foot. This is the moment depicted on Siborne's model. The second Old Guard column gave way and broke up in rout. Colborne of the 52nd Foot advanced diagonally across the field in pursuit, followed by the rest of Adam's Brigade and Halkett's Hanoverian Brigade. Wellington sent in Vivian's cavalry to support Adam's Brigade. They were followed by Vandeleur's Brigade making it a combined assault of Adam, Halkett, Vivian and Vandeleur which decisively attacked the French line in its centre.

This attack caused the French line to break. This resulted in the rest of the French army becoming outflanked. Wellington perceived this and rode to the centre of his position. He noted that the Prussians were again attacking Plancenoit and, saying "In for a penny in for a pound", he launched the counter-attack all along the line. The French, having seen the Imperial Guard routed and that their flanks and rear were threatened, broke up in panicked flight. They ran for the Brussels/Charleroi road back in the direction of the French border. The Prussians now broke through at Plancenoit and both allied armies met up on the Charleroi road somewhere south of La Belle Alliance. The Prussians then took over the pursuit and the battle ended.

However, some of this does not pan out when recreated on the model.

The problem Siborne faced was what I would call 'Spitfire Syndrome'. Almost every German pilot shot down in the battle of Britain claimed that he was shot down by a Spitfire, when in fact the majority were despatched by the less glamorous Hurricane. At Waterloo every battalion wanted to claim that it had defeated the French Imperial Guard or, if they had themselves been driven back, then it was the Guard who drove them back. To accommodate these claims Siborne, not wishing to cause any offence to his fellow officers, some of whom were very senior indeed, had the Guard attack in two columns and defeat Halkett's Brigade before being itself defeated by the British Foot Guards.

The Dutch Belgians and the Nassau Brigade do not get a look in. They either break and run away or stand still and take no part in this part of the action. They naturally complained about this. The Dutch Belgians in particular felt that they did play a major part in the defeat of the Imperial Guard's first column. From this has developed the various versions of this final French attack and how it was conducted. All of these new versions fall into the same trap that Siborne fell into. They are trying to make the French attack fit the sensitivies of the defending troops, be they British Guard or Belgian militia.

Mark Adkin has the Guard attacking in Square, with five battalions attacking on a 600-yard wide front with three battalions waiting in reserve. These are then attacked by all and sundry, the Guards, the 52nd Foot, the 95th Rifles, numerous batteries of British artillery, the 33rd, 69th, 30th and 73rd Foot, plus

Detmer's Brigade and the Belgian battery of Krahmer and de Binche. Well no-one can complain about that as every one has a hand in the defeat of Napoleon's elite troops, who just happen to have marched forward in a conveniently suicidal formation.

That is not what happened.

The Imperial Guard was certainly beaten and ran back in confusion and disorder. Wellington certainly broke the French line in two when he counter-attacked after the defeat of the Imperial Guard. But had there been a strong reserve of Imperial Guard available then the gap would have been closed and the 52nd Foot driven off.

The French army finally broke up and routed when its line was ruptured. Having been penetrated, the French line was vulnerable to an attack on its flank and rear. You can see on pages 261 and 263 the different versions in map form. The photographs on the preceeding and following pages show how the model depicts each version.

The question is did the rupture occur solely at the French centre where, following the defeat of the Imperial Guard, Wellington launched his counter-attack? Or did it happen further to the east in one or even two places where the Prussians broke through?

Other eye witness accounts, as described by Mark Adkin, have the Guard attacking in square across a wide front with a strong reserve also in square further back.

In this version Detmer's Dutch Belgian Brigade attacks on the flank of the British line whilst Kramer's and de Binche's batteries pour grapeshot into the Guard squares.

The Prussian version of events

The Prussians knew nothing of the attack of the Imperial Guard as this took place out of sight of their forces. Their perspective was based upon what they experienced directly in front of them.

We left the Prussians being driven back by two battalions of the Old Guard and their supporting units from Lobau and the Young Guard. Blucher began to reorganise his forces. He sent a messenger, a Captain von Scharnhorst, to intercept Ziethen on the Ohain road. His orders were to direct him to join Blucher at the Paris wood to support the attack on Plancenoit. They met at the road junction near Chapelle St Jacques where Lieutenant Colonel von Reiche received the order to turn to the south. Reiche, however, explained that he had arranged things with Muffling and that they were desperately needed by Wellington.

A heated debate took place but Scharnhorst would not hear any argument. He was carrying the order of the Field Marshall and that order could not be overturned by a Lieutenant Colonel. During the argument Steinmetz rode up and ordered Reiche to comply with the Field Marshall's order and back up the column, then march south towards Plancenoit. Before they could move very far, von Ziethen arrived. After

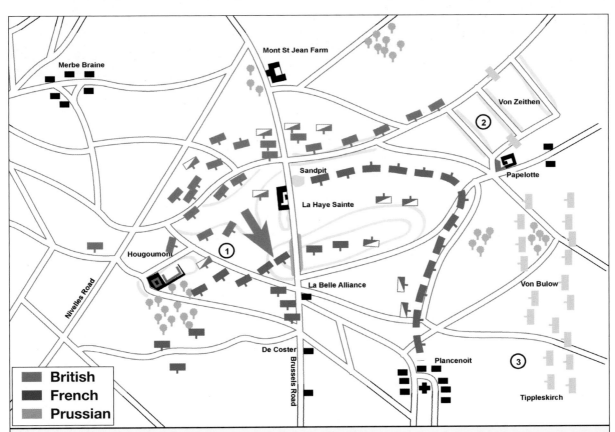

Siborne's view. (1) The British Guards and the 52nd Foot have broken the French Guard. Steinmetz is approaching Papelotte (2) whilst Tippelskirch is getting ready to assault Plancenoit (3). Siborne moved the Prussian figures back on his model. Since his model did not extend that far east, they were removed from the battlefield.

The meeting on the Ohain road between Steinmetz, Scharnhorst, Muffling and Von Ziethen. The advanced guard of the 1ˢᵗ Division are waiting for orders about the direction in which they are to march.

pleading from Muffling, who had returned to see where they were, he overruled Scharnhorst, and thereby Blucher, and continued the march onwards towards Papelotte.

On arriving at Ter Le Haye, a hamlet just east of Papelotte, Steinmetz's 1st. Brigade mistook the Nassau defenders for French. This was not too surprising since they were wearing French uniforms.

A minor skirmish broke out with casualties on both sides, which was only stopped when Muffling once again intervened. They then advanced, driving the French, the real French this time, out

of the houses around Papelotte farm, which the soldiers of Durutte's Division had occupied. Prussian skirmishers continued to advance against Durutte's main line whilst their cavalry and a battery of artillery moved on behind Papelotte to link up with Wellington's main position.

Now, according to David Hamilton-Williams, Steinmetz delivered the killer blow to Napoleon's army. They formed up in a Prussian Brigade attack column and came crashing out of the Ohain dip to sweep into Durutte's line, shattering it completely. Behind Steinmetz came Lutzow's cavalry Brigade of 1,300

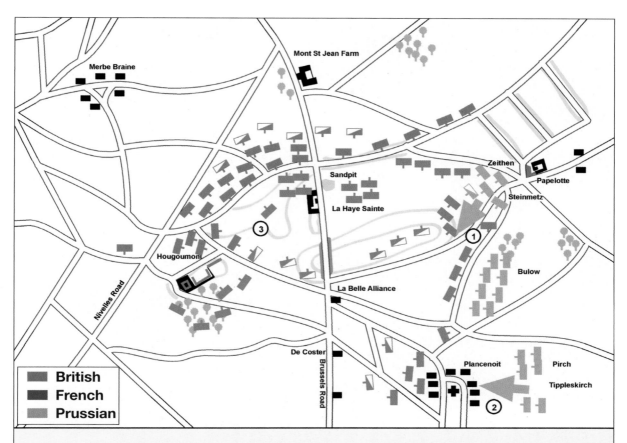

The Prussian view. (1) Steinmetz breaks through the line, outflanking the whole French army. (2) Tippelskirch attacks Plancenoit, driving out the Guard. (3) At the same time the French Guard make their attack on Wellington's line and are driven off by the British Guards and the 52nd Foot.

troopers and behind them came von Treskow's Brigade of cavalry with another 2,000 troopers. These turned left and right, rolling up both de Erlon's and Lobau's lines, causing confusion and panic in the French ranks. It is assumed by David Hamilton-Williams, and others, that Napoleon's supposed 'Voila Grouchy' order had disillusioned the French troops when they realised that the approaching troops were in fact Prussians not French.

As you now know, I doubt that any such order was ever sent, but something made the French withdraw away from the Steinmetz's attack which widened as it moved further and further towards La

Belle Alliance a mere 1,000 yards away. Wellington saw this happen from where he stood at Maitland's position. From there he ordered the general advance of the whole line. He could see that Steinmetz had broken Napoleon's line and put the battle beyond doubt. Steinmetz now turned south in compliance with Blucher's earlier order and attacked Plancenoit from the northeast. Just prior to Steinmetz's attack Tippelskirch's 5th Brigade supported by the remnants of Bulow's 14th and 16th Brigades, launched the final attack on Plancenoit village from the east. The 25th Regiment of the 5th Brigade played the

Steinmetz's Brigade attacked the Nassau troops in Ter Le Haye by mistake, causing and taking several casualties in the process.

leading part in the assault. One battalion pushed the Grenadiers of the Old Guard out of Chantelet. The other drove the rest of the Old Guard, together with the remnants of the Young Guard, out of the village and back towards the Charleroi road.

Wellington was now able to advance and join in the pursuit of the French army, which had been beaten by the arrival of Steinmetz, von Lutzow and von Treskow in the northeast and the devastating attack by Tippelskirch at Plancenoit from the east.

That is the version as seen by the Prussians, or rather how it is nowadays portrayed by more modern historians. But does it stand up to scrutiny?

Well actually no, it does not.

The two versions are based upon eyewitness and post-battle regimental reports. The eyewitness reports can only say what their eyes actually saw. In most cases this was precious little. Regimental reports are not particularly objective historical documents. See for example the differences between the official history of the 95th Regiment at Waterloo, with the recently discovered letter from Barnard about the number of troops who ran away when attacked. The truth can, however, be found in the casualty

Steinmetz's Brigade advancing in a Prussian brigade attack column out of the Smohain dip towards Durutte's Division.

Tippleskirch drives into Plancenoit with the 25th Regiment leading the way, as displayed in the original layout of Siborne's model. The Imperial Guard, both the two battalions of the Old and eight of the Young Guard, still defend the village yet fail to drive off Tippleskirch or cause even minor casualties.

returns. It is these factual records that are much more reliable than versions written for posterity by biased officers of the regiment in which they served. Why are the casualty returns more accurate? Because the returns have nothing to do with the casualties. They have everything to do with money.

I, myself, was the first person since 1820, when the volume was sealed with sealing wax, to see the medical records of the Scots Greys for the period of Waterloo. What I hoped to find was how each person had been wounded: musket ball, sabre cut, cannon ball etc. What I

actually found was an accounts book that listed the name of each soldier killed, wounded or missing, how much they owed the regiment and who they said would pay if they died or went missing!

That is one reason why these records are more reliable. No sentimentality here; just pure accounting. So what do the casualty returns tell us about the final attack made by Steinmetz, Lutzow, Treskow and Tippelskirch?

Steinmetz arrived at Ter Le Haye and got into a fire fight with the Nassau battalion. Then he sent in his skirmishers against Durutte's Division and drove them out of Papelotte and onto the plain beyond. There he formed his Brigade into a Prussian Brigade attack column and drove into Durutte's Division, which was still some 2,800 strong, allowing for losses and some redeployment to the centre of the French line. Steinmetz had only a few more men at just over 3,000. Steinmetz is supposed to have smashed Durutte's Division into rout, then turned south and joined in the fighting at Plancenoit.

In doing all of this fighting Steinmetz's 1st. Brigade only suffered in total, 300 casualties of which 111 went missing. Only 31 soldiers in Steinmetz's 1st. Brigade were killed and 158 wounded. The brigade comprised six battalions and two Jaeger units of nearly a battalion strength between them. This means that on average each battalion suffered 4 killed, 23 wounded and 16 missing. I do not believe that there is anyway that a brigade can attack a formed French infantry division that returns fire, drive it from the field, and suffer so few casualties.

In this instance the opposing forces are virtually at parity, whereas earlier at Plancenoit 25,000 Prussians attacked half that number and suffered nearly 5,000 casualties. The numbers simply do not stack up. However Steinmetz was supported by two cavalry brigades; maybe that made the difference.

Major General von Treskow's 1st Cavalry Brigade comprised four regiments of cavalry numbering some 1,370 troopers. Lt. Colonel von Lutzow himself was taken prisoner at the battle of Ligny; part of the brigade never reached the field of Waterloo and took no part in the battle. Von Treskow's Brigade and part of Lutzow's 2nd Cavalry Brigade that 'slashed into de Erlon's and Lobau's Corps' suffered 2 killed and 11 wounded.

Elsewhere on the field the Prussian reserve cavalry was engaged with the French. They fought at Plancenoit although not in any particularly dramatic fashion. There were no recorded charges with typical Napoleonic clashes, such as were seen when the British cavalry charged the French at 2.00pm. Yet the Prussian cavalry fighting here suffered 519 casualties.

Von Treskow's Brigade comprised four regiments of cavalry. Lutzow's cavalry at Waterloo comprised three regiments. These seven regiments each suffered on average less than one killed and less than two wounded. Overall the brigade suffered only 2 killed and 11 wounded. This indicates that the brigade did not take part in any aggressive action at the battle. Steinmetz's great attack is a myth. It never happened as it has been described; the casualties suffered make that clear.

But what of Tippelskirch and his attack on Plancenoit?

Once again the casualty returns tell the story. The 25th Regiment led the attack and claim that they drove out two battalions of the Old Guard from defensive positions. That is the same Old Guard which only an hour before routed 20,000 Prussians from the field. The 25th Regiment suffered no men killed and only eight men wounded. The 5th Westphalian Landwehr, who formed the rest of the 5th Brigade, suffered 2 killed and 8 wounded with a further 7 missing. The 7th Brigade under von Brause suffered 1 killed and 4 wounded. In total,

Even as displayed by Siborne in 1838 the Prussian attack at the crucial hour does not include Steinmetz's Brigade. The troops seen here looking south towards Plancenoit as Siborne's model showed when first displayed, are all from either Bulow's 4th or Pirch's 2nd Corps. Steinmetz, according to Siborne's original view, was not on the battlefield at this time.

therefore, the 2nd Corps suffered a mere 3 killed and 20 wounded with a further 7 missing, a total of 30 casualties. They suffered these in capturing the defended village of Plancenoit from 10,000 elite French infantry. I do not think so.

However the mysterious 8th Brigade, which according to most reports never arrived at the field of battle, suffered 28 killed, 119 wounded and 63 missing, a total of 210 casualties. Clearly the reports of the latter stages of the Prussian action at Waterloo are not complete or accurate.

We shall see on the model what most probably took place, and very interesting it is too.

Chapter Twenty Four

The Last Attack of the Imperial Guard and the
Rout of the French Army
(as it most probably occurred)

Napoleon watches as the Guard file past to assemble alongside La Belle Alliance before launching their final attack on Wellington's line.

To understand the attack of the Imperial Guard we need to forget about what the allies were doing and concentrate on the French plan.

Two battalions of the Imperial Guard Grenadiers and Chasseurs had just routed ten times their number in Plancenoit. Napoleon had seen this happen from his vantage point near La Belle Alliance. He was very satisfied but not surprised; it was after all as he planned it.

Wellington had been ground down and was on the verge of collapse. The Prussians had blundered into his line and had been routed from the field for their trouble. Now it only remained for the rest of the Imperial Guard to finish off Wellington. Then he could turn on the Prussians in force and crush them utterly.

Napoleon ordered the remaining eight battalions of the Old Guard to assemble near La Belle Alliance, ready to make the final onslaught on the already shaken and weakened Anglo Netherlands line. Napoleon was there. He helped organise the column that was sent into the attack. Forget any ideas about him being in a state of anxiety and so sending in the Guard piecemeal. Rumours of this are in the book written by Montholon and they are nonsense. Napoleon was about to win the battle. He was in command. He

The gap between Foy's and Bachelu's Divisions was the only place where the Guard could attack without getting tangled up with another corps right in front of the enemy line. Bachelu can be seen just south of La Haye Sainte, ahead and on the right of the Imperial Guard infantry, whilst Foy is in the Hougoumont orchard.

The position between La Haye Sainte and Hougoumont just as the Guard begin their advance. Wellington's line is thinned but the Dutch Belgians of Detmer and D'Aubreme's Divisions are advancing in support.

was not under threat from either Wellington or Blucher. He was winning.

Napoleon's Guard marched forward in one huge column heading straight for Wellington's line between Hougoumont and La Haye Sainte. Why attack this part of the line? The reason is clear from the model.

The reason the Guard attacked up the slope between Hougoumont and La Haye Sainte was because there was a gap between the edge of the Hougoumont orchard and the division formed to the left of the Brussels road, Bachelu's Division. In such an attack the last thing

you want is any confusion. The gap meant that the column could reach the allied line without passing though another division or corps of French infantry. That is why they did not march directly up the Brussels road and attack the weakened part of the allied line. If they had attacked in the centre then they would have got mixed up with de Erlon's infantry, thereby causing confusion and possible defeat.

The single column of Imperial Guard, consisting of seven battalions, marched straight along the track leading to Wellington's position. There was only one battalion in reserve, standing in square by the cutting in the Brussels road. At the same time as the Guard advanced, Bachelu also advanced in attack columns slightly ahead of the Guard. He attacked the allied line from the crossroads to the 'Y' shaped junction in the Ohain road. Bachelu arrived before the Guard. If there was any reason for the defenders to believe that they were the Guard, because they saw bearskins, then it may have been the Carabineers of the 2nd Light Infantry Regiment. They wore a similar uniform to the Chasseurs of the Guard including a bearskin cap, and in some reports this light infantry regiment

formed part of Bachelu's Division.

Halkett's Brigade consisted of the 30th, 33rd, 69th and 73rd Foot Battalions. They had suffered badly at Quatre Bras with the 69th losing its colours to the French cuirassiers. At the critical moment when the Imperial Guard and Bachelu attacked, Halkett was off the field having been wounded twice. Colonel Elphinstone of the 33rd Foot commanded the brigade at that time. As Bachelu advanced, the squares of the 30th and 73rd Foot withdrew and collided. Panic ensued and the whole brigade ran to the rear.

It is claimed by Siborne that they then, with some good humour, halted, restored

Halkett's Brigade sees enemy columns appear out of the mist and assume that they are Imperial Guard. They edge back and collide, causing them to panic and run from Bachelu's line infantry regiments.

Halkett's 30th and 73rd Foot Regiments retreat in disorder from Bachelu's attack whilst Detmer comes to the rescue (below).

order and advanced once again to the front to engage the second column of the Imperial Guards. This however does not ring true. It is most probable that the brigade retreated in some disorder, maybe even in rout, from the French attack. Because of this they wanted to claim that it was the Imperial Guard who threw them back and not ordinary French line infantry.

Halkett's Brigade ran back and in doing so they unnerved the Brunswicker's and Nassau troops stationed to their left. Wellington himself rode up and stopped the Brunswickers from routing. He ordered the cavalry behind them to close ranks to stop any infantry from getting to the rear. It is a credit to these troops that they did not flee when Halkett's Brigade ran. Siborne gave the credit to Wellington but the troops themselves also deserve their fair share of the credit.

Detmer's Dutch Belgian Brigade advanced against Bachelu and plugged the gap left by Halkett. This was the reverse of the earlier situation when Bijlandt broke and Kempt and Pack moved into the gap.

Now Detmer, with the support of Krahmer's battery, fired into the packed ranks of Bachelu's Division. They wavered and fell back. A bayonet charge by Detmer's Brigade drove them off into the fog in confusion.

Wellington calls the Foot Guards to their feet and orders them to fire into the packed ranks of the French Guard.

Wellington, meanwhile, rode back to Maitland's Foot Guards who were lying down behind a low bank protected from the cannonade flying overhead. The guns ceased fire. Wellington rode up to Bolton's battery, now commanded by Captain Napier, and told him to look out to his left as the French would soon be upon him.

On came the Imperial Guard, marching in perfect order confident of victory. As they approached to within fifty yards of the Foot Guards Wellington called out 'Now Maitland, now's your time' and then 'Up Guards, make ready —- Fire!'

With this order Wellington brought the final attack of the Imperial Guard to a crushing halt. The British Foot Guards at this time numbered about 1,500 muskets. They were well trained to fire three and even four rounds per minute. That is six thousand shots per minute. A general-purpose machine gun (GPMG) fires 600 rounds per minute. The firepower brought to bear on the column of the Imperial Guard was the equivalent of ten machine guns firing at a dense mass of men at a range of fifty yards.

At the same time as the Foot Guards stood up and fired into the face of the column, the 52nd Foot swung round the

The Imperial Guard was attacked in both front and flank by the British Foot Guards and the 52nd Foot. To the left Bachelu has retired back into the smoke, away from the canister fired from Krahmer's battery whilst on the right of the picture, the 23rd Light Dragoons engage the French cavalry supporting the Imperial Guard's left flank in the attack.

The whole field, at the moment when the British Foot Guards stood up and poured a volley into the French Imperial Guard.

low knoll by the Nivelles road and brought its 1,000 muskets to bear directly onto the flank of the column. They poured in a volley, then another and another. The column convulsed under the weight of shot fired at it.

Napier's five guns, one having been disabled, poured canister and shot into the massed French ranks. Suddenly Lord Saltoun seeing that the French column was on the point of breaking shouted 'Now's the time boys' and they dashed forward with levelled bayonets.

No troops, not the French Guard nor the British Guard nor any troops, could withstand such an onslaught of firepower and shock tactics. Stunned and dazed by the carnage, they broke and ran from the bayonet charge coming from both front and flank.

Both the Foot Guards and the 52nd Foot followed up the fleeing Imperial Guard, the Foot Guards at the charge, the 52nd in a steady line. Whether it was the 52nd Foot that the Guards saw coming out of the mist and mistook them for another French column I do not know but something spooked them and they fell into disorder and ran back to the ridge. The claim that they then re-formed and drove off another attacking column does not stand up to scrutiny; there was simply not enough room on the battlefield nor enough time in the action for that to happen.

But where were the French cavalry during all of this? A remnant of cuirassiers did charge a battery on the left flank of the Guards column but these were counter-charged by a squadron of the 23rd Light Dragoons and driven off. The left flank of the Guard column was left exposed, because any supporting cavalry were squeezed out by the proximity of the infantry in the Hougoumont enclosure and the King's German Legion positioned in square behind it. Stripped of flank protection and having the few cavalry that did get through driven off, the flank of the column was easy prey to Adam's advancing 52nd Foot.

What is less easy to explain is the fact that when Adam advanced his brigade diagonally across the field, their right flank was equally exposed and yet did not come under attack by cavalry or infantry. The reason why no infantry attacked is because Bachelu was attacking in support of the Guard on their right flank and Foy was engaged in the Hougoumont wood area. But the lack of cavalry action on this flank is less easily explained, unless we accept that the French cavalry by this time was a spent force incapable of direct action because of its earlier exertions.

Napoleon is alleged to have said, in the book written by Montholon on St Helena, that it was the lack of a cavalry reserve that lost him the battle. Had Guyot not advanced into the mouths of Mercer's guns then they would have been available to threaten the advance of the 52nd Foot and maybe the Imperial Guard could have rallied. This does have a ring of truth to it. But they were not there or at least they were not there in sufficient force to stem the allied advance.

With the Imperial Guard driven off, Wellington dashed forward, sending out orders left and right to follow up the advance of Adam's Brigade. Vivian and Vandeleur advanced and so did Halkett's

'La Guarde recule' Shattered by the musketry and the bayonet charge, the Guard breaks and runs back. Cambronne's square is easily visible trying to stem the rout which flows around him, having taken Bachelu's Division along with it.

Hanoverian Brigade, Du Platt's King's German Legion, Grant's and Dornberg's cavalry and behind them the reformed Brigade of Maitland's Foot Guards. Everything before them gave way and put up little resistance, shocked by the defeat of the Imperial Guard infantry. The rest of the army lost its will to fight on.

Wellington raced back to the centre, where La Haye Sainte had just been recaptured, and surveyed the scene. He could see that the French army, outflanked by his advance in the centre, was falling back all along the line. He claimed that he could also see that von Bulow was attacking Plancenoit and that von Ziethen had come up on his left flank, making that side secure. Even from the high position at the crossroads it is not easy to see any more of Plancenoit than the church spire, so Wellington could not be certain, other than from the frequent gun flashes, about what was happening in the Plancenoit area. He could see left towards Papelotte and Ziethen's Brigade approaching. In any event he felt confident enough in his position to order a general advance all along the line and in so doing brought the battle to an end. The French were

The 52nd Foot advance, supported by Halkett's Hanoverian Brigade and the advancing British cavalry. The rout begins to spread eastwards to include part of de Erlon's Corps, whilst part of Foy's light infantry in the Hougoumont enclosure also breaks and runs. Abandoned guns begin to litter the battlefield.

utterly defeated.

Napoleon saw the defeat of his Old Guard with disbelieving eyes. Impossible, it could not happen. But it had, now to stem the rout he needed troops, he needed cavalry, he needed something. Given enough time he could have gathered sufficient troops around him to stop Adam's advance and allow time for the Guard to re-form. He still had plenty of artillery and if he could gather sufficient cavalry then all was not lost.

Had the Imperial Guard advanced in squares, as depicted by Mark Adkin, then Napoleon would have had a reserve, behind which the broken troops could have rallied. The fact that they did not implies that there was no infantry reserve there to stem the rout.

Wellington was experienced enough to see the same thing that Napoleon saw. Time was of the essence, the counter-attack had to be in force but also well co-ordinated. Wellington sent Sir Colin Campbell forward to catch up with Sir Hussey Vivian with an order telling him not to attack before the infantry came up. Clearly Wellington was well aware of his cavalry's weakness. They could charge and they could fight but they could not

ABOVE: Wellington, by his tree at the bottom right hand corner of the photograph in the rear of La Haye Sainte, looks towards the Prussian position and orders a general advance.

BELOW: Napoleon takes shelter in the last square of the Guard near the house of Decoster on the Brussels road. The routing French cavalry swirl around him, unwilling to stop despite the best endeavours of the Generals and the Emperor himself.

control themselves and they could not hold onto ground. Vivian, however, pointed out that the infantry of Adam's Brigade had advanced so quickly that it was getting into open order and, if French cavalry attacked them, they would be badly mauled. Campbell agreed with Vivian's assessment. Vivian continued his advance.

Behind Vivian came more cavalry and more infantry. Even guns were being limbered up to take part in the advance, but not Mercer's, which had been shot to pieces. It was this counter-attack that finally broke Napoleon's army and caused the rout that spread from the centre to the flanks like wildfire. All along the line the French turned about and ran. From La Haye Sainte to Papelotte the line advanced and the French fell back, mostly in disorder. Later at Genappe the road was clogged with abandoned guns and carriages that had withdrawn from the battlefield. Clearly some troops left the field in good order but were eventually scattered by the Prussian pursuit. The Grand Battery fell to the advancing allied line, which was joined on its left by Steinmetz's 1st Brigade and Treskow's cavalry. Together they advanced across the plain, the French running, as fast as they could ahead of

Tippleskirch's 5th and 7th Brigades, supported by the 8th Brigade, attack Plancenoit. The rout of the French left and centre is already in full swing. Soon the majority of the troops in Plancenoit will join in the flight before the Prussians get to the village.

them, for the ever closing gap between the British and Allied left wing and the advance of the Prussians at Plancenoit.

On the high ground above Plancenoit, Bulow had re-formed his battalions but was relieved to see the approaching brigades of Pirch's 2nd Corps. Pirch had managed to get to the battlefield with three Brigades, 5th, 7th and the 8th. They had been placed under the command of Von Brause since they had lost two commanding officers in two days.

Tippelskirch and Von Brause launched their attack on the village. Lobau and the Young Guard were already joining the rout and were heading back to the Charleroi road and then heading south back to France. The Old Guard, however, were not so ready to run. They would fight on.

The 8th Brigade entered the village and came under a fusillade of fire from the churchyard. House to house fighting ensued. Musket butt and bayonet met boot and sabre but the numbers of Prussians could not be held back for long. The surviving few hundred Guardsmen retreated in good order from the village, their colours intact, their square invulnerable. The 25th Regiment outflanked the village to the south whilst other regiments of 2nd Corps moved around the north. 2nd Corps had suffered 240 casualties from these 500

Prussian cavalry at the top of the picture and British cavalry to the lower left pursue the fleeing French troops past La Belle Alliance.

ABOVE: When the Prussians made their final attack on Plancenoit the French army was already in rout. Only the two Old Guard battalions remained in the village and it was they that caused the casualties 2ⁿᵈ corps suffered in this final assault.

BELOW: The last of the Guard from Plancenoit retreat up the hill towards the Brussels road pursued by the Prussians from 2ⁿᵈ corps.

Guardsmen, a ratio of one casualty for every two Frenchmen engaged. This was the same ratio of casualties for the Prussian troops in general, 14,000 French causing 7,000 Prussian casualties.

British, Hanoverian and Prussian troops met just south of La Belle Alliance and the escape route for the French to the South slammed shut. Once this occurred, no French northeast of La Belle Alliance should have escaped. But the fact that they did escape is yet more evidence that the rout spread from the western centre to the eastern flank, rather than the other way around. If the Prussians had broken through earlier then the escape routes would have been closed much sooner. Neither Lobau nor de Erlon would have got away.

And that is pretty much what Siborne says.

The fact is that Siborne's version of events stands up to examination and scrutiny much better than the more modern versions. They simply do not stand up to the test.

I would ask you to consider these points and draw your own conclusions

Did Steinmetz in a Prussian Brigade column break through Durutte's Division in a straight fight and suffer so few casualties? Certainly not! At Plancenoit the kill rate of the French was one Prussian casualty caused for every two Frenchmen involved in the action. At Ligny it was one for every four engaged. The difference was the intensity of the fight and the fact that at Ligny the French were attacking and at Plancenoit they were defending. Steinmetz suffered one casualty for every ten Frenchman engaged, assuming that is that he did not suffer any other casualties anywhere else in the battle.

Yet we know he suffered some when they attacked the Nassau Battalion in Ter Le Haye. Had they been in a fight with Durutte then they would have suffered at least 1,000 casualties and would most probably have been thrown back on the defensive. Behind Durutte lay the Grand Battery. Just by turning the end battery to face east Steinmetz would have been further cut down by canister fire. In the rear of the Grand Battery were Jacquinot's Lancers and Chasseurs a' Cheval. What would they have done to Steinmetz's advance? The claims simply do not stack up when put to the test.

The same is true of the final attack on Plancenoit. 10,000 elite troops defending Plancenoit would have decimated Pirch's 2nd Corps, causing at least 3,000 casualties, probably nearer 4,500. This would have shattered the Prussian attack, sending them reeling back. How did these claims come to be so wrong? The claims were made from the Prussian point of view. The Prussians did not lie in what they said. From their point of view they advanced against the French and the French gave way in panicked rout. They would naturally believe that it was their advance that caused the French to rout, rather than events that happened in the French rear, which were out of sight of the Prussians. After the battle the reason for the rout was sought.

The answer proffered was that Napoleon had sent out false reports that Grouchy had arrived, and when the

Wellington and Blucher meet at La Belle Alliance and agree that the Prussians alone should continue the pursuit of the beaten French army, in order to reduce the incidents of friendly fire.

French army saw that it was the Prussians they broke and fled. But this does not, in my opinion, stand up to scrutiny as we have seen earlier. But even if it were true who would be the first to break and run? Why would it be Durutte's men who broke and ran? They of all troops had been on the right flank all of the day. They knew that the Prussians were attacking from the east and had been engaged in attacking Plancenoit since 4.30pm. They also knew that the Prussians were in the Frichermont wood and Chateau. Why was it a surprise to them to find out that more Prussians were arriving from Ohain?

None of this stands up when examined. But the Prussians reported in good faith and sincerely believed that they had driven off the French from both Papelotte and Plancenoit.

Chapter Twenty Five

The Conclusion About the Charges Against Siborne

We have come a long way in our quest for the truth about whether William Siborne was guilty of the charges made against him. The battle of Waterloo, like any battle, is a complex affair involving tens of thousands of people across miles of open countryside, all acting out some dramatic event at the same time and each action affecting everyone else on the field of battle. Siborne took on the task of sifting through this complexity. He researched the minutia of events in order to bring some semblance of clarity to the battle so that future generations could understand better what happened.

Naturally what he wrote is open to interpretation as is every other word written on the subject, including this work of mine. Healthy debate is fine. I do not agree with Siborne on the formation and events at the crisis when the Imperial Guard attacked Wellington's line. I have outlined my differences in this book. I have every right to put forward my version of the event as no one knows for certain what happened. But I might not be right; Siborne might just as well be right in his version, as I or any other author might be right in theirs.

But the accusations against Siborne go beyond healthy debate and enter the realm of a personal attack against the integrity of a man long since dead. That is why we have to return to the charges in order to see if Siborne deserves the criticism heaped upon him.

Did Siborne suppress evidence, to enhance the performance of the British army to the detriment of the Prussians?

I do not believe so. There is no evidence whatsoever to support this claim. Siborne must surely be found not guilty of this charge.

Did he suppress evidence to the detriment of the Netherlands army?

Once again, I believe he did not. He might not have been fair to the Dutch Belgians, and more of that later, but he did not suppress evidence. Of that we can be sure.

Did Siborne distort history for his own financial gain?

Absolutely not! If he had been in the least bit devious, or at least if he had a commercial brain cell in his head, then he would have exploited the controversy to its fullest extent and made a fortune. Siborne was treated shamefully by the Government of the day and he could have made a scandal out of it. Newspapers, then as now, would have loved it and they would have paid him for it. The other side might well have bought him off. None of this happened. Siborne was a simple man, obsessed with the battle and its accurate portrayal. His integrity stands intact despite the attacks made upon it.

Did Sir Hussey Vivian and others pay Siborne in order to have their part in the battle highlighted?

No they did not. Siborne told his story of Waterloo as he saw it and not as anyone else saw it. He did not take any bribes.

Did Siborne remove the Prussians from his model because of pressure from the Duke of Wellington in order to diminish the Prussian role in the battle?

No he did not. He goes to great length in his history to explain why he removed the Prussian troops from the model and points out that if they had been as he originally placed them, then neither Lobau nor de Erlon would have escaped. He believed, after years of controversy and study that the defeat of the Imperial Guard took place twelve minutes before the Prussian's final attack on Plancenoit. It may have been twelve, it may have been ten but the events did not happen at the same time.

Was the Prussian 1st Corps further forward in reality than Siborne shows them to be in his model?

As explained above, von Ziethen's Corps advanced against a retreating French force, which was already running away because of the defeat of the Imperial Guard and the advance of Wellington's centre. Siborne's model depicts the moment of the defeat of the second column of the Imperial Guard. At this time Durutte was not in flight and had Ziethen's Corps been further forward, in range of Durutte's muskets, then Steinmetz's 1st Brigade would have suffered more casualties than it did. They were not, therefore, any further forward than as they are shown on the model at the time it depicts.

And were the Prussians' 4th and 2nd Corps attacking Plancenoit at the same time as the Imperial Guard were being defeated by Wellington on the ridge between Hougoumont and La Haye Sainte?

No, they were not. If they had been then they too would have suffered dreadful casualties from the defenders in the village.

Was Siborne unfair to the Dutch Belgians and their part in the battle?

Well almost certainly, yes he was. But that is not a charge levelled against him here. If it is to be levelled against him then in his defence he was not unfair through any malice, but rather because of the evidence presented to him at the time.

Siborne was not aware of the panic and rout of the 95th Rifles from the sandpit during de Erlon's attack. But in any event, when the data is analysed, it becomes clear that in terms of troops missing at the end of the battle there were proportionally more Dutch Belgian troops that went absent without leave than there were British. This was the general impression of the British troops on the day and they told Siborne of it time and time again. Siborne repeated the claims and denigrated the Dutch Belgians, sometimes fairly, but in other instances unfairly. The following chart shows the analysis of the proportion of troops missing for each contingent in the Anglo-Netherlands Army.

Nationality	troops engaged	missing	%	ratio
British	21,024	580	2.75%	1 in 36
KGL	5,298	214	4.0%	1 in 24
Nassau	2,880	172	6.0 %	1 in 16
Hanover*	10,258	369	3.6 %	1 in 27
Dutch Belgians	16,607	1,368	8.23%	1 in 12
Brunswick	5,452	544	10.0%	1 in 10

*The Hanover troops do not include the Cumberland Hussars. When they are included the ratio jumps to 1 in 12.

It is clear, therefore, that a soldier was three times more likely to go missing from the Netherlands Dutch Belgian contingent than he was from the British contingent.

The overall impression Siborne gives in regard to this matter is supported by the facts.

Chapter Twenty Six

The Victors and the Vanquished

Waterloo has been described as the battle Napoleon lost rather than a battle anyone won. It has also been described as a German victory and of course as Wellington's finest victory.

We shall deal with each one in turn.

Napoleon, Ney and Grouchy

Napoleon is often blamed and often excused for the failure at Waterloo. Other villains are Ney and Grouchy. When Napoleon's actions and plans are seen in detail on the model one can see his genius in action and much of the criticism falls away. Was Napoleon ill at Waterloo? There is no evidence from his plans and actions to indicate anything but a clear and precise military mind in action.

Napoleon is criticised for four major events at Waterloo;

His diversionary attack on Hougoumont

The cavalry charges

The last desperate attack of the Imperial Guard

His failure to order Grouchy to the battlefield earlier.

As we have seen, his diversionary attack was well conceived and executed. It is only from the British side that the criticism is made. As they saw it, Napoleon tied down too many troops fighting against a few Guardsmen in the Chateau and orchard. But that view is flawed. Napoleon's diversionary attack pinned down the whole right wing of Wellington's army. It kept Wellington's attention focused on his right, when the main attack was being made in the left centre. One up to Napoleon; nothing wrong in the attack on Hougoumont.

The cavalry charges are also viewed as disastrous errors made by Napoleon and Ney. Once again this comes from the

British perspective. Wellington would never conceive of sending in cavalry alone, against formed infantry with artillery and cavalry support. It would be suicide. Well, for British cavalry it would be suicide. They would have charged bravely but they would never have been seen again. One need only look at the Charge of the Light Brigade at Balaclava to see what would have happened. The brigade was destroyed. But what if the Heavy Brigade at Balaclava had charged as well after the Light Brigade had disabled the guns? We might have seen a different story had that happened. British cavalry was renowned for its bravery and its foolishness.

French cavalry were a different force altogether. As we have seen, the massed cavalry charges were planned and successful. Viewed from this perspective it is clear that neither Ney nor Napoleon, nor anyone else made a mistake in thinking that the British were falling back, and that was why they charged. View it from the perspective that the armoured cavalry were the shock troops of Napoleon's army designed to do exactly what they did and you get a different picture.

Was the attack of the Imperial Guard a last desperate gamble at the expense of his best troops? The attack of the Guard was, in my view, a well-planned and executed attack. It should have broken through any European infantry line that had been subjected to the grinding down process Napoleon inflicted upon Wellington's line throughout the afternoon. This was not a mistake; it was not a gamble.

But why was Grouchy not ordered to Waterloo earlier than he was and in a more clear and precise manner?

The Grouchy incident is not a matter for the trial of Siborne as it does not come up in the accusations against him. Much could be written on the subject and yes, with hindsight, it would have been wise to bring Grouchy closer to Waterloo earlier in the day. However, Napoleon was extremely confident of winning the battle right up until de Erlon was defeated. There was no need to divert Grouchy to Waterloo only to arrive after Wellington had been defeated and driven off to the west. It is only after 2.00pm that Grouchy can be regarded as being needed at Waterloo and by then it was probably too late.

Did Napoleon lose the battle of Waterloo or did superior numbers, brought to the battlefield by Blucher and his Prussians beat him?

Blucher, the Prussians and the German victory

When analysed it can be seen that Blucher was, throughout the campaign, dancing to either Napoleon's or Wellington's tune. At no time until after the rout of the French army was Blucher wholly in command of events affecting his army and indeed his country. Blucher was just as humbugged by Napoleon as Wellington was on 15th June when Napoleon arrived in force at Charleroi. The Prussians were badly defeated at Ligny. But they deserve great credit for keeping the remains of their army together on the march to Wavre.

From Wavre to Waterloo their performance does not do them any credit at all; it was a shambles. Once they arrived on the battlefield their performance was not very impressive either. They suffered a greater ratio of casualties to troops engaged than the Anglo Netherlands army. This did not result from the intensity of the fighting but rather the inexperience of the Prussian army. 30,000 men of Bulow's Corps suffered 5,461 casualties at the hands of 10,000 French troops in four hours. They lost 18% of their troops and suffered a kill ratio of one casualty for every two enemy against them. Contrast this with Wellington's performance where we see 15,000 casualties from 67,000 troops engaged, 22%, but with a kill ratio of one casualty for every five enemy troops engaged. Furthermore, Wellington's army was engaged for more than twice as long as Bulow's forces. It is also true that when the two battalions of the Imperial Guard threw the Prussians out of Plancenoit, they were driven back five hundred yards or more in disorder, possibly even rout.

Had the situation been reversed, with 67,000 Prussians facing 72,000 French for four hours, then it can be argued that they would have suffered 36,000 casualties and would have been driven from the field long before the Anglo Netherlands army could have got to the battlefield.

It is hard to see how the claim that Waterloo was a German victory can stand up to any detailed analysis of the day's events. The Prussians were driven out of Charleroi. They were defeated at Ligny by a numerically inferior French force. Then, driven north to Wavre, where they were reinforced by 30,000 fresh troops.

Von Thielmann's 3rd Prussian Corps was defeated at Wavre on 19th June. At Waterloo the 30,000 fresh troops of Bulow's Corps were driven off in rout from Plancenoit, once again by a numerically inferior French force.

The remaining Prussians of Pirch's 2nd Corps only took the village once the French army had been routed by Wellington. Victories are not won by losing battles. What is clear, however, is that if the Prussians had been left to their own devices to face Napoleon alone, then Prussia would have been defeated in detail. Fortunately the Prussian role was not one of supreme commander but rather loyal ally. In that role they did as much, if not more, than one could reasonably expect from the circumstances they were in.

On the other hand……

The Prussian contribution to the campaign as a whole was immense. Without Prussia acting as an ally in Belgium, Britain would have had to evacuate the mainland and cross the sea behind the protection afforded by the Royal Navy. In the campaign, Prussia recovered after the defeat in the field at Ligny and did not abandon her ally. They manoeuvred in co-operation with Wellington and did arrive at the battlefield 'in a most decisive and timely manner' *Wellington despatch*. The performance of the Prussian army on the battlefield, whilst not impressive, did engage 14,000 of Napoleon's troops. This denied Napoleon the use of these against Wellington. There is a general assumption that had these 14,000 men been available to Napoleon then he would have won at Waterloo. Thus, in this regard, the Prussian intervention saved Wellington from defeat. Once again the assumption does not stand up to scrutiny, as we shall see when we examine Wellington's performance in the battle.

The Prussians did take over the pursuit, a role in which Wellington's armies had always been hopeless. The pursuit did great damage to the French cause. However, the pursuit would have taken place in any event and Napoleon would have fallen as a consequence of the Battle of Waterloo. But the pursuit could not have taken place without the victory at Waterloo. The battle was neither a Prussian nor a German victory.

Wellington, Picton and Uxbridge

Many writers have praised Wellington and some have seen his actions at Waterloo as faultless. I do not see his actions as faultless as he did make mistakes. Clearly, Napoleon held the initiative on actions on the field. But the initiative was handed over to Napoleon by Wellington when he chose his battlefield and decided how he intended to fight his battle. Wellington did make mistakes but it was Wellington himself who said that after all he was only a man.

There is no doubt in my mind that the victor of Waterloo was Wellington for two reasons.

Firstly it was the army system he created and honed to perfection in the Peninsular War. His emphasis on firepower and shock as opposed to the mass de decision of Napoleon's military

concept, the line against the column, won on the day.

Secondly it was the man himself, being at the critical point more often than not, and making the correct military decision amid the noise and confusion of battle. Wellington achieved this clarity of thought with men falling all around him at a rate he had never experienced before. That was the other fundamental reason for the victory.

Take away either of these two pillars of the Anglo Netherlands army's performance and the whole will crumble, in the face of Napoleon's brilliant plan and forthright execution of his attacks at Waterloo. Few understood it at the time. They could not see the joint effect of firepower and shock, delivered at the right time by a master tactician against a numerically superior enemy.

Added to this was the performance of Picton and Uxbridge. Napoleon's plan had duped Wellington into concentrating on Hougoumont, whilst the main attack went in to the east of La Haye Sainte. Wellington arrived at the centre but too late to make effective decisions. The critical decisions were made by Picton and Uxbridge who, acting on their own initiative, brought Napoleon's carefully made plans crashing down in ruins. To Uxbridge, and his heavy cavalry, and Picton with his excellent infantry, must go the credit for foiling Napoleon's grand battle plan, with Wellington taking some of the credit for his masterful deployment.

The Prussian advance had reduced Napoleon's army by 14,000 men and if these had been available could Napoleon have beaten Wellington?

The answer is still no. The addition of Lobau's Corps to de Erlon's attack would not have ensured victory, as they would have been swept away, as was de Erlon, by Uxbridge's cavalry charge.

The Young Guard and Lobau would have been able to launch another infantry attack after, or in conjunction with, the cavalry attacks. However this would have faced exactly the same problem that the Old Guard faced. It would have to march straight into the mouths of the British muskets. They would have been blown away in the same way as the other French infantry forces that attacked that day. Once again mathematics make the position clear. At the end of the battle, Wellington still possessed 15,000 British trained infantry, who were more than enough to deal with an extra 14,000 French troops.

The aftermath

After all wars the military of all nations study what happened to see if anything is to be learned from it. The Prussians, Russians and Austrians made their studies and one man in particular, Carl von Clausewitz, put it down in writing in his book 'On War'. Clausewitz saw the need for a high command structure trained to move vast armies in well ordered formations, properly supplied in order to deliver the mass de decision at the right place at the right time. Clausewitz was an admirer of Napoleon's system and, by and large, European armies followed Prussia's lead and continued to model their armies on the Napoleonic French system.

Britain developed its army in a different way. It followed the success of the Peninsular war and of Waterloo. It increased the amount of light infantry and improved the firepower of its infantry line. It did not follow the mass de decision concept of columns, or masses of men, marching rapidly across open country driving away the opposition by sheer weight of numbers.

The two systems clashed only once again during the 19th century, and that was in the Crimea at the battles of Inkerman and Balaclava. At Inkerman the British line, without senior officers present, crushed Russian columns that outnumbered them two to one. At Balaclava the thin red line, both British and Turkish infantry, brought the Russian cavalry to a halt with devastating musketry volleys. This was the history of the British Army throughout the 19th century and into the 20th.

Europe clung to the Napoleonic mass de decision until the dawn of the First World War. It was here, at the early battles that Britain's 'contemptible little army' came face to face with the German mass de decision at Mons and brought it to a sharp stop by its tremendous firepower. By this time, British firepower had risen to rifle fire of fifteen rounds per minute and machine gun fire of 500 rounds per minute. A battalion of five hundred men at Waterloo could deliver 1,500 to 2,000 rounds per minute. By the battle of Mons, the same unit armed with Lee Enfield rifles and two Lewis Guns could fire 8,500 rounds per minute from guns that could penetrate two or three men marching in close order, and could kill a man with an aimed shot at 500 yards. The slaughter was horrendous. A

German officer reported back that every British soldier was armed with a machine gun!

But Mons was a British defeat; the retreat to the Marne a dreadful experience. At the Marne, the French, with British support, finally stopped the German advance with firepower. Its effectiveness in defence led to the rapid development of trench warfare and all of the horrors that entailed.

Wellington's method, indeed Wellington's secret, served the British army for over one hundred years to the nation's benefit and their enemy's detriment. It was only after Mons that the Germans realised that the mass de decision could not work against massive firepower. A lesson the Imperial Guard learnt to their cost at Waterloo.

The French did not learn the lesson even then. They went as far as sending their troops into the attack in the First World War without bullets, convinced that the bayonet and French élan would suffice. No wonder they were slaughtered.

Perversely, the British forgot Wellington's lesson and went over to the mass de decision, which they called the 'big push'. This culminated in the disaster at the Somme on 1st July 1916, one hundred and one years after Waterloo. What would Wellington have done in the First World War? He would have dug in as at Torres Vedras and let the navy blockade defeat Germany, which in the end is what it did.

Wellington at Waterloo displayed his genius for tactics and energy. Here, facing each other, were the two great military leaders of the age. The difference between the two was only Wellington's tactical ability, fighting on the ground he chose and the effectiveness of the British trained (both British and German born) infantry and courageous, if uncontrollable, British cavalry.

Napoleon was the great master of strategy and he showed at Waterloo every bit of his genius. His choice of army, designed to lure the allies into accepting battle, his initial attack at Charleroi, which humbugged both Wellington and Blucher, his crushing defeat of Blucher at Ligny, ruined only by the failure of de Erlon to attack when and where Napoleon ordered him to, all show Napoleon at his best. Then suddenly the momentum of his attack falters. Wellington escapes from certain defeat by a masterful retreat in the face of an overwhelming enemy. The weather came to his assistance but he would in any event have made his escape to the Waterloo position virtually unscathed.

The position Wellington chose was exactly what he needed for the battle he planned to fight. He was imposing his will upon Napoleon by forcing him to attack him frontally, and on Blucher by forcing him to advance to his aid. Wellington was stretched to the limit by Napoleon's brilliance. The diversionary attack on Hougoumont worked in the French favour. The attack of de Erlon's Corps should have succeeded but failed because of the actions of Uxbridge and Picton. Above all, it failed because of the reverse slope tactics that the field of Waterloo, chosen by Wellington, made possible.

The grinding down phase was the most testing time Wellington had ever experienced. But he was up to the challenge, being everywhere at the right moment, making the right decision at the right time under enormous strain in a hail of gunfire. The final attack of the Imperial Guard was met, as were all of the others, by Wellington's line beating Napoleon's column. And then the counter-attack, 'in for a penny in for a pound' he said and launched his remaining troops at the very heart of the French position. The French collapsed under this assault and the battle ended with the Prussians renewing their advance on the French right flank.

At the end of the day it was Wellington who won and, whether you are an admirer of Wellington or not, that fact is difficult if not impossible to shift. Blucher could not have won without Wellington, but Wellington would not have been defeated without Blucher.

Waterloo was his battle, Waterloo was his victory, Wellington's victory.

Ponder, reflect and cast your vote

And so I ask you to cast your vote and make your comments on the website.

www.whowonwaterloo.net

(see password instructions on inside front cover)

You are the jury. It is for you now to debate in open forum on the web site if you feel that there is evidence to prove, on the balance of probability, that Siborne is guilty or innocent of the charges made against him.

At the end of the day History is His-Story. This is my version of that history, a version formed out of years of study, reading and re-creation of the battle in miniature. This now is your chance to make it your story. Have courage! I have said many things in this book that are open to challenge and I am not concerned about being proven wrong, provided that evidence is offered and not just a different opinion. Nor do I mind being persuaded by an opinion that is backed up by logical and convincing argument.

Remember it is my intention to publish the results of the trial in another book. I hope to include the best comments from the website in that book with the name of the person making the comment in print, if, that is, they wish their name to appear.

I hope that you will take part. I hope that you will add by your comments to the sum of knowledge about this monumental event. History is never a closed book. It is for us all to make sure it is kept open and filled with interest.

End

APPENDIX

The Waterloo Despatch

The Waterloo despatch is the most contemporary document of the battle of Waterloo in existence. It was written on the night after the battle ended. Wellington returned to his headquarters in Waterloo village at around midnight. He ate a late supper and then tried to go to sleep. He was soon woken up by Dr. Hume who informed him that Gordon, one of Wellington's young aide de camps, was dead. Wellington then began to write the despatch a mere five to six hours after the battle had ended. He did not finish it that night. On the morning of the 19th he left for Brussels and finished the despatch there. He gave the despatch to another aide, Major H. Percy, who left for London. The despatch was published in the Times on 22nd June as reproduced (in original text) below.

Waterloo, June 19th 1815

My Lord, – Buonaparte having collected the 1st. 2nd. 3rd. 4th. And 6th. Corps of the French army and the Imperial Guards, and nearly all of the cavalry on the Sambre, and between that river and the Meuse, between the 10th and 14th of the month, advanced on the 15th and attacked the Prussian posts at Thuin and Lobez on the Sambre, at daylight in the morning.

I did not hear of these events till the evening of the 15th and immediately ordered the troops to prepare to march, and afterwards to march to their left, as soon as I had intelligence from other quarters to prove that the enemies movement on Charleroy was the real attack.

The enemy drove the Prussian posts from the Sambre on that day: and General Zieten, who commanded the corps which had been at Charleroy, retired upon Fleurus: and Marshal Prince Blucher concentrated the Prussian army upon Sambref, holding the villages in front of his position of St Amand and Ligny.

The enemy continued his march along the road from Charleroy towards Bruxelles, and on the same evening, the 15th, attacked a brigade of the army of the Netherlands, under the Prince de Weimar, posted at Frasnes, and forced it back to the farm house on the same road, called Les Quatre Bras.

The Prince of Orange immediately reinforced this brigade with another of the same division under General Perponcher, and in the morning early regained part of the ground which had been lost, so to have command of the communication leading from Nivelles to Bruxelles, with Marshal Blucher's position.

I in the meantime had directed the whole army to march upon Les Quatre Bras, and the 5th division under Lieut. General Sir Thomas Picton, arrived at about half past two in the day, followed by the corps of troops under the Duke of Brunswick, and afterwards by the contingent of Nassau.

At this time the enemy commenced an attack upon Prince Blucher with his whole force, excepting the 1st and 2nd corps; and a corps of cavalry under General Kellerman, with which he attacked our post at Les Quatre Bras.

The Prussian army maintained their position with their usual gallantry and perseverance, against a great disparity of numbers, as the 4th corps of their army , under General Bulow, had not joined, and I was not able to assist them as I wished as I was attacked myself, and the troops, the cavalry in particular, which had a long distance to march, had not arrived.

We maintained our position also, and completely defeated and repulsed all the enemy's attempts to get possession of it. The enemy repeatedly attacked us with a large body of cavalry and infantry supported by numerous and powerful artillery; he made several charges with cavalry upon our infantry, but all were repulsed in the steadiest manner. In this affair His Royal Highness the Prince of Orange, the Duke of Brunswick, and Lieutenant General Sir Thomas Picton, and Major General Sir James Kempt, and Sir Denis Pack, who was engaged from the commencement of the enemy's attack, highly distinguished themselves, as well as Lieutenant General Charles Baron Alten, Major General Sir C. Halket, Lieutenant General Cooke, and Major General's Maitland and Byng as they successively arrived. The troops of the 5th division and those of the Brunswick corps were long and severely engaged, and conducted themselves with the utmost gallantry. I must particularly mention the 28th, 42nd, 79th and 92nd regiments and the battalion of Hanoverians.

Our loss was great as your Lordships will perceive by the inclosed return and I have particularly to regret his serene highness the Duke of Brunswick , who fell fighting gallantly at the head of his troops.

Although Marshal Blucher had maintained his position at Sambref, he still found himself much weakened by the severity of the contest, in which he had been engaged, and as the 4th corps had not arrived , he determined to fall back and concentrate his army upon Wavre; and he marched in the night after the action was over.

This movement of the Marshal's rendered necessary a corresponding one on my part; and I retired from the farm of Quatre Bras upon Genappe, and thence upon Waterloo the next morning, the 17th, at ten o'clock.

The enemy made no effort to pursue Marshal Blucher, on the contrary, a patrole which I sent to Sambref in the morning, found all quiet, and the enemy's videttes fell back as the patrole advanced. Neither did he attempt to molest our march to the rear, although made in the middle of the day, excepting by following with a large body of cavalry, brought from his right, the cavalry under the Earl of Uxbridge. This gave Lord Uxbridge an opportunity of charging them with the 1st. Life Guards, upon their debouch'e from the village of Genappe, upon which occasion his Lordship has declared himself to be well satisfied with that regiment.

The position which I took up in front of Waterloo crossed the high roads from Charleroy and Nivelles, and has its right thrown back to a ravine near Merbe Braine, which was occupied; and its left extended to a height above the hamlet of Ter la Haye, which was likewise occupied. In front of the right centre near the Nivelles road, we occupied the house and garden of Hougoumont, which covered the return of that flank; and in front of the left centre, we occupied the farm of La Haye Sainte. By our left we communicated with Marshal Prince Blucher at Wavre, through Ohain; and the Marshal had promised me, that in case we should be attacked, he would support me with one or more corps, as might be necessary.

The enemy collected his army; with the exception of the third corps, which had been sent to observe Marshal Blucher, on a range of heights in our front, in the course of the night of the 17th and yesterday morning: and at about ten o'clock he commenced a furious attack upon our post at Hougoumont. I had occupied that post with a detachment from General Byng's brigade of Guards, which was in position in its rear; and it was for some time under the command of Lieutenant Colonel Macdonel, and afterwards of Colonel Home: and I am happy to add that it was maintained throughout the day with the utmost gallantry by these brave troops, notwithstanding the repeated efforts of large bodies of the enemy to obtain possession of it.

This attack upon the right of our centre was accompanied by a very heavy cannonade upon our whole line, which was destined to support the repeated attacks of cavalry and infantry occasionally mixed, but some times separate, which were made upon it. In one of these the enemy carried the farm house of La Haye Sainte, as the detachment of the light battalion of the legion which occupied it had expended all of their ammunition, and the enemy occupied the only communication there was with them.

The enemy repeatedly charged our infantry with his cavalry, but these attacks were uniformly unsuccessful, and they afforded opportunities to our cavalry to charge, in one of which Lord E. Somerset's brigade, consisting of the life guards, royal horse guards, and 1st dragoon guards, highly distinguished themselves, as did that of Major general Sir. W. Ponsonby, having taken many prisoners and an eagle.

These attacks were repeated till about seven in the evening, when the enemy made a desperate effort with the cavalry and infantry, supported by the fire of artillery to force our left centre near the farm of La Haye Sainte, which after a sever contest was defeated, and having observed that the troops retired from this attack in great confusion and that the march of general Bulow's corps by Euschermont upon Planchenarte and La Belle Alliance had begun to take effect, and as Marshal Prince Blucher had joined in person, with a corps of his army to the left of our line by Ohain, I determined to attack the enemy, and immediately advanced the whole line of infantry, supported by the cavalry and artillery. The attack succeeded in every point; the enemy was forced from his position on the heights, and fled in the utmost confusion, leaving behind him, as far as I could judge, one hundred and fifty pieces of cannon, with their ammunition, which fell into our hands. I continued the pursuit till long after dark, and then discontinued it only on account of the fatigue of our troops, who had been engaged during twelve hours, and because I found myself on the same road with marshal Blucher, who assured me of his intention to follow the enemy throughout the night; he has sent me word this morning that he had taken sixty pieces of cannon belonging to the Imperial

Guard, and several carriages, baggage &c. belonging to Buonaparte, in Genappe.

I propose to move this morning, upon Nivelles, and not to discontinue my operations. Your Lordship will observe, that such a desperate action could not be fought, and such advantages could not be gained, without great loss; and I am sorry to add, that ours has been immense. In Lieut. General Sir Thomas Picton, his Majesty has sustained the loss of an Officer who has frequently distinguished himself in his service, and he fell, gloriously leading his division to a charge with bayonets, by which one of the most serious attacks made by the enemy on our position, was defeated. The Earl of Uxbridge, after having successfully got through this arduous day, received a wound by almost the last shot fired, which will, I am afraid, deprive his majesty for some time of his service.

His Royal Highness the Prince of Orange distinguished himself by his gallantry and conduct till he received a wound from a musket ball through his shoulder, which obliged him to leave the field.

It gives me the greatest satisfaction to assure your Lordship, that the army never, upon any occasion, conducted itself better. The division of the guards, under Lieutenant General Cooke, who was severely wounded; Major General Maitland and Major General Byng, set an example which was followed by all; and there is no officer, nor description of troops, that did not behave well.

I must however, particularly mention, for his Royal Highness's approbation, Lieutenant General Sir H. Clinton, Major General Adam, Lieutenant General Charles Baron Alten, severely wounded; Major General Sir Colin Halket, severely wounded; Colonel Ompteda, Colonel Mitchell, commanding a brigade of the 4th division; Major General Sir James Kempt, and Sir Denis Pack, Major General Lambert, Major General Lord E. Somerset; Major General Sir W. Ponsonby, Major General Sir C. Grant, and Major General Sir H. Vivian; Major General Sir O. Vandeleur; Major General Count Dornberg. I am also particularly indebted to General Lord Hill for his assistance and conduct upon this as upon all former occasions.

The Artillery and Engineer departments were conducted much to my satisfaction by Colonel Sir G. Wood and Col. Smyth; and I have every reason to be satisfied with the conduct of the Adj. General Major Gen. Barnes, who was wounded and of the Quartermaster General Col. Delancy who was killed by a cannon shot in the middle of the action. This officer is a serious loss to his majesty's service, and to me at this moment. I was likewise much indebted to the assistance of Lieutenant Colonel Lord Fitzroy Somerset, who was severely wounded, and of the officers composing my personal staff, who have suffered severely in this action. Lieutenant Colonel Sir Alexander Gordon, who has died of his wounds, was a most promising officer, and is a serious loss to his Majesty's service.

General Kruse of the Nassau service, likewise conducted himself much to my satisfaction, as did General Trip, commanding the heavy brigade of cavalry, and General Vanhope, commanding a brigade of infantry of the King of the Netherlands.

General Pozzo de Borgo, General Baron Vincent, General Muffling. And General Alvoa, were in the field during the action and rendered me every assistance in their power. Baron Vincent is wounded, but I hope not severely; and General Pozzo di Borgo received a contusion.

I should not do justice to my feelings or to Marshal Blucher and the Prussian army, if I did not attribute the successful result of this arduous day, to the cordial and timely assistance I received from them.

The operation of General Bulow, upon the enemy's flank, was a most decisive one; and even if I had not found myself in a situation to make the attack, which produced the final result, it would have forced the enemy to retire, if his attacks should have failed, and would have prevented him from taking advantage of them, if they should unfortunately have succeeded.

I send, with this despatch, two eagles*, taken by the troops in this action, which Major Percy will have the honour of laying at the feet of his Royal Highness.

I beg leave to recommend him to your Lordship's protection. I have the honour, &c.

(Signed)   WELLINGTON

P.S. Since writing the above, I have received a report, that Major General Sir William Ponsonby is killed, and, in announcing this intelligence to your Lordship, I have to add the expression of my grief, for the fate of an officer, who had already rendered very brilliant and important service, and was an ornament to his profession.

2ⁿᵈ P.S. I have not yet got the returns of the killed and wounded, but I enclose a list of officers killed and wounded on the two days, as far as the same can be made out without returns; and I am very happy to add, that Colonel De Lancey is not dead, and that strong hopes of his recovery are entertained.

*This is the text that was printed in The Times. Intriguingly, Wellington's original text stated there were three eagles. What happened to the third?

Bibliography

I have read hundreds of books on the subject of the Napoleonic Wars. For simplicity I list here those books that have some relevance to the specific subject of the Battle of Waterloo.

1815 The Waterloo Campaign - The German Victory - Peter Hofschröer

A desperate Business – Ian Fletcher

A Model Victory – Malcolm Balen

Adventures with the Connaught Rangers – William Grattan

Artillery and Equipment of the Napoleonic Wars – Terence Wise

Borodino – Christopher Duffy

Decisive battles of the Western World (vols. 1&2) J.F.C. Fuller

Following the Drum – Annabel Venning

History of the Waterloo Campaign – Captain W. Siborne

Hougoumont The key to Victory at Waterloo– Julian Paget and Derek Saunders

In the service of the King – William Thornton Keep

Journal of the Waterloo Campaign – General Cavalie Mercer

La Grande Armee – Georges Blond

Lady de Lancey at Waterloo – David Miller

Letters from the Battle of Waterloo – Gareth Glover

Memoirs of a French Napoleonic Officer – Jean Baptiste Barres

Napoleon – John Bowle

Napoleon as a Military Commander – James Marshall Cornwall

Napoleon at Bay 1814- F. Lorraine Petre

Napoleon on Napoleon - Edited by Somerset de Chair

Napoleon Surrenders – Gilbert Martineau

Napoleon's Cuirassiers and Carabiniers – Emir Bukhari

Napoleon's Dragoons and Lancers – Emir Bukhari

Napoleon's German Allies (1,2,3 &4) – Otto von Pivka

Napoleon's Guard Cavalry – Emir Bukhari

Napoleon's Guard Infantry (vols. 1&2) – Philip Haythornthwaite

Napoleon's Hussars – Emir Bukhari

Napoleon's Light Infantry – Philip Haythornthwaite

Napoleon's Line Chassuers – Emir Bukhari

Napoleon's Military Machine – Philip Haythornthwaite

Napoleonic Wars Data Book – Digby Smith

Napoleons Army – Col. H.C.B. Rogers

Napoleons invasion of Russia – George F. Nafziger

On the fields of Glory – Andrew Uffindell and Michael Corum

On war – Carl von Clausewitz

On Wellington – Jac Weller

One Hundred Days – Alan Schom

Redcoat – Richard Holmes

Rifleman Harris – Edited by Christopher Hibbert

Rifles – Mark Urban

The Age of Elegance – Arthur Bryant

The Anatomy of Glory – Henry Lachouque and Anne S.K. Browning

The Battle – A new History of Waterloo – Allessandro Barbero

The Campaigns of Napoleon – David Chandler

The Diary of a Cavalry Officer 1809-15 – Lieut-Col. William Tomkinson

The Eagles Last Triumph – Andrew Uffindell

The Legend of Napoleon – Sudhir Hazareesingh

The letters of Private Wheeler – Edited by B.H. Liddell Hart

The Napoleonic Wars – Gunther Rothenberg

The Notebooks of Captain Coignet – Captain Jean Roche Coignet

The Peninsular War – Charles Esdaile

The Prussian Army – David Nash

The Waterloo Campaign – Napoleon Bonaparte

The Waterloo Companion – Mark Adkin

The Waterloo Letters – H.T. Siborne

The Waterloo Medal Roll – Military Reference Book

Uniforms of Waterloo – Philip Haythornthwaite

Voices of Thunder – Gareth Glover

Warfare from Waterloo to Mons – Michael Glover

Waterloo – Andrew Roberts

Waterloo – Commander Henry Lachouque

Waterloo In the footsteps of the Commanders – Jonathon Gillespie-Payne

Waterloo New Perspectives – David Hamilton-Williams

Waterloo the Hundred Days – David Chandler

Wellington at Waterloo – Jac Weller

Wellington Pillar of State – Elizabeth Longford

Wellington the Years of the Sword – Elizabeth Longford

Wellington's Regiments – Ian Fletcher

Wellington's smallest Victory – Peter Hofschröer

Who Killed Napoleon – Sten Forshufvud

Who was Who in the Napoleonic Wars – Philip Haythornthwaite

INDEX